Janitors, Street Vendors,
and Activists

Janitors, Street Vendors, and Activists

The Lives of Mexican Immigrants
in Silicon Valley

Christian Zlolniski

UNIVERSITY OF CALIFORNIA PRESS
Berkeley / Los Angeles / London

*58604774

University of California Press, one of the most distinguished university presses in the United States, enriches lives around the world by advancing scholarship in the humanities, social sciences, and natural sciences. Its activities are supported by the UC Press Foundation and by philanthropic contributions from individuals and institutions. For more information, visit www.ucpress.edu.

Parts of chapter 2 originally appeared in a different form in "Labor Control and Resistance of Mexican Immigrant Janitors in Silicon Valley," *Human Organization* 62, no. 1 (2003), and in "Unskilled Immigrants in High-Tech Companies: The Case of Mexican Janitors in Silicon Valley," in *The International Migration of the Highly Skilled*, ed. Wayne Cornelius, Thomas J. Espenshade, and Idean Salehyan (San Diego: Center for Comparative Immigration Studies, University of California, San Diego, 2001). Some of the material presented in chapter 3 initially appeared in different form in "The Informal Economy in an Advanced Industrialized Society: Mexican Immigrant Labor in Silicon Valley," *Yale Law Journal* 103, no. 8 (1994), reprinted by permission of The Yale Law Journal Company and William S. Hein Company from *The Yale Law Journal*, vol. 103, pages 2305–2335.

University of California Press
Berkeley and Los Angeles, California

University of California Press, Ltd.
London, England

© 2006 by The Regents of the University of California

Library of Congress Cataloging-in-Publication Data

Zlolniski, Christian.
    Janitors, street vendors, and activists : the lives of Mexican immigrants in Silicon Valley / Christian Zlolniski.
        p.   cm.
    Includes bibliographical references and index.
    ISBN 0-520-24641-1 (cloth : alk. paper) — ISBN 0-520-24643-8 (pbk. : alk. paper)
    1. Mexicans—Employment—California—Santa Clara County—Santa Clara Valley.   2. Alien labor, Mexican—California—Santa Clara County—Santa Clara Valley.   3. Unskilled labor—California—Santa Clara County—Santa Clara Valley.   I. Title.
    HD8081.M6Z556   2006
    331.6'272079473—dc22   2005008439

Manufactured in the United States of America

15 14 13 12 11 10 09 08 07 06
10 9 8 7 6 5 4 3 2 1

This book is printed on New Leaf EcoBook 60, containing 60% post-consumer waste, processed chlorine free; 30% de-inked recycled fiber, elemental chlorine free; and 10% FSC-certified virgin fiber, totally chlorine free. EcoBook 60 is acid-free and meets the minimum requirements of ANSI/ASTM D5634–01 (*Permanence of Paper*).

To my parents, Miroslaw y Natalia

Contents

Illustrations and Tables

Figures

Tables

Acknowledgments

It is a great pleasure to thank all the people who helped me in the process of completing the project on which this book is based. First, I am deeply thankful to the dozens of Mexican workers and families who opened their homes and shared their lives, troubles, and triumphs with me in San Jose. Santiago generously offered me his insights on his life and experience as a janitor in Silicon Valley, and I truly enjoyed his wit and sense of humor. Anselmo, Jose, and Miguel always found the time to talk to me and engage in long conversations despite their tight schedules and demanding night-shift jobs. Martha and Agustín shared their home and meals with me on many occasions, introduced me to many neighbors in Santech, and invited me to numerous community events in the barrio and elsewhere. Doña Teresa and Amparo warmly received me at their homes, offered me their hospitability, and shared their lives with me. After their arrival in San Jose, Silvia and Fernando helped me to learn firsthand about their experience of adjusting to the life of newcomers in the United States. Joel's family made me feel at home every time I visited them, and I have fond memories of the many evenings I spent with them. Quina, Edelmira, Dolores and Zeferino, Xotchil, Alfredo, and many other former residents of Santech, whose names cannot all be listed here, offered their hospitability during my stay in San Jose. Doing fieldwork among them was a source of inspiration and joy, and I treasure the friendship that has grown with many of them throughout the years. I also thank Salvador Bustamante, Guillermo Barroso, and the organizers of Local 1877 for their time and generosity, as well as Corazón Tomalinas, the group People Acting in Community Together, and its community organizers in Santech. I hope I have conveyed their views and actions fairly. In San Jose, Jesús Martínez Saldaña offered me his guidance, generosity, and friendship, introduced me to important leaders in the Latino community, and gracefully shared his deep knowledge about Mexican immigrants in Silicon Valley. My friends Ervin Barrios and Omar Nuñez were a source of intellectual stimulus, and together we shared many laughs. Rafael Morales gave me the opportunity to work as a volunteer in his program, which I truly enjoyed. During fieldwork, I benefited from stimulating intellectual exchange with Daniel Dohan and Mary Pearman. After I left the field, Daniel continued his encouragement of my book project, while his own book comparing poverty among Mexican immigrants in San Jose and Mexican Americans in Los Angeles was an inspiration and model for a superb ethnography.

Several institutions have helped support my research financially. I thank UC Mexus and the California Policy Seminar for providing financial support for fieldwork in the initial phase. A Visiting Research Fellowship at the Center for U.S.-Mexican Studies at the University of California, San Diego, allowed me to write up the results of the initial phase of the study and, ever since, has always been supportive of me as a former fellow. El Colegio de la Frontera Norte (Colef) in Tijuana, where I worked for several years, allowed me to finish my dissertation with a lightened teaching load. While at Colef, I learned much from my colleagues about immigration and border issues. I also enjoyed the intellectual support and friendship of my fellow members of the Grupo de Tesis, Patricia Fernández de Castro, Alfredo Hualde, and Marie Laure Coubes, as well as Carmen Martinez and many other colleagues and friends.

This book is the product of a long process that started with my doctoral dissertation in the Department of Anthropology at the University of California, Santa Barbara. I am particularly grateful to the members of my dissertation committee for their support. Juan Vicente Palerm, chair of my committee, provided unconditional and consistent support throughout the years in more forms that I could enumerate here, and to this day has always been a model of commitment, honesty, and dedication both to the study of Mexican immigrants and to his students. Sandy Robertson has been consistently sympathetic toward my research interests since my early years in graduate school. I enjoyed his professionalism and serious scholarship and learned a great deal from his vast knowledge of the household from a cross-cultural and historical comparative perspective. Harvey Molotch enthusiastically endorsed my research, and his contribution concerning the impact of economic restructuring on urban issues helped shape my project, for which I am sincerely thankful. Mattison Mines was a cheerful supporter while I was working on the dissertation and always available to talk to me.

In the process of writing this book, I have received help from numerous people. My dear friend and colleague Annegret Staiger offered invaluable critical comments on numerous drafts of the manuscript. She was always there when I needed her, and her keen observations and intellectual and emotional support were critical to carry me through the end of this project. Roberto Treviño, a dear colleague and friend at the Center for Mexican American Studies at the University of Texas at Arlington, read, commented on, and patiently edited many chapters of this manuscript. His mentorship, loyal friendship, and support were invaluable in completing this book. I thank Manuel García y Griego and the members of the Interdisciplinary Faculty Seminar at the Center for Mexican American Studies for reading and commenting on different chapters of the book. My colleagues in the anthropology program generously allowed me to concentrate on my work by reducing my service load. My gratitude goes as well to Paul Durrenberger, Josiah Heyman, David Griffith, and James McDonald for their valuable comments on previous versions of chapter 3. In different ways, they represent a source of inspiration for the study of class, labor unions, economic restructuring, and poverty, as well as the control and stigmatization of immigrants by the state, all of which helped me to analyze and make sense of the lives of low-paid Mexican immigrants in Silicon Valley. Finally, I thank the anonymous readers of University of California Press for their constructive insights and suggestions. Needless to say the views presented in this book are my sole responsibility.

Last but not least, I am deeply indebted to my wife, Reina, without whose love and support I could not have completed this project. Her encouragement, patience, and willingness to put up with long days and weekends of work were central for the completion of the book and cannot be fully acknowledged here. Pilar Monreal, Juan Carlos Gimeno, and Ubaldo Martínez Veiga at the Departamento de Sociología y Antropología in the Universidad Autónoma de Madrid, Spain, have been a constant source of cheer since I began this study. Finally, I want to express my deep gratitude to my family in Spain for their unconditional love.

Introduction

In the midst of East San Jose, which contains the largest concentration of Latinos in the Santa Clara Valley of Northern California, lies Santech, my fictitious name for a poor urban community made up of barrack-like apartment buildings inhabited mostly by Mexican immigrants. The barrio consists of six blocks in a distinct, self-contained area surrounded by a larger neighborhood made up of modest single-family homes. The residents named the barrio after a public elementary school that most of their children attend. Next to the apartment buildings, and divided from them by a concrete wall, is a housing project for low-income Mexican American, Vietnamese, and other immigrants, surrounded by several well-kept grassy playgrounds.

When I first visited Santech, I was shocked by the disrepair of the neighborhood and its buildings: five of the barrio's blocks were lined with identical, blighted two-story buildings, some of which had been condemned by the local housing authorities. Everywhere were broken windows, walls with graying paint, damaged roofs, stairs with missing steps, and decks that looked as if they were going to collapse. On the ledges above the windows were cans, piles of scrap metal, bottles and glass, broken chairs, cardboard boxes, and other old items kept by the neighbors living upstairs. The front and back yards of the buildings, which looked as if they had been lawns at some point, were covered only by bare, hardened soil. The streets and parking lots were full of potholes, and behind the buildings the garbage containers were overflowing with rotting trash; abandoned refrigerators, mattresses, stoves, and ripped-up furniture lay piled next to them.

What impressed me the most on my first visits to this barrio was the striking contrast between the dilapidated landscape and its lively street life: dozens of children, some barely able to walk, were playing barefoot on the sidewalks and in the courtyards; groups of men were chatting outside their apartments; women were selling fruit, jewelry, and homemade confections door-to-door; vendors with pushcarts selling Popsicle-style frozen fruit pops were walking up and down the streets in search of clients; young men and women in work uniforms were going to or coming from work; and old men were pulling cans and glass bottles from the garbage containers for recycling. In the evenings, as I walked down the blocks, a blend of food aromas escaped from the apartments, and the loud sound of TVs, CD players, and radios invaded the streets. The exciting and busy life in the streets of this barrio contrasted sharply with the quiet pace of life I had observed in most residential neighborhoods of San Jose.

I initially thought that Santech might be an anomaly, a poor barrio in a region otherwise characterized by affluent suburban communities and a buoyant economy. After all, Silicon Valley is known internationally as the capital of the high-tech industry and considered an economic model that other regions should emulate. But I discovered that Santech was not an isolated case: scattered throughout the numerous metropolitan Latino neighborhoods in San Jose, and usually hidden behind areas of single-family homes, were several neighborhoods with similarly blighted barrack-like apartment complexes inhabited by Mexican immigrants. I also realized that the existence of these immigrant enclaves was not readily apparent to the typical Silicon Valley inhabitant. Many people who live in this region have never seen or heard about these barrios, and if they have it is usually through the dramatic stories about poverty, crime, or the activities of drug dealers and street gangs that occasionally have appeared in the local media.

A number of initial questions puzzled me: Why were these poor immigrant neighborhoods growing in a region like Silicon Valley, well known for its prosperity? Who were the people living in these neighborhoods, and how did they make a living in the midst of one of the most expensive regions in the United States? What attracted them to this particular region? What living arrangements did they form in their barrios? And what did Silicon Valley's economic success mean for the future of the low-income immigrants who lived in neighborhoods such as Santech?

Approach

This book is an ethnographic study of a group of Mexican immigrants employed in low-wage jobs in Silicon Valley. Focusing on Santech, I examine how structural economic and political forces in Silicon Valley work themselves out in the everyday lives of the barrio residents, and the varied ways in which the residents respond to these forces individually and collectively. I portray the experiences of these workers and their families in their own terms, linking those personal experiences to the broader economic, social, and political changes that have made these low-wage workers a key segment of the working class in Silicon Valley.

To provide a holistic portrayal of the lives of Mexican immigrants in Santech, I focus on three main areas—namely, work, including the formal and informal occupations by which these immigrants make a living; household organization, including the variety of domestic arrangements formed by these workers and their families; and community politics, by which the immigrants struggle to improve living conditions in their neighborhood. Rather than presenting only a snapshot of life in this community, I emphasize the constant processes of change, stress, adjustments, successes, and failures that characterize the lives of most people in the neighborhood.

In Silicon Valley, the forces of globalization and international immigration have created a new class of low-skilled immigrant workers, the contemporary proletarians of a postindustrial economy. Mexican and other Latino immigrants make up the core of this workforce—for example, the thousands of Mexicans who clean the office buildings of the large high-tech companies in Silicon Valley. For these workers, the wonders of Silicon Valley are visible and tangible but seemingly unattainable. Structurally located at the opposite end of the class spectrum from the techno-elite, Mexican and other Latino immigrants settled in the region as a direct response to the low-skilled manufacturing and maintenance jobs generated by the high-tech industries. Subcontracting, the process by which employers seek to reduce labor costs and enhance labor flexibility, is the central link that connects these workers with the area's high-tech companies. I argue that this organic articulation between the organization of production and immigrant labor permeates most aspects of immigrant workers' lives, from the survival strategies they develop to make ends meet, to the variety and instability of their domestic arrangements, to the severe problems they confront in barrios like Santech. The financial insecurity that characterizes the lives of many of these workers underscores the paradox of poverty in the midst of the affluence that has become a distinctive mark of Silicon Valley.

Yet this is just half the story. At the same time, the new economy also opened new, unexpected opportunities for Mexican immigrants in this region. The demographic consolidation of recent Mexican and other Latino immigrants—who form a central component of the local working class employed in low-skilled service jobs that cannot be sent abroad—has opened new opportunities for the politics of resistance and contestation by these workers in Silicon Valley. The newcomers have transformed labor and community politics and have infused new blood into labor unions and grassroots organizations in the region. As I document in this book, the janitors subcontracted by major high-tech corporations have organized one of the most successful union drives in recent times by capitalizing on the same kin and social networks used by their employers to hire and control them, all in the midst of a region well known for its strong antiunion political environment. Moreover, in Santech and similar neighborhoods, working poor immigrants, especially women, have mobilized through grassroots community organizations to struggle for better living conditions for their families. Union organizing and community politics are the main means by which the new immigrants make their political demands known and contest exclusionary notions of civic and political membership. In the process, they contribute to the transformation of working-class politics in the region. While the results of such political struggles are often mixed, even according to the immigrants themselves, and encounter important structural obstacles, their significance cannot be overlooked. These struggles speak of the opportunities, limitations, and contradictions created by the model of capitalist accumulation on which Silicon Valley's high-tech economy is based.

Ultimately, in this book I demonstrate the critical importance of examining immigrants' agency if one is to understand how they transform their workplaces and communities and, in doing so, affect the larger politico-economic structure of Silicon Valley. I show the multiple and complex ways in which global structural forces affect the lives of common immigrants, and how the latter respond to the consequences in the realms of their work, families, and communities. I also reveal the falsity of the claim that the new economy needs no unskilled labor, by uncovering the direct, real-life links between the glamorous world of microprocessors, virtual domains, and ever-changing computer technologies and the less-known world of mops, hard physical labor, and daily predicaments faced by thousands of low-skilled immigrants who keep Silicon Valley's economy running. My ethnographic study provides critical insights that help to elucidate the possibilities and limitations that the new economy brings to low-skilled immigrants today.

Theoretical Framework and Research Issues

Economic globalization, Saskia Sassen argues, has led not only to the transnationalization of capital but also to the creation of an internationalized labor market for low-wage immigrant workers (1999: 111). Yet economic globalization is not a unidirectional process. Along with new forms of labor exploitation, its contradictions generate new opportunities for social and political mobilization by immigrant and other disadvantaged workers (Burawoy 2000; Sassen 1999). Thus, not all low-skilled jobs in which immigrants are employed are the same. Even at the height of the information age, key regions in the United States require a large contingent of workers to create and maintain the material infrastructure upon which the new information economy is based (Sassen 1999: 101–2). Unlike many low-skilled jobs that can be and are often sent offshore when labor costs rise (e.g., in the garments industry), low-skilled jobs in the service sector cannot be so easily sent abroad. The structural indispensability of these jobs opens new economic and political opportunities for immigrants and other workers who can turn this situation to their advantage, changing globalization from an inexorable force to a resource that can advance their own interests (Burawoy 2000: 32; Sassen 1999).[1]

As the global capital of the high-tech industries in the world, Silicon Valley is an ideal site in which to examine from an ethnographic perspective this new economy's opportunities and contradictions for immigrants employed in the low-skilled service sector. Geographically located in Northern California, Silicon Valley is often regarded a paradigmatic example of the new U.S. economy, which relies on the high-tech industry to be an engine for economic development. Over the past few decades, this region has produced some of the most important technological developments in electronics and biomedical research the world has known (Kenney 2000; Hyde 2003). In the process, it has also become one of the most affluent regions in the world, producing new fortunes at a speed rarely seen in the old, smokestack industry era. The spectacular economic success of Silicon Valley has attracted the attention of numerous scholars who have discussed the technological, economic, social, and political factors that give this region a clear competitive edge over other high-tech regions (Saxenian 1994, 1999; Kenney 2000; Hyde 2003; Lee et al. 2000). A few anthropologists as well have described what life is like for the people who work and live in this mecca of the high-tech world, especially the scientists, venture capitalists, and high-skilled immigrants who were attracted to the region by its wonders (English-Lueck 2002). But the glamour that surrounds the public image of Silicon Valley has obscured the important fact that this region has also produced a large demand for low-skilled workers. As recent critical studies have shown, along with the well-known concentration of scientists, engineers, and highly-skilled technical workers, there are thousands of Mexican, Central American, and Asian immigrants employed in low-skilled manufacturing and service jobs (Matthews 2003; Hossfeld 1990; Benner 2002; Pitti 2003; Siegel 1995; Walker and Bay Area Study Group 1990; Martínez Saldaña 1993).

Despite the voluminous literature on the wonders of Silicon Valley, on the one hand, and its darker labor history, on the other, few ethnographic studies have examined the experiences of the thousands of Mexican and other Latino immigrants employed here in low-skilled service jobs. As a result, we know comparatively little about the lives of those immigrant workers and how they contribute to the maintenance of the giant material infrastructure of Silicon Valley's high-tech industry. What is life like for the thousands who work and live there amid extraordinary wealth? What economic and political opportunities has the new economy created for them? And what do the experiences of these workers and their families reveal about the dialectic between structural forces and the responses of immigrants as local actors in key regions of the global economy like Silicon Valley?

WORK

The impact of and responses to Latino immigrants' entrance into the restructured economy of the United States, defined by the shift from traditional to light manufacturing and service industries, has been the subject of several ethnographic studies (Lamphere, Stepick, and Grenier 1994; Ibarra 2000; Mahler 1995; Torres Sarmiento 2002). The use of low-skilled immigrants as a source for cheap and flexible labor in the new economy is a common theme explored in these studies. The expansion of labor subcontracting, by which many low-skilled jobs are out-sourced to independent contractors in agriculture and in manufacturing and service industries, has attracted the attention of anthropologists interested in issues of labor-management control and resistance. Several authors contend that large corporations subcontract to capitalize on immigrants' social networks for labor recruitment, training, and control; to deflect the responsibility to observe labor protection and laws; and to disguise highly unequal power relations.[2]

More recently, other authors have started to discuss the novel forms of resistance and collective organization by which immigrants contest exploitation under these labor regimes, thus shifting the attention to their political agency. For example, countering the common assumption that undocumented immigrants are unable or unwilling to organize, some scholars have documented the growth of political union activities by Latino and other immigrant workers in the recent past (Milkman and Wong 2000; Grey 1999). Some of these studies address the important issue of how immigrant's undocumented status affects their ability to join unions (Delgado 1993; Wells 1996; Lamphere, Stepick, and Grenier 1994). Others discuss how immigrants' kinship and social networks and their social and cultural practices shape their mobilization strategies as well as the demands they include in their labor union contracts (Milkman and Wong 2000; Wells 2000; Grey 1999). Together, these and other studies call attention to the important paradox of how one the most vulnerable segments of the working class has become one of the most politically active and constitutes the fastest-growing membership of the labor union movement in the United States today.

Despite the important contributions of these studies of labor control and the resistance of immigrant labor, other important issues have received scant attention. For example, little is known about how labor subcontracting affects client companies' ability to control and discipline their workers, and immigrants' ability to respond to managerial control. Also, while recent studies of union organizing by immigrants help us understand the structural conditions under which collective resistance takes place and may or may not succeed (Sherman and Voss 2000; Bonacich 2000; Zabin 2000; Fisk, Mitchell, and Erickson 2000; Delgado 1993; Wells 1996; Waldinger et al. 1996; Cranford 2000; Johnston 1994), they provide little information about how immigrants themselves experience this process, what motivates them to engage in this particular form of political action despite their precarious economic and political status, and what they expect from the unions they join.

In Silicon Valley, subcontracting is the principal form by which high-tech firms benefit from access to abundant, cheap, and flexible immigrant labor, which is accompanied by both authoritarian forms of labor control and modern forms of managerial control. Yet after several decades in place, this labor regime has generated its own limitations and contradictions, opening new economic and political opportunities for Latino immigrants. For example, the newcomers have colonized the building-cleaning industry by capitalizing on the opportunities provided by labor subcontracting and using its logic to their own advantage as the basis for collective mobilization. Working together with experienced Chicano leaders, recent immigrants have successfully organized into labor unions at the heart of one of the most politically antiunion regions in the country. Rather than taking immigrant workers' labor flexibility as a given, I discuss how work flexibility is constructed in the workplace, what specific mechanisms management uses to optimize immigrant labor, and how immigrants have responded to such methods of labor control by capitalizing on their own indispensability in order to unionize and fight for their labor and civil rights.

Another major labor market exists for many Mexican workers in Silicon Valley: the informal economy. For example, in San Jose, a city with low-wage and insecure jobs, as well as housing and living costs that are among the highest in the country, many Latino immigrants have few choices but to search for additional sources of income in the informal sector (Dohan 2003). The importance of the informal economy for immigrant workers in the United States has been extensively recognized in ethnographic anthropological and sociological studies (e.g., Stepick 1989; Fernández-Kelly and García 1989; López-Garza 2001; Briody 1986; García 1992; Moore and Pinderhughes 1993; Dohan 2003). From a broader theoretical perspective, some scholars maintain that labor subcontracting is a major force behind the growth of small, informal companies that employ undocumented workers. For example, the garment industry in Los Angeles relies on Mexican and Central American women employed in sweatshops or at home (Bonacich and Appelbaum 2000). Other authors highlight the role of the informal economy in supplying goods to immigrants and other low-income workers in poor urban neighborhoods (Sassen 1994; Raijman 2001). And still others interpret petty informal economic activities as a form of entrepreneurship for immigrants who are either left out of the formal sector or prefer them to low-paying and rigid jobs in the formal economy (Portes 1995: 30). In low-income Latino immigrant communities, most studies agree, the informal economy represents an important source of employment for undocumented workers and is a vital part of the survival strategies for working-poor families (López-Garza 2001; Chinchilla and Hamilton 2001; Dohan 2003; Zlolniski 1994; Moore and Pinderhughes 1993: xxxviii).

But while these and other ethnographic studies identify the conditions under which informal economic activities seem to flourish, they say little about the reasons that immigrants choose them and how immigrants themselves explain their choices (but see Dohan 2003; López-Garza 2001). Moreover, we know comparatively little about the internal organization of these activities and the complex labor arrangements behind them. I argue that the same forces that have propelled the growth of technologically advanced firms in industrial parks in Silicon Valley have also fueled the proliferation of informal economic activities in immigrant neighborhoods like Santech. The existence of the informal economy in this barrio is largely a result of the inadequacy of income from work in the formal sector as a viable path to financial stability and mobility. However, the informal economy in this neighborhood is not homogeneous but reveals a wide range of activities and workers: some workers run family-operated businesses, others are employed by local companies while disguised as independent sellers, and still others are immigrants with professional occupations who work underground. While for many immigrants the informal economy represents a source of supplemental income, for others it is an alternative to low-wage jobs in the formal sector. By examining some of these informal activities, I highlight the organic connection between these two sectors and explain how immigrants themselves respond to the comparative opportunities and limitations that jobs in both sectors offer.

HOUSEHOLD ORGANIZATION

The second focus of this study is the household.[3] In the field of immigration studies, the household has traditionally occupied a privileged place (Pessar 1999; Brettell 2000; Chávez 1990, 1992). For one thing, focusing on the household makes it possible to move beyond the image of immigrant workers as passive victims of economic forces beyond their control and to see how the household serves as a mediating institution between those structural forces and the choices and decisions of individual people (Pessar 1999: 55). Making the household a unit of analysis also allows us to examine family survival strategies and how the family serves to protect its members from hostile forces from outside (Pessar

1999: 60). It is not surprising, then, that the concept of "family economy" has been widely used to explain the adaptive strategies of low-
income Mexican and other Latino immigrants.[4] More recently, however, this perspective has been criticized for romanticizing the family
and ignoring important processes of gender inequality and social stratification (Hondagneu-Sotelo 1994; Pessar 1999; Rouse 1989). Challenging the dominant paradigm of the family as an indivisible unit coalesced
around altruistic economic and kin ties, several studies contend that it
also serves as a unit of exploitation and is often fraught by important
inequalities along gender, generational, and immigrant status lines
(Hondagneu-Sotelo 1994; Menjívar 2000; Mahler 1995; Rouse 1989).
For example, Patricia Pessar maintains that anthropological studies of
the survival strategies of immigrant families should focus not only on
the broad economic context in which immigrant labor is inserted but
also on the narrow political economy of the household itself (1999: 57).

Inspired by this approach, I examine the internal economic and
social arrangements of the families of Santech's Mexican workers who
are employed in low-skilled jobs in Silicon Valley. Global and regional
forces penetrate as far down as the household level, producing a set of
interrelated and unsettling effects. Most Mexican workers in Santech
who are employed in low-wage formal and informal jobs live in
extended family households, not because of cultural preferences, but to
compensate for their low earnings and to cope with the high housing
and living costs that prevail in this region. These extended family households absorb much of the cost associated with the subsistence and
reproduction of cheap and flexible immigrant labor. Yet often, rather
than becoming stable and well integrated, these domestic households
remain in permanent flux, with kin, fellow countryfolk, friends, and
boarders frequently moving in and out. In addition, immigrant families
in Santech are often plagued by issues of exploitation, power inequality,
and economic stratification that cannot be ignored without distorting
the internal dynamics within these households. Moreover, for undocumented immigrant women, the household can be both a bastion of
resistance against hostile external forces and an arena of inequality and
exploitation at the hands of family and other kin.

COMMUNITY POLITICS

Beyond the workplace and the family, the local community constitutes
a major arena around which the everyday lives of Mexican immigrants

in Santech revolve. Despite their precarious financial and legal status, or perhaps because of it, many of the people of this barrio actively partici- pate in grassroots organizing activities to improve education, housing, and safety in the community. While in the field, I was surprised by the commitment, determination, and passion with which many neighbors in Santech, especially women, engaged into different community organizing activities. My surprise resulted from the fact that Mexican immigrants, especially the undocumented, are commonly portrayed as people afraid or unwilling to participate in political activities.

Since the early 1990s, however, two bodies of literature have chal- lenged this view. The first is the literature on transnational immigrant communities, one of the most recent and influential theoretical approaches in the interdisciplinary field of immigration studies. Studies informed by this model have shown immigrants' ability to develop novel forms of political organization that trespass national state bound- aries in an era characterized by massive labor migration flows.[5] A second body of literature consists of the studies of local, nonelectoral, grass- roots community activities conducted by Latino and Latina immigrants, especially women, to channel their political demands (Pardo 1998a; Hondagneu-Sotelo 1994; Hardy-Fanta 1993; O'Connor 1990; Delgado- Gaitán 2001). As these studies show, women often use preexisting social networks of mutual support to mobilize for political purposes. Politics is thus deeply embedded in their kin and social networks, which play multiple economic, social, and political roles.[6] These studies challenge the image of immigrants, particularly women, as passive subjects and show the importance of community organizing as an arena for collec- tive resistance and political mobilization by disempowered peoples around issues other than labor concerns (Pessar 1999: 65; Brettell 2000: 112). Despite the accomplishments of these contributions, however, studies on grassroots political activism by Mexican and other Latina immigrant women often tend to romanticize these activities and under- estimate the structural limits that undocumented immigrants face in their civil struggles. Moreover, issues such as how undocumented immigrant women go about engaging in these political activities, and how women's political activism affects their position in the household, have often been overlooked.

Local political activities constitute the third focus of immigrants' lives in Santech.[7] Like union organizing, grassroots community organizing constitutes a central avenue though which low-income Latino immi- grants channel their basic civil and political demands as residents of Silicon Valley. Community organizing aimed at local political structures, rather than labor organizing aimed at the region's industrial structure, represents an important but overlooked form of political mobilization by disadvantaged immigrants in regions like Silicon Valley. Generally organized in an informal manner, these grassroots community movements are essential to understanding the political agency of the working poor, representing one of the "weapons of the weak" (Scott 1985) for immigrants in this region. Working mothers are the main organizers and leaders of these groups, often building coalitions with larger, well-established grassroots organizations with more experience and political clout, through which they channel local demands for the benefit of their families. In examining these grassroots community activities, I show how Santech's residents have become politicized, and discuss the opportunities and structural constraints that low-income immigrants and their families encounter while trying to integrate as full members of the local society in Silicon Valley. Examining the dialectics between these sets of opportunities and limitations helps us to move beyond rival theoretical models that portray immigrants either as passive subjects in the hands of structural capitalist forces or as active political actors able to contest and successfully circumvent the control of nation-states.

Together, work, family, and community reflect the opportunities, contradictions, and limitations generated by the structural dependence of Silicon Valley's low-skilled service sector on Latino immigrants. In this book, I show how global forces incorporate immigrants as an integral part of the working class through flexible labor regimes. This, in turn, opens new possibilities for workers to advance their financial goals and political claims. At the same time, I show that optimistic interpretations of this phenomenon are usually unmerited. Enormous structural barriers prevent this segment of the working class from capitalizing on such opportunities, and it is difficult for them to translate structural indispensability into power.

Organization of the Book

The book is divided into six chapters. In chapter 1, I situate this study by providing a brief history of the development of the high-tech economy in Silicon Valley and discuss the major factors that characterize the political economy of the region. Then, combining information gathered through ethnographic fieldwork with census data, I provide a brief portrayal of life in the barrio and its central demographic, economic, and social characteristics, contending that Santech is first and foremost the product of the growth of the high-tech industries and the demand for cheap immigrant labor in the region.

In chapter 2, I narrate the experience of a group of Mexican immigrants employed as subcontracted janitors by one of the largest high-tech corporations in Silicon Valley. I describe their working and labor conditions, their struggle to unionize, and the results and consequences of their actions. In so doing I discuss the relation between global forces that connect high-tech corporations to low-skilled immigrants, and the set of economic and political opportunities and constraints these workers face in this region.

Chapter 3 focuses on cases of immigrant workers employed in informal occupations in Santech and elsewhere in San Jose. I provide a full description of these activities, their inner organization and dynamics, the dilemmas these workers confront in the informal sector, and the motives that lead them to work in these occupations. In addition to illustrating the complex and rich variety of informal economic activities developed by Mexican workers, I discuss the critical role that such activities play for the subsistence and reproduction of immigrant labor employed in the formal economy of Silicon Valley.

Chapter 4 examines the household types formed by low-income Mexican immigrants in Santech. In it I describe the subsistence strategies organized by the members of these households, as well as the internal inequality, stratification, and exploitation that characterize some of these households. Through specific and detailed case studies, this chapter illustrates the multiple ways in which structural forces that characterize Silicon Valley's political economy penetrate and throw out of balance the households of Mexican workers, as well as the different ways that the members of these households respond to these unsettling effects.

In chapter 5, I discuss some of the community political activities conducted by Santech residents. I explain how these community struggles first started, how they unfolded over time, and the role that women played as community activists and leaders. Without painting a romantic portrait of immigrants' grassroots politics, I document how Mexican immigrants who are excluded from electoral politics struggle against racial and class discrimination, develop a sense of community, and seek to build a better future for their families and children. In so doing, they redefine their civil and political rights in the region.

In the conclusion, I summarize the major findings presented in the book and discuss their implications for immigrant workers at the heart of the low-wage sector of the new economy in global regions like Silicon Valley. In the epilogue, I document the most important changes that have taken place in the region since this study was conducted and focus on how the economic crisis of the high-tech industry that started in the year 2000, combined with the anti-immigrant backlash after September 11, has affected the lives of Mexican immigrants in the region.

Methods

This book is based on several years of ethnographic fieldwork I carried out among Mexican immigrants in Santech and other Latino neighborhoods in San Jose, the largest city in the Santa Clara Valley. The use of ethnographic methods allows the collection of detailed information about the history, lives, and experiences of undocumented immigrants who are difficult to reach with traditional research techniques, such as surveys and structured interviews (Chávez 1992; Mahler 1995; Dohan 2003). In addition to offering accessibility, ethnographic methods bring the human dimension of immigrants' experiences to the forefront, one of the trademarks of anthropological research on immigration (Foner 1999: 1269; Brettell 2000: 118). By documenting the creativity and ingenuity of immigrants' actions, ethnographic studies also counteract the excessive emphasis on macro-level processes that characterize structuralist-oriented approaches to immigration.

I conducted my first and most intensive stage of fieldwork between the fall of 1991 and the fall of 1993, during which I lived continually in San Jose. The second stage took place between 1994 and 1998; during the first year of this period, I returned frequently to Santech for additional fieldwork, and after 1995 I returned less frequently. Finally, I conducted follow-up fieldwork in San Jose in July 2004, when I examined the effects of the economic downturn and restrictive immigration policies on the lives of the people presented in this book.

I started my fieldwork by exploring different San Jose neighborhoods with sizable populations of Mexican immigrants, most of them located on the east side of the city. After touring these communities, I decided to focus on Santech for several reasons. The first was a practical one: I had already developed several contacts in this barrio and was becoming familiar with a number of workers and their families and the public officials working in the neighborhood. Second, unlike old Mexican American neighborhoods in San Jose, Santech was a modern barrio resulting from the population explosion that accompanied the high-tech industrialization of the Santa Clara Valley, which began in the early 1970s. The majority of people in this barrio were employed in the kind of low-wage service jobs that became a magnet for new immigrants in Silicon Valley in the 1980s and 1990s, just the kind of context in which I was most interested. Third, Santech was a small barrio with relatively well-defined physical boundaries that seemed to residents and city officials alike to have its own identity, which made it an attractive and manageable working site for an ethnographic study of this kind.

I originally gained entrée to Santech through a local government program that sought to address the problems of drugs, housing, and safety in this and other low-income neighborhoods in San Jose. Through the community meetings sponsored by this program, I met many residents in the barrio, who in turn introduced me to kin, friends, and neighbors in Santech. Soon afterward, I established my independent presence in the community by several means. For example, I helped people in the community with translations; immigration-related paperwork; job applications; government, school, and other official forms; and other matters, which contributed to my visibility in the neighborhood. I also taught English as a second language to a group of adults in Santech at their request, which further helped to establish a strong bond with them. All in all, this enabled me to build a large network of informants, contacts, and acquaintances in the community, a network that kept expanding over time. Although I selected my informants from the individuals I met through this snowballing technique, rather than through a statistically representative random sampling, I sought a selection that would illustrate the variety of cases and situations I encountered in Santech. Thus in addition to the vicissitudes of each particular case, my informants illustrate the common dilemmas, problems, responses, and situations experienced by people in this community.

In the field, I maintained an informal approach in my interaction with informants.[8] Participant observation, hundreds of informal conversations, and numerous open-ended interviews were the main techniques I used to gather the bulk of the information presented in this book. I spent most of my time interacting, observing, and participating in the daily routines of my informants in Santech. I visited them at their homes on a regular basis, accompanied them to their jobs whenever possible, and participated in many of their social and leisure activities.

While trying to follow a research guide and plan, I was flexible and let informants and daily events shape my research activities. This allowed me to pursue my own research interests while, at the same time, letting my informants guide me to what was important to them.

Although I focused on Santech, it was just one of multiple sites where I carried out my fieldwork. My interaction with the individuals in this book led me to such diverse places as clinics, government offices, nonprofit and charitable agencies, public schools, high-tech companies, lawyers' offices, swap meets, churches, courtrooms, city and county jails, offices of city officials, shopping malls, public parks, and houses of relatives and friends, as well as to other neighborhoods in Silicon Valley where some individuals moved after I originally met them in Santech. I also attended numerous baptisms, weddings, birthday and *quinceañera* parties (celebrating fifteen-year-olds' rites of passage), and other family celebrations and social events. This close, day-to-day interaction with numerous people in the community enabled me to collect detailed information about both routine and extraordinary events in their lives that constitute the prime material on which this book is based.

The information collected through participant observation and interviews was complemented with secondary data gathered from census, archival records, government and nonprofit organization reports, newspapers, and other documentary sources. These sources were valuable in providing background information about the history of Mexicans in the region, and the contemporary demographic, economic, and social characteristics of the larger Latino population in San Jose.

Building trust in ethnographic fieldwork is especially important when working with vulnerable sectors of the population like undocumented immigrants (Chávez 1992; Mahler 1995; Dohan 2003). Developing rapport was not, however, an automatic process. The political environment is hostile to Latino immigrants, and this made many Mexican immigrants, both legal and undocumented, feel vulnerable and suspicious of strangers like me who hung out in their barrios. Many people at first took me, a red-haired white person, for an Anglo outsider, and some suspected I was an undercover immigration agent or some other sort of government officer. Once they found out that I did not work for any government agency, that I was from Spain and spoke Spanish fluently, the initial anxiety some people felt about me, especially at the beginning of my fieldwork, was largely relieved.[9] After their cautious and logical initial reactions, many of the people I met opened their doors to me and were eager to talk about their personal experiences without much reserve, including delicate personal and family issues and work-related matters they encountered as undocumented immigrants. This, in turn, helped to relieve my own anxiety about how people would react to my interest and presence in their lives.

Not everybody in Santech, however, was eager to talk to me. Some of my initial contacts never developed further, some people were polite but zealous about their privacy, and still others avoided me altogether. Whenever this was the case, and no matter how interested I was in following particular case studies, I would retreat after I made what I considered to be reasonable efforts to gain their trust. This, and my continual contact with my informants and frequent visits to their homes and the neighborhood, served to gain the trust of other residents in the community and expand my circle.

Many of my principal informants whose lives are portrayed here were working mothers. This was not an accident. As Pierrette Hondagneu-Sotelo (1994) has shown, the multiple economic, social, and community political activities in which Mexican and other Latina immigrant women are often involved play a critical role in ensuring the stability of their immigrant families and developing roots in the United States. As will become clear in the chapters that follow, in Santech women are the true gatekeepers and centripetal agents that keep the families and community together. Thus, any research into informal income-generating activities, family, and community politics would be seriously flawed if the voices of these women were not incorporated in it. As I discovered, having a good rapport with them not only afforded the best and safe access to the community but also provided a window to many important community issues. Making my initial contacts through women in the neighborhood also greatly facilitated my access to their homes and families, without which I could not have conducted this study.

Establishing my identity as a researcher in the field was not as easy as, perhaps naïvely, I had anticipated. Despite the customary explanation I gave people when I first met them about the central purpose of my presence there, and despite my frequent reminders along the way, my public identity in the community was not the same to everybody. Thus some people referred to me as a "student," which was my occupation then, others called me "maestro"—a common designation people in Mexico use to refer to schoolteachers—and still others believed I was some kind of social worker associated with a charitable agency or a church, or just somebody eager to listen to or help them. What I learned was that, in the end, the reasons why I was there were less important to them than my involvement in the community and their day-to-day activities, and the rapport and mutual friendship that developed over time.

During the first phase of my fieldwork, I collected detailed information about twenty-five Mexican immigrant households in Santech, including their size and composition; the age, sex, occupation, and legal status of their members; how and when the individuals migrated to the United States; income and household budget arrangements; their use of welfare and charitable help; and many other issues related to their lives after they arrived in this country. I also collected information about dozens of workers employed as janitors in Silicon Valley, some of whom lived in Santech and others who lived in other Latino neighborhoods in downtown and East San Jose. In a second phase of my fieldwork, I focused on a small number of workers and families with whom I spent numerous hours in conversations and interviews, this time to develop an in-depth understanding of their particular cases. From this reduced number of workers and families, I selected the case studies presented in this book. In presenting them, I made a special effort to document the constant flux that characterizes the lives of these workers, including the frequent transformations of their households, their economic instability, the ups and downs of their jobs, and their continuous changes of residence within and outside the barrio.

While in the field, I used a notebook as my principal tool. After their initial reaction of surprise and amusement, my informants got accustomed to seeing me with a notebook all the time and did not seem affected by its presence. I rarely used a tape recorder, both because I did not feel comfortable with it as a research tool and because I felt that it could hinder my attempts to be unobtrusive and informal. Only after establishing a solid rapport with informants did I use a tape recorder for some interviews. Because of this, only in cases where I am sure my notes reproduce accurately what people said and how they said it do I use quotation marks or extracts; otherwise I paraphrase them.

As a narrative strategy, in this book I have tried to use an easy and direct style, reducing academic jargon to a minimum while, at the same time, addressing the theoretical issues relevant for this study. In some chapters, I have described events as I observed them in the field, producing a narrative from a combination of what Van Maanen calls "impressionistic tales"—stories organized around some key, dramatic events that convey the essence of an important experience—and "critical tales," which are cases I selected because of what they reveal about larger economic and political issues (1988: 101–3, 127–30). I used this technique particularly in the chapters on janitorial workers in Silicon Valley and the community organizing activities in Santech, both of which reflect different forms of resistance by immigrants as they responded to important events in their lives. In other chapters, I have followed a more conventional narrative strategy that focuses on the mundane, day-to-day activities of people in their working and family lives, an approach producing a narrative closer to Van Maanen's "realist tales" (1988: chap. 3). I used this strategy especially in the chapters about informal economic activities and about families, in which I have tried to convey the vicissitudes experienced by my informants in these two arenas through a detailed description of their normal activities and experiences. Overall, I have attempted to achieve a balance between the need to present this ethnographic study in a succinct, coherent, and organized form according to established academic standards, and my goal to document in their full complexity, richness, and diversity the experiences of Mexican immigrants in Silicon Valley as I observed and interpreted them. Finally, to protect the identity of the people portrayed throughout this book, I have used pseudonyms for both their personal names and the names of the bosses and the companies that employed them. In the quotes, all Spanish translations are mine.

CHAPTER I

Mexican Immigrants
in Silicon Valley

Capitalist development is by nature an uneven process, generating contradictions and inequality as well as a mix of exploitation and opportunity
in the economies of advanced and peripheral regions in the world (Blim
1992: 16). Silicon Valley in Northern California is no exception. In this
region, futuristic-looking buildings featuring advanced architectural
designs with glass walls, aluminum fronts, and dark-tinted windows
house the research and development facilities, assembly plants, and
administrative headquarters of the most prominent high-tech corporations in the world. Surrounded by neatly maintained lawns, these high-
tech buildings offer a sharp contrast with the smokestack factories of older
U.S. manufacturing centers. The names and logos of many high-tech
firms, such as Cypress Semiconductor, Sun Microsystems, Seagate Technology, Quantum, Solectron, and Siliconix, seem to capture the essence
of the high-tech dream and are reminiscent of those used in science-
fiction novels and films. Not far from these industrial parks lie exclusive
suburban residential communities with mansions and gardens that, surrounded by tall bougainvillea-covered walls equipped with sophisticated
surveillance systems, house the most privileged Silicon Valley professional
workers. These elite, socially homogeneous, and exclusionary residential
communities vividly illustrate the concentration of wealth created by the
high-technology economy in the region in the past few decades.

Yet at the heart of the world's high-tech-industry complex that created all this prosperity, there are also many urban neighborhoods where
poverty is palpable. An oddity at first glance to the casual observer,
these barrios contrast vividly with the affluence that characterizes life in

many suburban communities in the Santa Clara Valley. Mostly located on the east side of San Jose and in other pockets of the city, these neighborhoods are largely inhabited by Mexican and other Latino immigrant workers and families. These barrios are largely invisible to most people in Silicon Valley. They are partially obscured from view by the triumphal public image of this region as the center of technological innovation, a concentration of highly skilled and remunerated professional workers, and general prosperity. But how and when did these poor immigrant neighborhoods develop in the midst of such an affluent region like Silicon Valley in the first place? Who lives in these neighborhoods and how are they connected, if they are connected, to the region's mainstream economy? What is life like for the immigrant workers and their families who live in these neighborhoods? And what do these low-income communities reveal about the economic opportunities and contradictions generated by Silicon Valley's model of industrial development?

Santech, the low-income Mexican immigrant barrio where many of the people described in this book live, symbolizes the Latino immigrant neighborhoods that have emerged along with the demand for immigrant labor in recent history in the Santa Clara Valley. Working in the very low-skilled service occupations that have proliferated in Silicon Valley since the early 1980s, Mexican immigrants in Santech are part of a large contingent of flexible immigrant laborers employed in the maintenance of the region's high-tech industrial complex. Poverty in this neighborhood is not the result of immigrants' marginality to the valley's economy, but rather of the unequal employment opportunities generated by the high-tech industry. In this context, the residents of Santech have developed a variety of financial and social strategies to deal with the economic insecurity that results from these jobs. Collectively, they have joined different grassroots political groups to address the various problems that affect them as local residents. The ethnographic portrayal I present in this chapter challenges the customary idea that there is no room in Silicon Valley's advanced economy for a group of poorly educated immigrants. It reveals recent immigrants' opportunities and challenges, illustrating the paradox posed by the poor but vibrant Latino immigrant neighborhoods that have emerged in Silicon Valley in the midst of economic prosperity.

From an Agricultural to a High-Tech Region

Located at the southern tip of the San Francisco Bay in Northern California, "Silicon Valley" includes Santa Clara County as well as parts of the neighboring San Mateo and Santa Cruz counties.[1] The Santa Clara Valley—the heart of Silicon Valley—covers about 1,312 square miles. At its greatest width, it is approximately 20 miles across; it extends some 60 miles southeast from the salt marshes of the bay. The valley has about 1.7 million inhabitants, of whom 44 percent are white, 25 percent are Asian, 24 percent are Latino, and 3 percent are black (U.S. Bureau of the Census 2000). People of Mexican origin make up the bulk of the Latino population in the region. There are about 325,000 people of Mexican origin in Santa Clara County; they represent about 80 percent of its Latino population and 19 percent of its total population (U.S. Bureau of the Census 2000).

Prior to the arrival of the high-tech industries, the region was known as the "Valley of Heart's Delight" because of the variety of colorful orchard trees that covered most of it. Annually nourished by the flooding of the local Guadalupe, Los Gatos, and Coyote rivers, the valley's fertile soil, along with its mild climate, made the region an excellent location for agricultural production. The evolution of the region into a major fruit production center with orchard trees, vineyards, and nursery plants was the result of economic developments that occurred between the 1860s and 1880s. The arrival of the railroad during the 1860s transformed San Jose's economy and made possible the large-scale export of agricultural products to other parts of the country (Sánchez 1984: 5; Pitti 2003). Years later, the development of drying and canning processes to preserve fruits contributed to the further transformation of San Jose's agricultural production from grain to orchards and vineyards. By the turn of the twentieth century, the Santa Clara Valley was the most important fruit producing and canning center in the United States, supplying one-third of all California's produce (Sánchez 1984: 7–8).

In the 1950s, after several decades of vibrant agricultural activity, a gradual but crucial economic transformation began in the Santa Clara Valley, one that replaced its agricultural base with industrial microelectronic production. This transformation, which would have a dramatic and lasting effect on the region, resulted from political and economic forces in the aftermath of the Second World War, when the U.S. government made this region the center of the developing defense-electronics-research industry (Saxenian 1985: 103). Meanwhile, the food-processing industries experienced a sharp decline as cannery companies moved to rural areas in California and Mexico in an attempt to reduce operation costs (Zavella 1987: 162). In the 1960s and 1970s, the market for microelectronics gradually matured and then boomed, completing

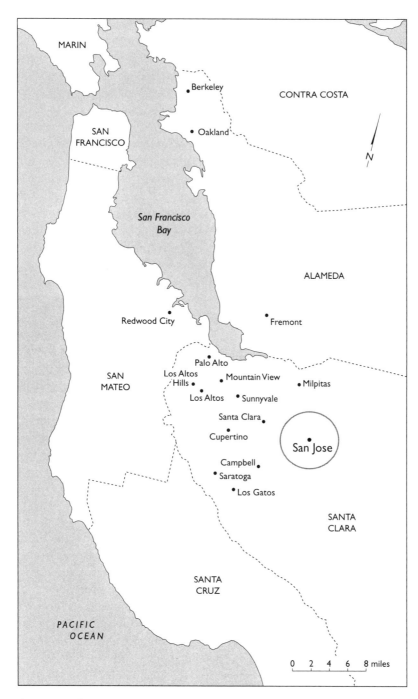

San Jose and vicinity

TABLE 1. Population in Santa Clara County and
the City of San Jose, 1900–2000

Year	Santa Clara County Population	San Jose Population
1900	50,216	21,500
1910	83,539	28,946
1920	100,676	39,642
1930	145,118	57,651
1940	174,949	68,457
1950	290,547	95,280
1960	658,700	204,196
1970	1,064,714	445,779
1980	1,265,200	625,763
1990	1,497,577	782,205
2000	1,682,585	894,943

SOURCE: Data from Martínez Saldaña 1993; and U.S. Bureau of the Census 2000.

the economic transformation of the Santa Clara Valley, which then became popularly known as Silicon Valley, the international capital of the high-technology economy.

The impressively fast industrialization of the Santa Clara Valley marked the beginning of an also explosive demographic and urban growth. As Table 1 shows, between 1950 and 1980 the population in Santa Clara County increased by about a million (from 290,547 to 1,265,200), and in San Jose by more than a half million (from 95,280 to 625,763), making this city the fastest growing in the country for several years in the 1970s. This demographic explosion produced a great demand for new housing and triggered rapid suburban growth. Massive suburban housing tracts promoted by private developers in San Jose and most other cities in the region rapidly replaced fruit orchards. Also as part of this massive suburbanization process, a large highway system, centered in San Jose, was built to connect the city to the major high-tech industrial parks and new residential suburban areas in the valley. To keep up with this rapid urban growth, the city of San Jose started an aggressive annexation campaign to buy land before private developers did. Between 1950 and 1970, the city government approved about 1,400 annexations, and San Jose's area expanded by more than 130 square miles (Rosaldo, Flores, and Silvestrini 1993: 6). Despite this strategy, San Jose soon became sprinkled with housing developments in unincorporated areas, many of which remained unincorporated for several years.[2]

Mexican Migration to the Santa Clara Valley

Mexican migrants have played a central role in the economic development of the Santa Clara Valley through its different historical stages. In fact, the migration of Mexican workers to the area, and their settlement patterns, have historically responded to changes in the region's political economy. When the Santa Clara Valley's position as one of the world's leading agricultural processing centers was consolidated in the 1930s, Mexican workers, both native and foreign born, soon became the backbone of the labor force employed in agriculture-related jobs, which led to the formation of a large Mexican working class (Pitti 1998: 146). A Mexican American journalist who grew up in the Santa Clara Valley in the 1940s and 1950s recalled that, at the time, the valley's canneries employed more than thirty thousand people during the peak season from mid-May to early September, most of them Mexicans from other parts of California; from Texas, Arizona, and New Mexico; and from several regions of Mexico (Juárez 1972, 1975).

Mexican agricultural and cannery workers started to settle down in new neighborhoods on the outskirts of San Jose. The largest and best known of these neighborhoods was the Mayfair District, an unincorporated area on the east side, outside the city limits, near local fields and canneries (Pitti 2003: 91–92). Sal Si Puedes (Get Out If You Can) was a little and heavily populated barrio on this side—the Mexican side—of town. An ethnographic study conducted in this barrio in the 1950s revealed a population made up of seasonal agricultural workers, or braceros, and cannery workers, construction workers, and casual laborers (Clark 1970: 74–76). For the most part, city officials blamed Mexican residents for the dilapidated condition of this barrio and ignored such problems as the housing shortage, poverty, and lack of public infrastructure (Pitti 1998: 210).

In response to their pressing needs, Mexican residents in East San Jose started to mobilize, first around labor issues and later around neighborhood- and community-related demands. In the 1940s and 1950s, for example, Mexican residents formed several civic and community groups, including the Community Service Organization, to improve living conditions (Pitti 2003: 149–65; Matthews 2003: 106–7). Mexican women were particularly active in community politics, and they frequently recruited other residents to join groups like the Community Service Organization and become involved in neighborhood meetings. The Catholic Church played a central role in facilitating these community efforts, emphasizing issues of social justice and the political rights of the working-poor Mexican population.[3] Together, these labor and community organizing efforts left an important legacy of political activism by the Mexican population in the Santa Clara Valley that would have important consequences for similar forms of union and community politics several decades later, when the region was deeply transformed by the high-tech industry (Matthews 2003; Pitti 2003).

When, in the early 1950s, the Santa Clara Valley started its rapid economic transformation from agricultural to microelectronics production, this change dramatically affected the nature of the labor demand in the region. The new high-tech economy attracted thousands of college-educated professionals, such as engineers, technicians, and managers, many of them immigrants from China, Japan, Korea, India, and Taiwan (Saxenian 1994; Alarcón 2000). But at the same time, the high-tech industry generated thousands of jobs in unskilled, low-wage occupations in electronics assembly and the service sector that became a magnet for Mexican immigrants (Walker and Bay Area Study Group 1990: 34).

In fact, the demand for low-skilled labor in manufacturing and service occupations fueled further immigration from Mexico and contributed to the rapid growth of the Latino population in the region.[4] This growth was particularly pronounced in San Jose, where, as Table 2 shows, the Latino population went from 14 percent to 22 percent of the total city population between 1960 and 1980. Indeed, after earlier waves of Mexican migration to the region (Pitti 2003), we can distinguish two major stages in the modern history of Mexican migration to the Santa Clara Valley. The first one took place between the early 1960s and the late 1970s, fueled by the booming electronics industry and the demand for immigrants to work in semiconductor processing and assembly jobs. The second wave of Mexican immigrants arrived in the 1980s and 1990s, this time attracted by the supply of unskilled jobs in various service industries. Mexican immigrants, many of them undocumented, became the bulk of the workers employed as janitors, gardeners, hotel housekeepers, fast-food and restaurant workers, maids, house cleaners, baby-sitters, and elder-care workers and in other personal service occupations.[5] By the mid-1990s, for example, there were as many janitorial workers—most of them Mexican immigrants—as computer engineers employed in Santa Clara County (State of California, Employment Development Department 1998), revealing the bifurcated labor demand fueled by the high-technology industries in the region.[6]

TABLE 2. Latino Population in San Jose, 1960–2000

Year	Latino Population	Percentage of Total Population
1960	28,596	14.0
1970	97,367	21.8
1980	140,529	22.3
1990	208,381	26.6
2000	269,989	30.7

SOURCE: Data compiled by the author from U.S. Bureau of the Census 1990, 2000.

The arrival and settlement of thousands of recent Mexican and other Latino immigrants left a strong imprint on the urban geography of San Jose. Traditional neighborhoods like the Mayfair District that had served as receiving enclaves for newcomers were severely damaged or destroyed by urban renewal projects. Capitalizing on the international reputation of Silicon Valley as the heart of the high-tech industries, local authorities launched a massive urban redevelopment plan in the 1970s to transform San Jose from an agricultural town to the financial and business capital of Silicon Valley. Their plan included new highways, office buildings, commercial centers, hotels, and other public facilities. These grand projects gradually but irreversibly led to the destruction of some of the oldest traditional Mexican neighborhoods (Rosaldo, Flores, and Silvestrini 1993; Flores 1987). By the early 1970s, for example, Sal Si Puedes, once the most vibrant Mexican neighborhood, had disappeared after most of its houses had been razed as part of urban renewal (Clark 1970: vii; Pellow and Sun-Hee Park 2002: 64).

Simultaneously, new Mexican barrios started to flourish in San Jose on the east side of town, accommodating the large number of Latino immigrants attracted by job opportunities. Among these was the Tropicana neighborhood, a collection of numerous subdivisions made up of modest single-family homes and apartment complexes, which in the 1970s became the major destination for newly arrived Mexican immigrants. Like residents of the Mayfair District in the 1940s and 1950s, residents of the Tropicana neighborhood also suffered from severe problems like substandard housing, deficient social and community services, and poverty. It was in this historical context that the new barrios, mostly made up of apartment complexes, became a symbol of the unequal occupational and income opportunities generated by the area's high-tech industries.

The Demand for Labor Flexibility

Silicon Valley is the most important high-technology industrial district in the world. An industrial district is a spatially located region specializing in the production of certain commodities and characterized by an agglomeration of firms, a shared set of social and cultural norms and sense of identity, and an institutional framework that defines the labor market rules to ensure its stability and reproduction over time (Markusen 1996). Silicon Valley has been characterized as a highly decentralized industrial system integrated by a variety of informal and formal networks, cooperative practices, and institutions that ensure a shared technical culture and fluid diffusion of technological knowledge, upon which the success of the region's economy depends (Saxenian 1994). Thus in the Santa Clara Valley, all the leading industrial sectors are linked with the high-technology industry complex: this complex accounts for 41 percent of total formal employment in the region (Benner 2002: 50). The geographic proximity of the valley's firms facilitates this cooperation, and high-quality educational institutions, venture capitalists, business associations, and service providers also are key parts of the technical infrastructure (Saxenian 1994; Hyde 2003).

From a historical perspective, the development of Silicon Valley took place in several stages. The high-tech economy first developed in the 1950s, when it became the target of federal investment for defense-related projects.[7] Later, in the 1960s, the local economy experienced an important transformation when the technology of the integrated circuit was developed, after which the semiconductor industry became the valley's leading industry. This industry is the oldest and most established in Silicon Valley, and it is one of the region's largest employment sectors.[8] The third phase in the history of the regional economy started in the early 1980s, when companies producing computer systems and their components became prominent and Silicon Valley came to dominate the production of semiconductors for personal computers (Hyde 2003: 13; Benner 2002: 66–69). During this phase, a large proportion of employment in electronics manufacturing was sent offshore to Asia and Mexico, where labor and production costs were considerably lower than anywhere in the United States.[9] The last phase in the development of the regional economy started in the mid-1990s, when software and Internet-related companies became the leading growth sectors. Increased access to the Internet created enormous business opportunities for new companies—the so-called dot-coms—that could provide the necessary software and technology (Hyde 2003: 14; Benner 2002: 63–66). Since the mid-1990s, the industry has been the engine of economic and employment growth in the region. At the beginning of the twenty-first century, however, this sector crashed when many Internet companies went bankrupt, leaving thousands of people unemployed and prompting an even stronger economic recession than the one experienced in the late 1980s with the decline of military-related investment.[10]

The development of the high-tech industrial complex in the Santa Clara Valley radically transformed the political economy in the region. There are four basic elements that define the economic and political framework in which the relations between capital and labor operate here. All these elements are central to understanding the structural context in which the experiences of low-skilled immigrants described in this book are situated. The first factor at the heart of the political economy in Silicon Valley is the continuous demand for labor flexibility. The need for flexible employees has resulted from strong competition in the region's high-tech industries, which depend on constant innovations in developing new products and services.[11] Subcontracting is commonly used in Silicon Valley to enhance labor flexibility and reduce operating costs. Labor subcontracting first started in the 1980s, when high-tech corporations began outsourcing lower-level building services and landscaping operations.[12] In the 1990s, this trend expanded and many manufacturing and administration service jobs were subcontracted; in many cases, contracted employees in the service sector took over jobs previously held by in-house employees (Benner 2002: 43). This explains the fact that, while job opportunities at the major firms in Silicon Valley were stagnant or declined in the 1990s, employment at contract manufacturers grew significantly.[13]

Competition among subcontractors is intense in both the low-skilled-service sector and electronics manufacturing, and the regularity of work at any given firm depends mainly on the employer's ability to obtain and retain production contracts.[14] Subcontractors and other labor intermediaries have radically transformed the contractual relationships between employer and employees regarding salaries, wages, benefits, and types of management practices (Benner 2002: 24). In all cases, subcontracted manufacturing and service workers are legally separated from the client firms that either design the products they make or own the buildings where they work, which prevents them from receiving the same wages and benefits as the employees in those high-tech firms.[15] Subcontracting is at the heart of the problems Mexican immigrant janitors in Silicon Valley face and has shaped their political responses.

A second characteristic of Silicon Valley's political economy is the significant income disparities in the region. The development of the high-tech economy attracted thousands of college-educated engineers, technicians, managers, and other professional workers, but at the same time it generated thousands of new jobs in unskilled, low-wage electronics-assembly and service-related jobs. Until the late 1980s, the result of this dual labor demand was an occupational structure strongly polarized along ethnic lines made up of highly skilled Anglo technical and professional workers, on the one hand, and low-skilled, low-wage minority manufacturing and service workers, on the other.[16] The economic boom of the 1990s created a tremendous number of employment opportunities for both skilled and low-skilled workers in the region, but it did not significantly alter this segmented labor market structure. While the high labor demand in the second half of the decade resulted in high wages for a large number of the region's workforce, most economic benefits went to a minority of highly skilled workers, and as a result, income distribution in Silicon Valley grew more unequal than in the previous decades.[17]

As in the past, economic inequality in the region largely overlapped with ethnic divisions. In 1990, for example, whites made up 81 percent of the managerial workforce and 71 percent of the professional workforce in high-tech employment. By comparison, Latinos made up 7 percent of employment in high-technology industries and constituted 14 percent of the labor force.[18] In the 1990s, Mexican and other Latino immigrants became the principal source for cheap and flexible labor in the low-skilled service sector. Yet rising labor demand was hardly reflected in higher wages, leading these workers to develop a series of individual and collective strategies to advance their interests (see chapter 3).

The third element characteristic of Silicon Valley's political economy is a strong antiunion environment: labor unions in the high-tech sector have traditionally been nonexistent (Saxenian 1994: 55; Hyde 2003: 154; Walker and Bay Area Study Group 1990: 34–35; Benner 1998). Behind this are large electronics corporations resolutely opposed to the development of a unionized labor force that could jeopardize the flexible production model on which they rely.[19] In the early 1990s, however, a notable exception to this trend occurred when janitorial workers who cleaned the office buildings of major high-tech companies in the valley started to organize under the leadership of Local 1877 of the Service

Employees International Union. Even though this group was success-ful, union organizing in the private sector was confined to this segment of the service industry and did not alter the opposition of high-tech companies to union organizing in the electronics industry, the core of the region's economy. In 1993, for example, the employees—many of them immigrant women—of a medium-size electronics company that manufactured personal-computer boards tried to organize into a union following the example of the custodial workers in the region. Soon afterward, the company declared bankruptcy and announced it was shutting down, sending a clear message to the larger community that Silicon Valley would continue being union-free and reassuring other electronics firms that no pro-union precedent would be set (Pellow and Sun-Hee Park 2002: 211).

Finally, the fourth defining characteristic of the industrial district in Silicon Valley is a spatial pattern of residential segregation that mirrors the economic and social inequality of the region. From its inception, the bifurcated occupational structure generated by Silicon Valley's high-tech economy critically shaped the urban geography and settlement pat-terns of workers in the region. AnnaLee Saxenian noted that the region's most affluent professionals and entrepreneurs, for example, settled in western foothill residential communities such as Los Altos, Saratoga, Palo Alto, and Los Gatos, all of which started growing in the 1950s as a result of the influx of scientists and executives who arrived to work in the microelectronics industry. In contrast, upper- and middle-class technical and professional workers settled in rapidly growing sub-urban communities like Cupertino, Mountain View, Sunnyvale, and Santa Clara, and assembly-line workers, craftspeople, and the thousands of unskilled service workers associated with the maintenance of the high-tech-industry complex settled in San Jose's minority neighbor-hoods, where housing remained more affordable (Saxenian 1985: 86, 87). This pattern of residential segregation in the region is still visible today. Wealthy, well-educated whites are clustered in the Palo Alto area and the foothills, while less affluent residents, including Latinos, are concentrated in Mountain View and San Jose (Pellow and Sun-Hee Park 2002: 68). Residential segregation has shaped the neighborhoods where Mexican and other Latino immigrants live and has been the impetus for the growth of poor immigrant barrios like Santech.

Together, all these trends both affect and mediate the experiences of the Mexican immigrant workers portrayed in this book. During the first stage of my fieldwork, in the early 1990s, Silicon Valley was still feeling the effects of the economic recession that had hit the region in the late 1980s when military spending declined after the end of the cold war. This economic recession had a direct and profound impact on the employment opportunities and labor conditions of low-skilled Mexican immigrants. During the second and less intensive phase of my research, in the mid-1990s, economic conditions considerably improved in the region, and this was felt by many of my informants as the supply of jobs increased. Wages, however, remained almost stagnant, unlike the cost of living, which soared throughout the rest of the decade. But while labor flexibility had an unsettling economic effect on many workers and their families in the 1990s, at a another level the rising demand for immigrant labor to fill low-skilled service jobs that could not be sent abroad created new and unexpected economic and political opportunities for Mexican and other Latino immigrants.

Santech: A New Mexican Barrio in San Jose

Santech is one of the numerous low-income immigrant barrios in East San Jose born alongside the economic and demographic explosion of Silicon Valley in the 1960s. Located in the southeast part of San Jose, the barrio is encapsulated in a residential area composed of modest single-family homes and a government project for low-income residents. As shown in Figure 1, the barrio consists of 96 fourplexes and 28 condominiums symmetrically aligned along six streets, four of which are parallel to each other, with the fifth and sixth perpendicular to the rest. All the fourplexes consist of small two-bedroom apartments, each of which contains a living room, a kitchen, one bathroom, and, in the case of the upstairs apartments, a small deck (see Figure 2). The apartment complexes are separated from the government project by a high cement wall that divides the population of mostly first-generation Mexican immigrants and Cambodian refugees in Santech from the second-generation Mexican Americans and Vietnamese residents who live in the housing project.

Since the 1980s the media and city officials alike have stigmatized Santech. For example, in 1985, a local newspaper in the city of San Jose published an article about Santech that described the barrio as a "Silicon Ghetto" plagued by poor housing, social problems, illiteracy, crime, and poverty. It labeled it an "Ellis Island" for Silicon Valley because of its large concentration of poor Latino immigrants and Cambodian refugees

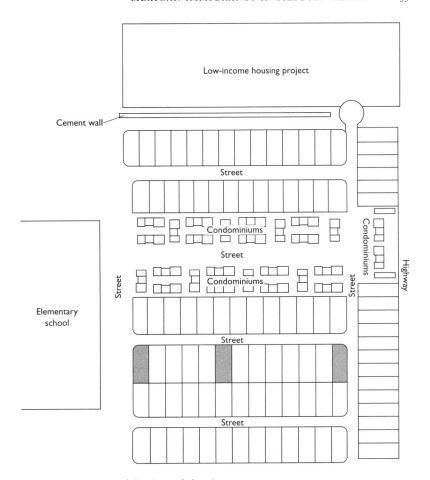

FIGURE I. Layout of the Santech barrio.

who did not speak English and who lived in isolation from the rest of the population. The sudden, unexpected discovery of Santech in the midst of Silicon Valley shocked many readers and prompted the publication of numerous articles in the 1980s and 1990s about this neighborhood. To address the problems in this and other poor immigrant neighborhoods, newspaper stories encouraged local government officials to take a firm stand with slumlords exploiting immigrants who barely spoke English, develop aggressive programs to curtail drugs and crime, and teach local residents the ropes of the American political and cultural system and the value of organizing to improve their own communities. But when and

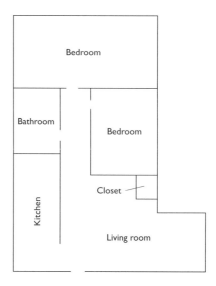

FIGURE 2. Layout of a typical
apartment in Santech.

how did Santech first emerge? Why did Mexican immigrants choose this
"Ellis Island" as an entry to Silicon Valley? And who were the people who
came to live to this neighborhood?

A HISTORY OF NEGLECT

Until the late 1950s, the land on which the barrio stands today was occupied by only a few scattered single-family homes. In the early 1960s,
however, San Jose housing officials rezoned this land for multiple-family
residential use. Shortly afterward, as the single-family homes were
demolished, a private development company began constructing fourplexes. Most of Santech's apartments were built between 1965 and 1971,
just as San Jose was experiencing rapid change and urban growth.

At first, Anglos who moved to San Jose to work in the burgeoning
electronics industry inhabited this neighborhood. By the mid-1970s,
most of the original residents had moved out to more affluent residential neighborhoods, and Santech became a low-income barrio for Mexican immigrants employed in low-paying electronics and service-related
jobs. In the early 1980s, Cambodian and Vietnamese political refugees

began arriving at the barrio in search of affordable housing after the U.S. government chose San Jose as one of the main resettlement sites for Cambodian and Vietnamese political refugees. By the end of the decade, capitalizing on government help and their own social networks, many of the Vietnamese and Cambodian families moved either to other neighborhoods in San Jose or to rural California towns. Then, in the early 1990s, a new wave of immigrant families arrived from Mexico and settled in Santech, representing about 75 percent of the barrio's population; Cambodians and Vietnamese made up about 25 percent.[20]

The most important public institution in Santech is an elementary school. Located at the heart of the barrio, the school has been the center around which much of the social and political life revolves. The history of the school, built in the early 1960s, mirrors that of the rest of the barrio. During the 1960s, white children represented more than half the student body, and Latinos made up less than one-third. In the mid-1970s, following the white flight from the area and the arrival of Mexican immigrant families, the proportion of Mexican children started to grow rapidly, reaching 50 percent by the early 1980s. A decade later, after many of the Cambodian families had moved out, the proportion of Mexican children continued to grow. By the early 1990s, Mexican students made up more than 60 percent of the school's population, with Cambodians making up one-third and whites dropping to less than 2 percent. The Mexicanization of Santech's elementary school reflected the shift toward a larger, settled immigrant population that had been attracted by employment opportunities in Silicon Valley and was made up of young workers with their families.

Shortly after it was built, Santech began suffering from important housing and infrastructure service problems, reflecting neglect by city officials. For many years, the barrio was classified as an "unincorporated" urban tract and received only basic services such as sewage, water, gas, and electricity, but not services reserved for fully incorporated tracts, such as street cleaning and public street lights; these arrived only in the early 1990s. The barrio did not have child-care centers, health clinics, playgrounds for children, parks, and other community services, nor did it have conveniences like food stores, laundries, and shops. Many apartment buildings rapidly deteriorated, making Santech one of the worst-kept areas in town (see Figure 3). Real estate speculation in San Jose, at a time when the demand for housing was growing greatly, contributed to this situation. Most of the apartment buildings were built by a private company, which, although responsible for their maintenance, started to

FIGURE 3. A decaying apartment building in Santech, 1993.

sell them to external buyers in the mid-1970s. The latter, seeking to turn a quick profit, resold them to other investors. By the end of the decade, there were more than seventy different property owners operating the apartments that a few years earlier had been owned and managed by a single company. Housing conditions in Santech continued to deteriorate, and the barrio became a port of entry for low-income, recent immigrants and political refugees who lived with their extended families in overcrowded apartments. The landlords, in exchange for not evicting them, demanded inflated rents without making necessary repairs and investing in the maintenance of their properties.

THE PEOPLE OF SANTECH

The area in which Santech is included contains about 4,050 people: 66 percent are Hispanic, 27 percent Asian, 5 percent white, and 2 percent black.[21] In reality, because this figure includes the residents of Santech and those of the adjacent housing project, the percentage of Mexicans in the barrio is most likely about 75 percent, as many Asian refugees live in the government-subsidized housing project. As in other Latino immigrant neighborhoods, many of Santech residents are young parents with children, composing a much younger group than the rest of

the general population in the city. For example, the average age of Santech residents is only 23.6 years, compared to 32.6 years in San Jose and
34 years in Santa Clara County; about 35 percent of the barrio's inhabitants are 18 years old or younger (U.S. Bureau of the Census 2000). In
addition, most people in Santech live in overcrowded conditions with
extended families and boarders, a factor that contributes to the barrio's
high population density. According to census data, there are five people
per household in Santech, compared to an average of about three people per household in San Jose and Santa Clara County (3.20 and 2.92
persons per household, respectively). Official statistics however tend to
underestimate the number of people per household in low-income
immigrant neighborhoods, including in other Mexican barrios in San
Jose (Dohan 2003: 233). According to a nonrepresentative ethnographic
survey I conducted of twenty-five households in the barrio, the average
household was composed of 7.7 members, and commonly ten to fifteen
people lived together in a two-bedroom apartment.[22]

Santech is also included among the neighborhoods with the highest
rates of poverty in San Jose. According to census data, about 30 percent
of the residents in the area where the barrio is located live below the
poverty line, compared to only 9 percent in San Jose and 7.5 percent in
the Santa Clara Valley. More revealing are the figures regarding average
personal income. Per capita income for people living in this area is only
about $9,000, compared to about $27,000 in San Jose, and $32,800 in
Santa Clara County (U.S. Bureau of the Census 2000). Because official
statistics generally undercount the number of people per household in
immigrant neighborhoods like Santech, the former figure overestimates
per capita income in the barrio. Among the twenty-five households
included in my survey of Santech, for example, per capita income was
only $4,696 in 1993 (Zlolniski, with Palerm 1996: 67).

The origins and educational backgrounds of the residents of Santech
are far from homogeneous, challenging simplified notions about Mexican communities made up of uneducated immigrants from rural areas.
The majority of Mexican immigrants in Santech come from traditional
migrant-sending regions like Michoacán, Guanajuato, Jalisco, and
Zacatecas. Although many migrated from rural parts of these regions,
others come from cities in these and other states, including Mexico
City, Guadalajara, Veracruz, Acapulco, and Ensenada, where they
worked in factory and service jobs. While many have completed only
elementary school, especially those who grew up on ranches in rural
areas, many others, especially younger immigrants, tend to be better

educated, having completed secondary education, the equivalent to high school in the United States. Still others are immigrants with professional and technical degrees, including schoolteachers, accountants, agronomists, nurses, white-collar office workers, and other professionals who, escaping the economic crises and currency devaluations in Mexico in the 1980s and mid-1990s, decided to try their luck north of the border.

The immigrant status of the members of many Latino urban immigrant neighborhoods in California tends to be heterogeneous (Dohan 2003; Hondagneu-Sotelo 1994; Menjívar 2000; Chávez 1992: 131), and the same is true of Santech. The issue of individuals' legal status often surfaced in our conversations or when those I interviewed asked me about the prospect of legalizing their status. The majority of adults I met in the neighborhood were undocumented immigrants; many others were legal immigrants who obtained this status after qualifying for the Immigration Reform and Control Act's amnesty program of 1986.[23] A few residents were naturalized U.S. citizens who, after five or more years of legal residency, had opted to become citizens. Others, especially young children, were natural U.S. citizens by virtue of having been born in this country after their parents migrated from Mexico. Because of this, the immigrant status of members of the same family often differed. An extended family frequently included undocumented immigrants, legal residents, U.S.-born and naturalized citizens, and children who, despite having spent most of their lives in the United States, were still undocumented immigrants because they were born in Mexico.

Regardless of their place of origin, educational background, labor experience, and immigrant status, most Mexican immigrants in Santech are employed in low-skilled jobs in Silicon Valley. For example, among the twenty-five households I surveyed, sixty-two people worked in low-wage jobs. Twenty-three of them were employed as janitors, by far the most common occupation among Mexicans in Santech. Nine workers, all of them women, were employed as electronics assemblers, and seven men in landscape maintenance. The rest worked in restaurants, construction, car washes, furniture stores, supermarkets, schools, and elder-care facilities, and a few women worked in the only cannery left in town. Most of these jobs are segmented along gender lines. Men are generally employed in janitorial, landscaping, and construction jobs, often under subcontracting arrangements, and women are usually hired to work in electronics assembly plants, canneries, and elder-care facilities or as janitors, house cleaners, or baby-sitters.

Many Santech residents also hold jobs in the informal economy—that is, jobs not reflected in official statistics and that escape regulation (Castells and Portes 1989). Informal economic activities are common in low-income Latino immigrant neighborhoods (López-Garza 2001; Hondagneu-Sotelo 1994; Dohan 2003). For example, women work as house cleaners, baby-sitters, and elder-care providers, and their employers pay them in cash to reduce labor expenses by avoiding paying taxes on these workers. Men often work in informal occupations to supplement income they earn in formal wage-jobs like building-cleaning and landscaping. Many of these informal activities are connected to the low-skilled maintenance sector of Silicon Valley's economy, of which they are an intrinsic part (see chapter 3).

Whether employed in formal or informal jobs, most Mexican workers in Santech earn minimum hourly wages or slightly above, depending on their occupation. By the mid-1990s, for example, those employed as janitors made between $4.25 and $6.25 an hour, depending on whether they worked for a union or nonunion company. In turn, women employed as electronics assemblers usually earned wages only slightly above minimum wage, as none of the firms in the electronics industry employed union workers. Women employed in elder care in the formal economy were also paid minimum wage and received no benefits when working part-time, while those who worked in the informal sector were often paid less than the minimum wage. Equally important, many of the jobs held by Santech residents are highly instable. This is especially true of janitorial, landscaping, and other service-related jobs, which can be transferred from one private contractor to another. As a result, many of the immigrant workers I met in Santech changed jobs several times a year, whenever they were laid off after their employers lost contracts with client companies. These changes, consequences of the pattern of poorly paid, flexible employment of Mexican immigrants, have a negative and destablizing effect on the budgets of these workers and their dependent families.

In many poor neighborhoods in San Jose and elsewhere in California, drug trafficking and other illicit activities are common (Dohan 2003), and the same is true in Santech. Drug-related crimes increased notably in the late 1980s as elsewhere in San Jose, a trend commonly associated with economic restructuring, poverty, and the subsistence strategies of low-income people in the underground informal economy (Moore and Pinderhughes 1993: xxviii). According to police and city officials, most people in Santech who sell drugs on the streets are small-scale dealers attracted to the barrio by its high transient rate, which makes tracking by residents and the police difficult. In other cases, members of households in the barrio sell drugs in small quantities for a profit.[24] While most residents I met in Santech were not involved in the drug-dealing business either as sellers or buyers, the pervasiveness of drug traffickers in the neighborhood has long been an important reason why many families move to safer neighborhoods when they can afford it, which contributes to further turnover in the barrio. There are also a few gangs in Santech. Gang fights occasionally break out between a Santech gang and a rival gang from the housing project next door. While, according to police authorities, fighting to control their respective territories for drug distribution is the most important reason for gang confrontations, tensions are also triggered by an open antagonism between Santech residents and those of the contiguous housing project. Some Mexican American residents of the housing project blame their neighbors in Santech for trespassing on their property and using the laundry rooms, green areas, and children's playgrounds, and others look down on Santech residents for being undocumented immigrants who invade the neighborhood and live in overcrowded, run-down apartments. In turn, some Santech residents refer to the people living in the projects as "lazy" people who prefer living off welfare instead of relying on a paycheck. Although this antagonism is not widespread among the residents of the two areas, there is an open rivalry between the gangs, who jealously keep an eye on their respective territories. This reflects the competition for scarce public resources between low-income Mexican Americans and Mexican immigrants living in the two areas.

DAILY LIFE IN THE BARRIO

Despite all the problems that come from living in a poor neighborhood like Santech, from the beginning I was surprised by the vibrant economic, social, and community life I encountered here. The everyday lives of the residents I met in this community reflect the multiple connections that link them with economic and political institutions and organizations in the broader Silicon Valley region, while the rhythm of daily life in Santech closely follows the work routines in which most of their residents are engaged. The following briefly describes the most common activities I observed on weekdays in Santech and the mixture of work, social, and community activities in the barrio.

Early on summer mornings, between 6:30 and 8:00, many residents leave for work in old, secondhand cars. Meanwhile, a few elderly Mexican and Cambodian men comb the parking lots and sort through garbage containers, looking for aluminum cans, glass bottles, metal pieces, and other materials to recycle for cash, getting a head start on outside competitors and trash collectors. Later in the morning, dozens of children come out of the apartments and hurry on their way to school, after which the streets of Santech turn quiet. In the meantime, women sweep the courtyards and stairs of their apartments and do other household chores, like cleaning and cooking, leaving windows and doors wide open to cool down the apartments.

As morning gives way to noon, the streets of Santech come alive again. Street vendors arrive peddling tortillas, vegetables, fruit, cheese, clothes, and a large variety of other products door-to-door. Others station their vans and pickups in front of apartment buildings and honk their horns, signaling clients to come down. Many women, after finishing part of their household chores, go shopping at the nearest supermarket, about a mile and a half from Santech. Some take the bus, others walk, and a few use their own cars. In the early afternoon, children begin returning home from school, and frozen-fruit-pop vendors gather along the streets trying to get their attention and business. By midafternoon, the first group of men and women return home from work, many still wearing their work uniforms.

In the early evening, the streets in Santech become animated once again when children come out of the apartments to play with their friends on the sidewalks, in alleys, and in courtyards, and teenagers gather on street corners and in parking lots to chat (see Figure 4). After dinner, some of the adult men gather in front of their apartments to talk and have a beer with their buddies while listening to Mexican music played by any of the numerous local radio stations in town. Some women visit their friends, others gather outside their apartments to keep an eye on their children playing in the streets, and still others stay indoors to watch their favorite Spanish TV soap operas.

Later in the evening, life in Santech picks up further when dozen of street vendors arrive to the barrio selling beauty products, cookware, jewelry, decorative household objects, insurance policies, pirated tapes, and other merchandise, giving the streets the appearance of an impromptu flea market. Meanwhile, residents who work the night-shift janitorial jobs have an early dinner and prepare the "lunch" they will eat at work on one of their breaks later that night. Some residents, especially women, attend community meetings organized by any of the several organizations and groups active in the barrio. A group of young missionaries from a Protestant congregation, dressed in suits, may come

FIGURE 4. Santech residents socializing.

to visit local residents and families they know, and to knock on the doors of other neighbors in search of new converts. In the midst of this busy time, the sound of TVs, radios, and boom boxes fills the air and the smell of food being prepared for dinner wafts out of the apartments.

As the sun sets, the pace of life in Santech slows down. Children return home and street vendors begin leaving the area. After dark, families lock themselves inside their apartments, some using sticks in the windows and chain locks on the main doors because door locks are either broken or missing. This is the time when, according to residents, much of the drug trafficking occurs in the backyards and parking lots. Police cars redouble their patrols along the streets and in parking lots in search of drug dealers, the well-maintained police cars offering a sharp contrast to Santech residents' old cars. Late at night, around three in the morning, the last wave of workers employed as janitors returns home visibly tired, after which the barrio remains quiet far a few hours.

COMMUNITY GROUPS

Residents of this barrio are also active in a wide variety of local community organizations and groups. Many participate in, for example, programs and community groups run by city government agencies, most of which first started in the early 1990s. One of the most popular government programs is Project Crackdown, an ambitious housing and neighborhood rehabilitation plan that addresses problems of housing, drugs, gangs, and crime in this and similar poor neighborhoods. Government workers actively recruit Mexican and other immigrants to participate in this project and help promote community action and a sense of pride in Santech. Another popular government program is Migrant Education, which provides educational assistance to children whose parents are or have been involved in agricultural work, and classes for parents to help them adjust to life in the United States.

Many Santech residents prefer to participate in nonprofit local organizations, some of which have goals similar to those of government-sponsored projects but use different means to accomplish them. The most influential of these is People Acting in Community Together, a multiethnic grassroots organization that, reflecting the legacy of community activism left by Mexican American organizations like Community Service Organization (Pitti 2003: 149–65), works to promote community organization and political mobilization among the peoples of working-class and minority neighborhoods in San Jose. People Acting in Community Together is one of the most important groups through which the residents of Santech expressed political and civil rights claims (see chapter 5). A third type of organization found in Santech consists of grassroots groups solely formed by local residents. Unlike the neighborhood groups put together by city officials and nonprofit organizations, these grassroots groups are the product of local residents themselves who get together to address their concerns. During the period of my fieldwork, Mexican residents in Santech organized to demand bilingual teachers in the local elementary school, protest against abusive landlords, complain about police abuse, and tackle other important issues. Women, especially working mothers, are usually the organizers and leaders of these groups. Unlike the first two types of community organizations, these grassroots groups are more difficult to identify and often remain invisible to government officials and outsiders alike. Yet, they play a central role in the political life of the community and are effective in mobilizing residents whenever an important occasion arises.

Not all people in Santech participate in grassroots activities, and in fact, only a few are engaged in any community groups. Moreover, some prefer to get involved in clubs and organizations formed by immigrants who share the same community of origin in Mexico, groups that sponsor social and sports events in San Jose to recreate their community ties and cultural traditions, a well-established tradition among Mexicans in the Santa Clara Valley (Pitti 2003). For example, some young Mexican workers I met in Santech who came from Nueva Italia—a town located in the Tierra Caliente region of central Michoacán in Western Mexico— had little contact with community activities and groups in the barrio. Instead they were actively involved in a local club composed of immigrants from their native town that sponsors a soccer team and organizes dance parties and other social activities in San Jose, and that maintains ties with the home community in Mexico. While only a few of the local residents I met in Santech were involved in this type of transnational organization, they represent yet another important facet of community life that transcends the spatial and social boundaries of this particular neighborhood, contradicting its characterization as a self-contained, isolated, and disconnected immigrant community in Silicon Valley.

In short, Santech is not a "silicon ghetto" of Third World immigrants with little education disconnected from Silicon Valley's economy, but is the result of a dramatic transformation of the Santa Clara Valley from agricultural center to high-tech industrial center. Contrary to common perception, the high-tech industrialization of the area did not lead to a decline in jobs for Mexican immigrants, but rather to a rising demand for Mexican immigrant labor to fill the thousands of low-skilled jobs generated in the electronics manufacturing and the service maintenance sectors. This structural economic transformation, along with urban renewal policies aimed at transforming San Jose into the "capital of Silicon Valley," destroyed old, traditional Mexican neighborhoods while giving rise to new Latino barrios for recent immigrants.

The political and economic forces that characterize Silicon Valley's industrial district both penetrate and are reflected in the lives of the people in Santech. Most Mexican immigrants in the barrio maintain a strong connection to the array of very low-paid service jobs that, according to government statistics, has proliferated at a rapid pace in the region since the 1980s. Unsurprisingly, many Santech residents are employed in low-wage jobs in janitorial, landscaping, electronics assembly, restaurant, personal services, and other occupations—often through subcontracting and other flexible employment arrangements— that link them to high-tech firms at the core of Silicon Valley's industrial district. At the same time, the existence of informal economic activities in the barrio reveals the creative adaptive strategies that many of its residents develop to deal with the consequences of low-paid and flexible employment. Thus the transition to a high-tech industrial economy did not break, but rather accelerated, the demand for Mexican immigrant labor, opening up new economic opportunities for recent immigrants. This transition also helped transform the inhabitants of Santech and similar immigrant neighborhoods in San Jose into the core of its working-poor population, all in a structural context of increasing economic and ethnic inequality, in which Latino immigrants are relegated to the bottom.

Despite poverty and Santech's troubled history, the residents of this barrio do not live in a social and political void. Instead, they have developed effective forms of community activism to confront the numerous problems that affect them and their families. Although community organizing among Mexican immigrants in the Santa Clara Valley is not new, the community groups and organizations formed by Santech neighbors illustrate the novel forms of collective political action that Mexican and other Latino immigrants in the region have developed in the recent past (Benner 2000; Martínez Saldaña 1993; Pitti 2003).

CHAPTER 2

The Subcontracting of Mexican Janitors in the High-Tech Industry

It is early afternoon on a sunny, hot summer weekday in 1992. Luis and his roommates are watching a rented movie on their VCR, comfortably seated on two sofas in the living room in the two-bedroom apartment they rent in Santech. A stereo with two big speakers and a bookcase with a few CDs complete the furniture of the living room. Born in Nueva Italia, a town in central Michoacán in Mexico, Luis is in his midtwenties and loves all kinds of technological gadgets like video and photo cameras and VCRs. His biggest passion, though, is soccer. An amateur player in Nueva Italia, he founded a soccer team shortly after arriving in San Jose in 1988, made up of friends and other immigrants from Michoacán, that competes in local tournaments in the region.

Around 4 P.M., Luis and one of his roommates go to the kitchen to fix lunch, as there is an agreement among the six who share the apartment that every day two of them will take turns cooking for the others. For the next forty minutes, they labor in the kitchen while joking and teasing each other. Today, they will have *caldereta*, a traditional Michoacán dish Luis learned from his mother that consists of ground beans and rice. When the food is ready, they all come to the kitchen, serve themselves, and start eating. They eat fast, as they have only forty minutes before going to work. When Luis finishes, he takes a quick shower and goes to his room to get dressed. When he comes out, he is wearing his usual work clothes: gray trousers, black tennis shoes, and a blue T-shirt. The shirt is worn, has a small hole on the left shoulder, and, on the left upper corner, his employer's name—Bay-Clean—is sewn on with black thread. Close to 6 P.M., Luis walks downstairs, goes to the parking lot where his car is parked, and warms the engine until his roommates join him. Leaving the parking lot, they cruise down a couple of Santech streets and then take a three-lane avenue that, after about a mile, puts them on the northbound freeway.

After about twenty-five minutes, Luis and his roommates arrive in the city of Cupertino and enter the big parking lot of a large, modern office complex. The five-building complex belongs to Sonix, one of the largest and most respected multinational electronics corporations in Silicon Valley. At this time, the parking lot is empty except for a few cars belonging to Sonix employees working late and those of the security officers in charge of patrolling the buildings. In a few minutes, dozens of cars full of Mexican workers arrive at the parking lot, all of them wearing blue Bay-Clean shirts like Luis'. Among them is Anselmo, a twenty-three-year-old native from the state of Veracruz who lives in San Jose's Tropicana neighborhood. Unlike Luis, Anselmo is more of a private person who prefers hanging out with close friends rather than engaging in big social events. He has a keen sense of humor and is very much liked by many of his coworkers. Shortly afterward, Don Manuel, as most of his friends call him, arrives. A tall, thin, half-bald man, Manuel comes from Guadalajara in the western state of Jalisco, where he worked as a taxi driver before migrating to California. In his midforties, Manuel is considerably older than the rest of his friends, some of whom like to tease him by calling him *tío* (uncle.)

Coming from different regions in Mexico, and with different educational backgrounds and work experience, Luis and his roommates, Anselmo, and Don Manuel nonetheless have something in common: they are part of a crew of about 325 janitors who clean the Sonix office buildings. None are Sonix employees; instead, they are employed by Bay-Clean, one of thirteen janitorial companies subcontracted by Sonix to clean the dozen or so buildings this multinational corporation owns in Silicon Valley. They are part of the estimated 12,000 janitors who work in the Santa Clara Valley alone, a large but mostly invisible army of janitors who, night after night, clean millions of square feet of research and development, office, industrial, commercial, and retail building space (State of California, Employment Development Department 1998).

When I first arrived in Silicon Valley, I was surprised by the high number of Mexican immigrants who worked as janitors. Some clean the buildings of high-tech companies in the northern part of the region, others the business offices and public buildings in downtown San Jose, and still others the small offices, corner markets, supermarkets, and other private businesses, all employed by any of the hundreds of small contractors that proliferate in the region. The first group, those cleaning the offices of high-tech corporations, offered an excellent opportunity to examine firsthand the paradox of the most technologically advanced companies relying on recent immigrants to perform low-skilled service jobs. Unlike assembly jobs in the electronics industry, cleaning jobs in Silicon Valley could not be sent abroad but only contracted out to local independent firms. I was interested in finding out how management used subcontracting to enhance labor flexibility, and in how this labor system affected work relations.

I was also interested in understanding why immigrant janitors in Silicon Valley were struggling to unionize, and what it was like for undocumented workers to get involved in this form of political activity. While recent studies of union organizing by immigrants help us understand the structural conditions under which such forms of collective resistance take place (Milkman, ed., 2000; Wells 1996), they provide little inside information about how immigrants themselves experience this process, what motivates them to engage in this particular form of political action despite their precarious financial and political status, and what they expect from the unions they join. To understand why and how these workers organized, we must go beyond a top-down approach that privileges labor unions' political strategies and instead examine how the workers' view of dignity and respect in the workplace shaped their political actions.[1]

Subcontracting and the Union's Response in the Building-Cleaning Industry

Few service sectors illustrate better the relationship between the development of the high-tech industry and the growth of low-skilled jobs that depend on immigrant workers than the building-cleaning industry. The rapid expansion of electronics plants and research and development facilities, and the overall economic development fueled by the high-tech industry, generated a strong demand for janitorial workers. Between 1965 and 1990, for example, the demand for janitors in the Santa Clara Valley grew fivefold (Mines and Avina 1992: 441). By 1995, there were an estimated 12,110 janitorial workers in the region, almost matching in number the 12,690 computer engineers working in Santa Clara County.[2]

But the concentration of Mexican immigrants in the building-cleaning industry in Silicon Valley was also the result of a major restructuring process. Up until the mid-1970s, workers employed as janitors in Silicon Valley's private sector fell under two main categories: in-house custodial workers, who were employed directly by the high-tech companies for whom they performed their services; and contract janitors, who were employed by independent janitorial firms. In-house janitors, who generally were not unionized, usually earned between $7.00 and $10.00 an hour, with benefits such as health insurance and sick leave similar to those provided to other low-skilled and semiskilled employees in high-tech companies. Labor conditions for contract janitors were not as good as those experienced by their in-house counterparts, but given that the industry was highly unionized, they were comparable to those in other unskilled or semiskilled occupations in the region. Wages for unionized janitors ranged between $5.00 and $7.50, and workers received ample fringe benefits, including health care, sick leave, paid holidays, and pension benefits (Zlolniski 2001). At the time, janitorial employment was an entry-level job for minority and immigrant workers, including Chicanos, Filipinos, Portuguese, and Mexican immigrants.[3]

In the late 1970s and increasingly throughout the 1980s—in the midst of an economic recession—high-tech companies and building owners sought to reduce operating and maintenance costs by contracting with nonunion independent firms that relied on cheap labor, mainly that of undocumented Mexican immigrants. This restructuring process was facilitated by nonunion firms' ability to use immigrants' social networks to recruit newly arrived immigrant workers, and by the lack of natural skill barriers that could have prevented the replacement of experienced custodial workers by recent immigrants without previous experience in this occupation.[4] Former in-house janitors were given early retirement packages, moved to other maintenance positions, or simply laid off. The restructuring of janitorial work lead to a sharp decline of wages and labor benefits for workers employed in the private sector.[5] By 1985, nonunion contractors were paying between minimum wage and $5.00 an hour, while wages mandated by the union contract ranged between $5.12 and $7.96 with ample benefits (Mines and Avina 1992: 442). Such differences were an incentive for many high-tech companies to shift from in-house to nonunion contract janitors. The group of settled immigrant workers who formed most of the workforce for unionized janitorial firms and held most of the in-house cleaning jobs experienced wage-depression and labor displacement by recent immigrants. Some of these janitors eventually become self-employed independent contractors, often upon request by the client companies that formerly employed them. Others were hired as supervisors by nonunion firms because of their experience, and others were retired in advance or left unemployed.[6]

By the late 1980s, the building-cleaning industry in Silicon Valley had been radically transformed into a labor niche for recent Mexican and Central American immigrants. In the early 1990s, more than 70 percent of janitors working for private contractors in Silicon Valley were Hispanic, and about 60 percent of them were foreign, non-U.S. citizens (Zlolniski 2001: 271). Moreover, 46 percent of contract janitors in the region were Mexican immigrants and 12 percent Central Americans; 44 percent of all immigrant janitors employed in Silicon Valley had arrived in the 1980s (Zlolniski 2001: 272). By then the annual income of janitors in the private sector was just above $12,000, compared to almost $20,000 for custodial workers employed in the public sector (Zlolniski 2001: 272).

In response to these developments, in the late 1980s the local union that represents janitorial workers in Silicon Valley—Local 1877—launched a campaign to organize workers who cleaned the buildings of large high-tech companies in the region.[7] This was part of a wider "Justice for Janitors" campaign organized by the Service Employees International Union to organize immigrants and other low-wage workers in major U.S. cities in order to press big buildings' owners to employ unionized janitorial contractors rather than nonunionized cleaning firms.[8] In Silicon Valley, the Justice for Janitors campaign focused on reaching out to immigrant workers.[9] In addition, to accomplish its goal, Local 1877 used innovative and confrontational tactics, including corporate campaigns, consumer boycotts, grassroots organizing, and coalition building. By the early 1990s the campaign had made important inroads, organizing thousands of immigrants employed as janitors in Silicon Valley, especially those subcontracted by the largest high-tech companies. Despite this success, Local 1877 was not able to bring wages back to what they were before the industry was restructured in the 1980s (Johnston 1994: 169).

Mexican Janitors at Sonix

Luis first arrived in Silicon Valley in 1988, unaware of all these structural developments. Before migrating to the United States, he had never heard of janitorial work. He believed he would be a farmworker like his older brother, who had migrated to the United States before him, or a restaurant worker like many of his friends from his hometown in Michoacán. But after his arrival in San Jose, Luis worked as a janitor. He worked first for Atlantis Maintenance, a large janitorial firm cleaning the buildings of a giant international pharmaceutical company headquartered in Silicon Valley. Two years later he was laid off, and through a friend he found another cleaning job, at Bay-Clean, one of the numerous cleaning companies contracted by Sonix. At Bay-Clean, Luis was hired as a "utility worker," a position one level above that of entry-level janitors. As a utility worker, he was in charge of waxing floors, shampooing carpets, stripping and buffing floors, cleaning windows, and other "special" tasks, for which he earned about $.75 more per hour than a regular janitor. The duties of rank-and-file janitors like Anselmo, Don Manuel, and others included emptying trash cans from all offices; vacuuming carpets; cleaning restrooms; sweeping and mopping floors; dusting desks, chairs, bookcases, and other office furniture; and cleaning and setting up conference rooms. They were also in charge of cleaning all meeting rooms, halls, elevators, stairs, lunch rooms, cafeterias, and kitchens in the various Sonix buildings where they worked.

Like many other high-tech corporations in Silicon Valley, Sonix had employed its own in-house custodial workers for several decades. This abruptly changed in 1989 when, to reduce costs, the company started replacing them with subcontracted janitors furnished by independent contractors. To Sonix, outsourcing cleaning and other maintenance operations was but one more step along the path of decentralization that had begun in the 1970s, when it, like many other corporations in Silicon Valley, started sending manufacturing operations abroad (Hossfeld 1990). In-house custodial workers at Sonix were given the option of either being trained to work in shipping and receiving or being given a compensation package with an early-retirement plan. The company's incentive to use subcontractors was obvious: while in-house custodial workers earned an average of $10.00 an hour plus insurance and received a generous benefit package, subcontracted janitors at Bay-Clean were paid an average of $5.50 an hour and received no health insurance or any other benefits. Moreover, according to Sonix's managers, outsourcing considerably reduced administrative costs: the maintenance cost of in-house cleaning workers was $1.15 per square foot in 1989; independent contractors offered to do the job for as little as $.06 cents per square foot. By the early 1990s, Sonix had contracts with more than a dozen independent nonunionized cleaning firms, mostly small- and medium-size companies that relied almost exclusively on Mexican immigrant workers like those employed by Bay-Clean.

But at Sonix, the replacement of in-house janitors by subcontracted workers was not based on economic reasons alone: the company also saw it as an opportunity to enhance the flexibility of custodial labor itself. Sonix considered small, nonunion companies without a complex bureaucratic structure to be the ideal vehicles to accomplish this goal. According to the Sonix managers I interviewed, small- and medium-size contractors offered two important advantages. First, the maintenance managers of each Sonix building had the option of selecting their own janitorial contractor, which was in line with the decentralized organizational culture that characterized this company. Second, the owners of these cleaning companies often had direct control over their workers, without the thick managerial structure of large cleaning firms, making it easier for Sonix managers to work in close contact with them. Bay-Clean, for example, employed 275 workers, who constituted a thin layer of managers, most of them Koreans, and a large base of workers, most of them Mexican and Central American immigrants and a few Koreans. In most of Sonix's buildings, Bay-Clean maintained one manager and one or two shop-floor supervisors who acted as intermediaries between Sonix maintenance managers and the janitors. On the shop floor, however, Sonix managers worked hand-in-hand with the principal managers of Bay-Clean, to whom they transmitted their requests, while supervisors were in charge of implementing their orders and overseeing janitors' work routines. When I interviewed an upper-level Sonix manager, he summarized the advantages of the arrangement in this way:

> We prefer working with small janitorial companies because they allow for more flexibility and better service, as for example when we request a non-scheduled service and have janitors respond promptly. . . . They are managed by their own boss, who normally is on the site, which makes communication between these companies and us very easy, and which leads to a very good service. . . . The better the relationship between Sonix and these companies' owners, the better the quality of the service and the lower the cost. . . . [In short,] with these companies we had instant service.

Sonix managers also valued Mexican immigrants because they viewed them as highly motivated workers. They especially appreciated Mexican janitors' willingness to change their work routines whenever they were asked to do so, their readiness to work overtime even with short notice, and their ability to send relatives or friends to substitute for them at work whenever they were sick or after they quit their jobs. From the Sonix managers' perspective, Mexican janitors' social practices and customs were not obstacles to developing a homogeneous, disciplined, and well-trained custodial workforce. Rather, they were regarded as some of the most valuable assets janitors brought to the workplace and, if wisely used, could enhance labor flexibility and productivity.

Despite shifting to a subcontracting system, Sonix management still maintained a great deal of control over the organization of janitorial work and the daily activities of the workers employed by Bay-Clean and other small cleaning companies. This was done by, among other means, placing some of Sonix's former in-house janitors in supervisory positions, especially those who were fluent in Spanish, to serve as intermediaries between the new workers and Sonix management. Mario, a Mexican employee in his thirties who had been born in Mexico and raised in the United States and who was fluent in both English and Spanish, held one such position. After Sonix laid off most of its in-house custodial workers, Mario was promoted first to the position of maintenance supervisor and then to assistant manager. Sonix's top maintenance manager regarded him as a valuable asset not only because of his language skills but also because of his knowledge about the Mexican janitors, including the regions they migrated from, how they found jobs, where they obtained fake green cards in order to work, and even where and with whom they lived in San Jose. In short, Mario's role at Sonix was that of an ethnic broker unhampered by "language and cultural barriers," in the words of Sonix's manager, who helped the company develop and tailor training methods and work plans for Mexican janitors.

Subcontracting also allowed Sonix to delegate the legal responsibility for determining the labor conditions of, and the immigration status of, janitorial workers to its contractors, an important factor after the passage of the Immigration Reform and Control Act in 1986, which threatened sanctions against employers of undocumented workers. Three Sonix managers whom I interviewed estimated that about 80 percent of the janitors employed by its cleaning contractors were undocumented immigrants. In their opinion, the solution was to legalize their immigration status and pay them higher wages, allowing a legal and more stable workforce that would diminish the high employment turnover among workers. Yet they saw the wages and labor conditions of janitors as the sole responsibility of the companies that directly employed them, not the legal or moral responsibility of Sonix. In short, subcontracting allowed Sonix access to a reliable source of abundant, cheap Mexican immigrant labor without the financial costs and legal risks of directly employing them, and permitted the corporation to retain a great deal of control over the subcontracted janitors and their activities in the workplace.

JANITORS' VIEWS ON BAY-CLEAN

Unlike Sonix's managers, who had a positive view of the subcontracting arrangement with Bay-Clean, the janitors employed by this company had a negative opinion of their employer. Most Mexican janitors with whom I talked were angry about the working conditions and their supervisors. They complained about their low and stagnant wages; many of them had been working for this company for several years without a wage increase. For example, Luis, who had been working for Bay-Clean for more than two years, had not seen a wage increase, nor did he envision seeing one any time soon. Workers were also upset by the fact that the paychecks they received every ten days often bounced, and that they had to wait several days before cashing them, which threw their otherwise precarious budgets out of balance.[10] Others resented not having employment benefits: Bay-Clean workers did not have health insurance or any other benefits, as this was a nonunionized cleaning company. This made janitors like Don Manuel, who lived with their wives and children in San Jose, feel especially vulnerable.

Many of the Bay-Clean janitors also openly expressed their dissatisfaction about the poor working conditions they had to endure. They complained about inadequate equipment and cleaning supplies and the fact that they were required by their supervisors to scrimp on cleaning supplies such as paper, chemicals, and plastic bags to help the company keep expenses down. For example, Anselmo explained to me that in his building, instead of regular towel paper used in janitorial work to dry tables, sink, and other surfaces, he and his work crew were given napkins that Bay-Clean regularly took from the Sonix cafeteria run by an independent vendor. In other cases, workers themselves were instructed by their supervisors to take the napkins and risked being caught by Sonix's security officers, who routinely patrolled the buildings. Whenever I asked why they would not just ask for additional cleaning supplies, Anselmo and other workers told me they were afraid of doing so because their supervisors would angrily respond that they spent too much and the company needed to reduce expenses. Anselmo commented, "They [supervisors] keep demanding that we work harder and faster, but they do not give us the materials to do it. They want us to clean with only water and expect that everything shine!"

Janitors at Bay-Clean were also upset about the poor condition of the uniforms they had to wear at work. Upon being hired, each janitor was given one shirt, most often a used one, and was responsible for washing it. Some workers felt ashamed wearing shirts in poor condition, because they believed this projected a poor and humble image of themselves and their employer to the white-collar Sonix employees who worked at night. Frustrated, some would tear up their worn shirts hoping to get new ones, only to find that the shirts they received as replacements were also used and, in some cases, in even worse shape than the originals.

But the one factor that consistently came up in my conversations with Bay-Clean janitors, and that seemed to upset them the most, was the lack of respect with which their supervisors treated them. The janitors angrily complained about insults, threats, unfair treatment, and the general contempt with which they were treated and interpreted it as a direct assault on their personal dignity. Luis considered this lack of respect to be an open form of racial discrimination by their Korean supervisors. Others complained that Bay-Clean supervisors favored Korean employees by using a double standard that assigned Mexican workers the hardest chores, such as cleaning the kitchens and bathrooms, while giving the few Korean janitors the lightest and easiest tasks. They also protested that, whereas Korean workers were often promoted to supervisor after a few months of employment, Mexicans never reached that position, a situation they found especially offensive. The common feeling of being discriminated against because of their ethnicity was captured in a comment by Jesús, a young worker employed by Bay-Clean: "When a Korean janitor is first hired, they pay him $6 an hour; but if the new worker is Mexican, he only gets $5. I do not have conclusive proof, but we know this is the case. Moreover, supervisors don't check the areas and work of the Koreans, but they always check ours, and Koreans always get smaller areas than we do."

Many of the Mexican workers thus interpreted the harsh working conditions they experienced in this company as an issue of racial discrimination. Luis, for example, was convinced that Koreans used racial solidarity to protect and benefit themselves while discriminating against Mexican janitors.[11] What seemed to infuriate Mexican workers was that racism was being perpetrated against them not by American employers but by Korean immigrants, who, in their view, should not feel entitled to more rights than Mexicans. In one of the numerous conversations I had with Anselmo, he commented, "After all, they [Koreans] are also immigrants who are invading here [the United States] like us, and they want to step on us. . . . It is one thing to be exploited by the country's own people, and quite other to be exploited by other immigrants. . . . That is too much!"

The workers' negative feelings about Bay-Clean contrasted sharply with the positive opinion they had of Sonix. Neither the poor labor conditions nor material conditions at work were, in their minds, attributable to Sonix. For one thing, they considered Sonix managers to be more humane and respectful than their direct supervisors at Bay-Clean. Because of this, some workers would seek to cultivate personal relationships with Sonix managers in their buildings so they could seek their support in the event they had serious problems with their supervisors. In fact, most workers I interviewed at Bay-Clean considered their poor wages, lack of benefits, and overall harsh working conditions as the sole responsibility of Bay-Clean, and they channeled their anger correspondingly. According to Don Manuel, for example, Bay-Clean's usual shortage of supplies, old and deteriorated cleaning equipment, and lack of a clear and transparent policy regarding wage raises, promotions, and the distribution of workloads were all clear indicators of this company's "poor, unprofessional management." To him, it was a sad irony to have come all the way to the United States only to end up employed by what he considered to be a "third-world, pedestrian" company like Bay-Clean, which was "not up to the task of working for a [prestigious] company like Sonix." Subcontracting at Bay-Clean thus pitted immigrants against each other, making many Mexican janitors blame their harsh labor and working conditions on race.

JANITORS REBEL AGAINST BAY-CLEAN

After several years of employment at Bay-Clean, tired, frustrated, and with no hope that their situation would improve in the near future, a group of janitors contacted Local 1877 in 1992 to serve as an intermediary between Bay-Clean workers and their employer. The response they received from Local 1877 was clear: to solve your problems in the long run, you must organize and join the union. To that end, Luis, Anselmo, Don Manuel, and about half a dozen other Bay-Clean janitors started promoting the union's cause among their peers. This was not an easy task. Sonix buildings were dispersed among several sites and cities in Silicon Valley, making it particularly difficult and time-consuming to disseminate information about the union. More important, this group of workers had to overcome the initial skepticism of their peers, whose response was cautious at first. Many were recent immigrants who had never heard of the union and were afraid of getting involved in any political activity that could jeopardize their jobs or, worse yet, get them deported. Others had doubts about the union's motives, and still others were not aware they had the right to organize even if they were undocumented workers.

To win their confidence, Local 1877 implemented two main strategies. The first consisted of paying close, personal attention to workers like Luis and Anselmo, who were among their most visible leaders, and assigning a team of six union representatives to work in this campaign. Luis, Anselmo, and about a half dozen other janitors started meeting in secret with union officials on the weekends, afraid that Bay-Clean's supervisors would find out and fire them. For each of these meetings, union representatives would call workers by phone and even give them a ride if they did not have their own transportation, a personal attention workers greatly appreciated. The second strategy consisted of capitalizing on immigrant kin and social networks as a recruiting tool. Rather than relying on an impersonal campaign for signing up workers, union organizers took a more efficient approach, mobilizing the same social networks that held these workers together and that Bay-Clean used to recruit and replenish its workforce. For example, Local 1877 decided to help sponsor the soccer team founded by Luis. Many of the Bay-Clean workers had come from the same town that the team represented, and the team already brought them together on the weekends for games and other social events.[12] With time, this labor-intensive approach, combining personal attention to workers with the mobilization of their kin and social networks, paid off, and the movement grew from half a dozen workers to a solid core of about twenty actively involved workers supported by the majority of Bay-Clean janitors.

After several weeks of intense organizing, the union campaign at Bay-Clean picked up steam and entered a frantic and intense phase, with leaders like Luis and other sympathizers going through a roller-coaster experience as the campaign unfolded. One of the most dramatic and critical moments I witnessed was a rally that Bay-Clean workers conducted in front of the company's administrative office, coordinated by Local 1877.

One afternoon, about twenty-five workers and five union representatives showed up at Bay-Clean's headquarters. The company's president, Charles Choi, a middle-aged Korean entrepreneur, was visibly surprised by the workers' visit. The standoff that followed revealed the symbolic struggle to establish the significance of this encounter and the terms on which this meeting should be conducted. Trying to deny any formal status to their meeting, Bay-Clean's president declined to receive workers inside the company's office and asked them to stay in the parking lot, addressing them from the back door. He persistently tried to convince workers to meet privately with him without the presence of union representatives. Talking to both his employees and the union organizers, he argued, "Just as you have been meeting on Saturdays with the union, I want an opportunity to meet with you alone. . . . Like a family who deals with its problems in private first, before airing them in public, this is an internal company issue that I would like to treat directly with you. . . . If later you are not satisfied, then you can look for external support." Then, addressing the union representatives, he added, "I should be given an opportunity to talk with my workers before involving a third party. First you have to give me a chance; you have to be fair."

Joaquín, a Bay-Clean employee in his early twenties who was one of the most outspoken critics of the company's policies, replied, "You had plenty of time to talk to us and never did. . . . If you want to speak to us alone, you can look for us at night at Sonix's parking lot after we get out of work. Now, we are with the union, and today's meeting is with the union, and us, so we want them [union representatives] to be present."

A long debate followed about who would be the legitimate translator between the Bay-Clean president, who did not speak Spanish, and the janitors who did not speak English. Choi refused to accept a Chicana union official proposed by workers as their translator, and instead insisted in using one of his own clerical employees who was fluent in Spanish. In turn, workers vehemently opposed the proposal and refused to listen to his employee, arguing that "he was part of the company's staff and could not be trusted." Whenever the company's officer translated his boss' words, workers either ignored or booed him. At other times, there were two translations going on simultaneously, one by the Bay-Clean official and the other by the union representative. Through her, the janitors aired their complaints about the bad and discriminatory treatment they had to endure every night at work, demanded the removal of some of the company's "abusive supervisors," and questioned the racially discriminatory policies implemented at work. They also threatened a two-day strike if Choi did not meet with them at the union's office to discuss their demands. After about two hours of tense discussion, overwhelmed by the size of the workers' visiting party and their determination, Choi reluctantly agreed to hold a meeting in two weeks with a group of workers and representatives of the union to discuss their grievances. For Bay-Clean janitors, this was a symbolic victory because, overcoming their fears, they had finally confronted their boss on his own turf, something they had never anticipated doing when they first started to organize.

Two weeks later, at the long-awaited meeting with Bay-Clean's president, Luis, Anselmo, and three other workers who had been elected by their peers to represent them in this meeting presented their demands. Held at Local 1877's office in San Jose, the meeting was attended by two officials of Bay-Clean, including its president; three union representatives; and eleven workers participating as observers. As I sat in this meeting, Bay-Clean's workers first presented their demands on wages, benefits, and material conditions at work, including the establishment of a plan for wage increases based on seniority, the establishment of health insurance as part of workers' contracts, and access to cleaning supplies to do their jobs. What galvanized most of the workers during the meeting, however, were issues of racial discrimination and the conditions they endured in their day-to-day interaction with the company's supervisors. Thus, their second set of demands included an end to racial discrimination in the workplace, the establishment of a transparent policy regarding the distribution of the workload, the promotion of Mexican janitors to supervisory positions, and an end to derogatory treatment by the company's supervisors.[13]

Workers spoke openly about discriminatory treatment by their Korean supervisors night after night, the supervisors' demeaning attitude, and the workers' determination to get rid of those whom they considered the most unfair and hated supervisors. Guillermo—a young, outspoken, articulate Mexican worker, one of the leaders chosen by his peers and designated by the union to lead the campaign—captured the importance this issue held for Bay-Clean workers. Addressing the Bay-Clean president, he told him, "You should have brought your supervisors with you to this meeting; they would know what we are talking about. . . . We want you to fire some of our supervisors. To us this is not a joke, because it is we who have to work and put up with them eight hours a day. . . . These supervisors don't know about human relations and treat us like animals; they threaten and try to intimidate us all the time!" Then, stressing their resolution to put an end to racial discrimination in the workplace, he added, "We want Latinos in supervisory positions. Why aren't there any? You don't need to speak English to be a supervisor in this job. . . . Besides, our Korean supervisors don't speak English either."

Overwhelmed by the workers' resolve, and in an effort to cool down the union's campaign, Bay-Clean's president requested time to investigate the janitors' complaints about abuses by the company's supervisors and think about their demands. After the meeting was over, workers were visibly frustrated that the meeting had not produced clear and immediate results, and they interpreted Choi's resolution as a distraction tactic. Yet they were also clearly relieved about finally having directly expressed their grievances to their boss. They were especially proud about having showed him that, despite their undocumented status, they were not willing to tolerate the demeaning treatment they were subjected to at work. Their resolve surprised not only Bay-Clean's president but also the union organizers, who, at least up to that point, seemed more eager to talk about wages and labor conditions than to deal with the thorny issue of racial discrimination in the workplace.

The turning point in the Bay-Clean workers' campaign to unionize, however, was the corporate campaign organized by Local 1877 targeting Sonix rather than Bay-Clean, modeled on a favorite political strategy of the new labor movement in the United States (Sherman and Voss 2000). A few weeks after the initial meeting, the union organized a larger public demonstration in front of one of Sonix's major administrative buildings in Silicon Valley. This was a difficult and stressful moment for janitors like Luis and Anselmo, who had actively participated in the campaign. Several Bay-Clean workers told me that, unlike at the rally at Bay-Clean offices, they were afraid of marching in front of Sonix's buildings because they believed they could be identified by Sonix's managers, who supervised their work every night. Moreover, many workers did not identify Sonix as the source of their problems, and this march did not appeal to them as much as the rally organized to protest at Bay-Clean.

As a result of fear and lack of motivation, only a handful of workers attended the demonstration. Despite the poor attendance by Bay-Clean workers, the rally was a political success due to the support of the Cleaning Up Silicon Valley Coalition, a broad community coalition made up of local labor and community leaders, representatives of religious groups and nonprofit organizations, university students, and sympathizers from

FIGURE 5. Mexican workers in a Justice for Janitors march against
a Silicon Valley cleaning contractor.

other unions (see Figure 5). Attended by about fifty people and the local
media, this rally presented the plight of the janitors cleaning Sonix buildings as an issue of social justice for the working poor in Silicon Valley and
emphasized the economic, social, and ethnic inequality that characterized the region.

Because Sonix was afraid of negative publicity that could affect its
public image, this political strategy produced immediate results. A few
days later Sonix publicly announced the decision to "consolidate" its janitorial contracts and deal with a single, large, unionized cleaning company with a good reputation in the industry. The news was well received
by Bay-Clean workers, including Luis, Anselmo, Guillermo, and Don
Manuel, who had actively participated in the union campaign from the
beginning, especially because the new cleaning company agreed to hire
them to continue cleaning Sonix's buildings. This put an end to a long
campaign that, with dozens of meetings, intensive organization, two
public rallies and several other events, boosted workers' morale: they felt
more optimistic about their future in a union company that promised
better wages and working conditions than Bay-Clean had.

Scientific Management
and Workers' Resistance at Sonix

The use of scientific management techniques with immigrant workers in technologically advanced industries has been considered a characteristic of the flexible specialization model of the new economy (Lamphere, Grenier, and Stepick 1994; Hossfeld 1990). But ethnographic study of how such techniques are implemented in the workplace, and how immigrant workers respond to them, has received scant scholarly attention. Again, the experience of the janitors at Sonix, one of the most advanced high-tech companies in Silicon Valley, helps to illuminate this issue.

Headquartered in Europe, Service International, the new cleaning contractor hired by Sonix to take the place of Bay-Clean, had a profile rather different than that of Bay-Clean. Unlike the latter, which got most of its business from a single client, Service International was one of the largest building-cleaning companies in the world. Although it had begun operation in Silicon Valley in 1991, by the end of that year it was already ranked among the five largest janitorial firms in the region. Because of that and the fact that it was a union company, the switch to Service International translated into immediate and tangible benefits for the janitors who cleaned Sonix's buildings. The starting wage for regular janitors went from $5.50 an hour at Bay-Clean to $6.10 at Service International, and wages for utility workers like Luis went up from $5.80 to $6.80 an hour. Moreover, custodial workers were now entitled to fringe benefits, including health care (after three months of employment), sick leave, and a one-week paid vacation after their first year of employment with the company. Equally important, they were protected by the union from potentially unfair labor practices, a reassuring feeling after the numerous abuses they had endured at Bay-Clean.

From the perspective of the Sonix managers I interviewed, however, this change was responsible for a decline in the quality of the cleaning service. The switch from a local, nonunion company like Bay-Clean to a giant cleaning company like Service International had brought important changes in the organization of janitorial work and the management methods used at Sonix. Sonix managers complained that, unlike small cleaning contractors, Service International had a single, centralized managerial system that offered less flexibility and slower response from its workers.[14] In the view of Sonix's managers, the challenge was to recover the flexibility that had been lost or, in the words of their principal maintenance manager, "to consolidate [janitorial services] without losing quality."

To accomplish this goal, Sonix decided to implement a modern scientific managerial system known as Total Quality Management (Dennis 1995). Broadly defined, the aim of this system is to increase productivity by assigning workers new duties, promote cooperation among coworkers, and require them to perform a variety of tasks following detailed instructions about how to do each of the jobs assigned (Parker and Slaughter 1988; Dennis 1995). In Sonix's case, the central goal was to recreate flexibility in the workplace and prevent janitors from hiding behind the bureaucratic structure of Service International. To do so, a team of Sonix managers developed a booklet titled *Cost Effective Housekeeping*, which applied the philosophy of Total Quality Management to cleaning services in the company, providing specific and detailed instructions about how to implement this approach and how to measure workers' performance. In one of its opening paragraphs, the booklet presented the economic rationale behind subcontracting: "[Sonix] has been a leader in the use of QUALITY improvement programs in the product assembly production areas for years. We have demonstrated that the same concepts may be applied to a service organization as well. . . . Faced with continued budget pressure to reduce staff levels and expenses for housekeeping supplies while improving the level of services, we decided to try a Total Quality Control (TQC) approach" (emphasis in original). The booklet went on to explain how to implement the new management method, emphasizing the importance of both instilling the philosophy in workers' minds and promoting the concepts of teamwork and competition:

> We then developed a "Team Concept" with the custodians. They were delegated more responsibility and authority to analyze the condition of an area of the building and decide what to clean and what not to clean. . . . For years now, they have been assuming that they had to "clean everything every day" and they were doing their best to do so. . . . [They were] "willing workers" at their best. . . . One very strong lesson that was learned in this experience is the importance of workers involvement and "buy-in" of the concepts. In order to develop a sense of trust, it is important to have a few quick success stories and then celebrate them as a group with individual recognition to those that put forth that extra effort on a day to day basis.

Sonix pressed Service International to modify its bureaucratic approach and institute a more flexible system for janitors to use in the workplace. Given that Sonix was Service International's largest client in the region, the latter was eager to accommodate these demands. According to Service International's top regional manager, whom I interviewed,

the first step in getting workers involved was to eliminate the stigma usually associated with janitorial work. In his view, the key was to make
employees feel they had a respectable occupation and to motivate them.
"[That is why] we do not call our employees 'janitors,' because that is a
word with negative connotations. We prefer to call them 'service
employees' because it gives them higher self-esteem and tells [them] that
they are important to someone else and the company," he added.

The janitors were much less enthusiastic about the new managerial
system than the managers of Sonix and Service International were. As
Service International took over, the janitors found that their workload
had notably increased. The cleaning company had reduced the number
of workers per building as a strategy to compete with other companies
for Sonix's contract. While Bay-Clean had employed 275 janitors at
Sonix, Service International used only 240 workers. In the office complex where Luis worked, for example, the number of janitors decreased
from 65 to 44. The consequences of this reduction fell directly upon the
janitors' shoulders, each of whom now had to clean areas considerably
larger than when they worked for Bay-Clean. Reflecting on this issue a
year after they had started working for Service International, Anselmo
explained to me the increasing pressure they felt on the job and how this
affected their work:

> [At first], the only thing we felt was work, pure work, because they [Ser-
> vice International] doubled the cleaning areas of almost every janitor—
> things that we did not do before and now we have to do, [though] of
> course, less thoroughly. But in any case it was more work, bigger areas, so
> at the beginning the only thing that we felt was more work. . . . Before,
> with Bay-Clean, we were twenty-three people in my building, and with
> Service International we are only seventeen, and two of them are "utility
> workers." So it was as if they had taken out eight workers and divided their
> work among us. Because of this, the quality of the job was pretty
> bad. . . . Sometimes I was ashamed because they [Sonix managers]
> blamed us for not cleaning well. . . . Mr. Lozano [a Sonix maintenance
> manager] blamed that on the union, asking whether this is what we
> wanted the union for.

In addition to an increased workload, the janitors at Sonix confronted
an intensification of work as a result of the new scientific management
system. At first, following the logic of the new management system, Service International instructed janitors to modify their working routine in
order to redistribute the additional workload that resulted from reducing the number of cleaning workers. Then Service International

instructed them to clean less thoroughly in order to cover a larger area during their regular eight-hour shift. After some weeks, however, the company started receiving complaints from Sonix maintenance managers about the quality of their work. In response, Service International's managers began pressing janitors to clean more thoroughly in order to meet Sonix demands, further increasing their workload. Don Manuel, commenting on the contradictory orders they received from their supervisors, asked ironically, "What do they want, quantity or quality?" Anselmo, reflecting on the changes brought about by the new Total Quality Management system, commented, "My [supervisor] thinks he is clever because at first his policy was to tell us not to worry about the extra area we have to clean, not to worry about leaving it perfect. But after only a few weeks, he and the other [supervisors] started pressing us. They are assigning us more things to do and telling us now that we have to clean better." And in a humorous tone, he pointed to the inconsistency between Service International's discourse on professionalism and daily practice at work. "For example, this week we were shown some videos to teach us how to do our job properly that lasted about 30 to 45 minutes," he said. "I was laughing because, in the video, the person who is cleaning does everything very methodically, very slow, but in our work we have to hurry up every night to clean all the area we are assigned."

Confronted with increasing pressure at work and unwilling to surrender to the logic of the new system, Service International's janitors started to engage in creative tactics of work avoidance, which, following Deborah Reed-Danahay, I call "microresistance strategies." These include a wide range of skillful actions whose goal is to "make do" in difficult situations.[15] For the janitors, these tactics sometimes consisted of helping each other to get an extra break from work away from the attention of their supervisors. Other tactics involved collaboration among coworkers to resist the individualization of work and competitive spirit promoted by the new method. Another tactic involved finishing work routines and then resting during unscheduled breaks while other workers took turns as lookouts. Some workers preferred dealing individually with pressure at work. Anselmo, who at the time was going to school in the afternoons to earn a high school certificate, proudly told me about his own microresistance strategies:

> There are several offices in the building where I work that nobody except me and the security officer have the keys for—even my foreman does not have the keys. When everybody else is emptying trash cans, I finish my

area fast, and when I finish I lock myself into one of those rooms and have a garbage can and my cleaning things ready just in case. And then I start doing my homework until I get bored, sometimes [for] an hour, sometimes [an] hour and a half. Where do you think I read the books for school? In school? No, . . . everything I do here. You see, it's *maña* [ingenuity], and look, I have never had problems. . . . I do this at that time because that is when everybody else is working hard and the supervisor cannot imagine that, early on, somebody is already taking a [unscheduled] break.

Often, workers' cynicism, resistance tactics, and spontaneous rather than well-organized collective strategies hindered the ambitious plan of implementing a Total Quality Control system at Sonix. But it is important not to misinterpret janitors' actions. Rather than functioning as a reaction to the scientific managerial system, or as resistance to capitalist discipline, the janitors' reactions were a critique of their employer's failure to meet its own standards and to transform the workers into well-trained, well-equipped, professional custodial workers. In other words, janitors at Service International were not protesting the attempt to transform them into professional "custodial employees" but rather the fact that the company *failed* to effect this transformation despite its official discourse. In spite of the wage increase and access to some basic benefits, many janitors at Service International openly expressed disappointment about what they referred to as the "low professional standards" of this cleaning company, which to them was not much different from their former employer. In their view, most building-cleaning companies were "cut of the same cloth," regardless of the companies' management discourse on professionalism. Workers' reactions seemed to express a critique of the mismatch between their own models of American modernity embodied by Sonix, on the one hand, and the harsh working conditions they endured while employed by cleaning companies like Bay-Clean and Service International, on the other. In the meantime, the system of subcontracting contributed to mask the relation between these two apparently disconnected realities.

The INS Comes on the Scene: Structural Limits to Agency

When examining issues of management control, labor discipline, and resistance in the context of immigrant labor, the role of the state in shaping immigrant workers' opportunities and constraints cannot be overlooked. Yet, how specifically the state, by means of immigration and labor policies, shapes workers' ability to resist as political actors is a matter of discussion (Rouse 1992; Heyman 1998). The last twist in the story of the janitors who cleaned Sonix buildings has direct implications for this issue.

In the summer of 1995, a short twenty months after the janitors first started working for Service International, this company received a letter from the Immigration and Naturalization Service (INS) announcing it planned to conduct an audit to check the work-authorization documents of the company's employees. Two weeks later the INS conducted the audit; within two months, it informed Service International about all workers whose papers did not match the government's records. Shortly after that, Service International sent a letter to all workers identified by the INS as having invalid papers, giving them one week to bring valid work permits or otherwise be laid off after signing their resignations. A few weeks later, about four hundred janitors employed by Service International, including most of those employed to clean Sonix offices, were laid off because they lacked work permits.

Janitors' reaction to this sudden and unexpected ending to their short tenure at Service International was a combination of disappointment, anger, and resignation. Although all were familiar with stories of friends and acquaintances who had lost jobs because of the INS, some of whom had been deported, they could hardly believe that this time it had happened to them. In my conversations with Luis, for example, he resisted believing that the INS was solely responsible for what had happened. Like many others, he suspected the INS letters were either false or the outcome of a plot by their employer to replace them with a new cadre of janitors without seniority at entry-level wages and few benefits, with the consequential financial savings for the company. Other workers believed in the authenticity of the INS investigation but were convinced their employer had taken advantage of the situation to get rid of them to hire new, less costly workers. Ironically, but not surprisingly, the new janitors hired by Service International were Mexican workers like them—some were even their relatives or acquaintances—and also undocumented. Commenting on the rationale for signing their resignations, Anselmo explained,

> [At that point] we did not have other alternatives but to sign our resignations. [At first] we were not going to sign—we all felt pretty strong about it. But at the end we realized that we could not win. [Moreover,] if we did not sign, they [Service International] would not pay us the last week and vacations they still owed us—because they owed us vacations and many days of work, almost two weeks of work—so to make sure that

we would get paid, we decided to sign. . . . When we went to the office
to pick up our checks, we saw the company was hiring new workers, most
of them just like us with no papers, because many had just arrived, and
we wished them good luck.

Jobless, without the possibility of applying for unemployment compensation because of their status as undocumented immigrants, and
pressed by immediate financial needs, many workers started immediately to look for new jobs. With the help of Local 1877, some found
employment in other unionized cleaning companies in the region,
where they had to start as entry-level workers at the minimum wage
stipulated in the union contract. Others were less fortunate and took
jobs in nonunionized janitorial companies that paid significantly less
than their previous employer and offered no benefits. Don Manuel
could not find work in the building-cleaning industry and ended up
working temporarily as a cook's helper in a fast-food restaurant. While
looking for new jobs was stressful, most former Service International
janitors were particularly sad and frustrated because of losing all the
working benefits they had won after a hard union struggle at Bay-Clean,
which was supposed to improve their jobs and bring them stability.

In addition to labor disenfranchisement, the intervention of the INS
also had another crucial effect: it undermined trust established between
workers and the union, which was the basis for the Justice for Janitors
campaign at Bay-Clean. Many janitors were disappointed with the union
because it did not support them precisely at the time they needed it most.
When their employer asked them to prove their legal status or lose their
jobs, several workers asked Local 1877 to intervene on their behalf, only
to find out that the union could do nothing about it because this was an
immigration rather than a labor issue. To workers like Luis, the fine legal
line between the two realms was difficult to understand and seemed artificial because, as he reiterated several times to me, being laid off was foremost a labor issue.

Janitors' alienation from Local 1877 was also the result of an important structural limitation often faced by labor unions that represent low-
income immigrants: they must choose between to investing resources
in organizing more workers and concentrating their resources on ser-
vicing and consolidating the existing membership (Fisk, Mitchell, and
Erickson 2000: 207–11; Durrenberger and Erem 1999). To solve this
dilemma, Local 1877 had proposed—before janitors at Service International lost their jobs—that they develop a system of stewards, so that
workers could represent themselves and handle most problems in the
workplace. Many janitors, however, interpreted this plan as a sign of

lack of support and commitment by the union. Having limited English and little familiarity with labor law, they expected the union to play an active role in dealing with their problems at work.

Moreover, having grown accustomed to receiving a great deal of personal attention during the union campaign, janitors at Service International resented the reduced assistance they received after they joined Local 1877. Luis, for example, who at the time was a steward, interpreted the union's proposal as a sign that it was abandoning them to their fate. "Now the union does not want to hear about problems at work because one is already paying the [union] fees. . . . Once you are inside, they do not have time for you. . . . What is the point of naming people like me as [the] union's delegates if the company does not allow you to do your job as such? The supervisor has orders to not let you do your job as the union wants, so we cannot do anything—and if you do, they fire you, as simple as that." Then in a critical tone, reflecting a common feeling among his peers about the union, he added, "I am disappointed because the union was not what we thought it was. The union helps you when they are interested in the worker; then when everything is done, when the worker has done his part of the fight, they [union representatives] do not care anymore for him, they do not pay us the same attention."

Most Local 1877 representatives I interviewed were aware of the janitors' feelings and complaints. They recognized the effects of an organizational strategy that concentrated much of the union's attention at one point on a group of workers in a given company, and that, after it had succeeded, focused on a different target company while barely able to meet the legitimate needs of the thousands of new union members. Facing increasing demands by their supervisors at Service International, on the one hand, and finding it continually more difficult to access their union representative, on the other, Luis and his workmates became increasingly frustrated with Local 1877. Disenchanted, many workers who had been among the initial leaders of the Justice for Janitors campaign at Bay-Clean—including Luis, Anselmo, Guillermo, and Don Manuel—distanced themselves from the union even before losing their jobs. They stopped attending its meetings and responding to Local 1877's calls to support public rallies on behalf of other workers contracted by nonunionized cleaning companies in the region.[16]

The case of the janitors at Sonix offers a prime window on issues of labor flexibility and political resistance in one of the largest low-skilled service industries in Silicon Valley. At Sonix, contracting out building-cleaning and other services was but the next step in a decentralization strategy that first began when this company started sending manufacturing operations abroad. This shift from a vertical to a decentralized, flexible organizational structure at this and many other high-tech companies—rather than the immigration of Mexican and other Latino workers per se—was the crucial factor that led to restructuring the building-cleaning industry in the region. This shift fueled the proliferation of independent, nonunion contractors like Bay-Clean, which, relying on undocumented immigrant labor, offered competitive contracts to Sonix and other companies.

Sonix's replacement of in-house custodial workers with immigrants employed by independent contractors also led to the subproletarianization of custodial work. In other words, subcontracting led to a redefinition of custodial work, from an entry-level, stable, in-house occupation for minority and immigrant workers to an unstable, low-paid, low-status occupation for Mexican and other Latino immigrants, especially undocumented workers. By the time Luis, Anselmo, and Don Manuel arrived in Silicon Valley in the early 1990s, custodial work had already been redefined.

In addition to reducing labor costs and increasing labor flexibility, subcontracting allowed Sonix to retain control over the organization of custodial work, including work routines and management techniques, as well as the subcontracted immigrants themselves. This is what I call indirect rule, an organizational system in which a client company, while contracting with an independent service provider, is able to shape that provider's organization of production and methods of labor control in the workplace. Subcontracting also played a major role in shaping workers' class consciousness by coming between the structural conditions of janitorial work and the subjective perception of janitors themselves. Workers who cleaned Sonix's facilities were eager to protest the inhumane conditions at work, which they blamed on their employer; they rarely made a connection between such conditions and Sonix, which was Bay-Clean's primary client. Their failure to make this connection can be seen as resulting from the fact that labor subcontracting masks power relations in the workplace, in the process shaping workers' ethnic and class consciousness. The janitors' spirited reaction against Bay-Clean, and their interpretation of labor relations at work in racial terms, shows the effects of subcontracting on workers' class consciousness. The contracting system pitted Mexican and Korean workers against each other and, in doing so, helped mask the connection between janitors' poor labor conditions and Sonix. This seems to confirm the decontextualization of class relations that characterizes labor relations in today's global economy, in which capital and its workforce become more and more remote from each other, contributing to the fragmentation of class consciousness and to class antinomies (Comaroff and Comaroff 2001: 12–13).

But while first part of this chapter speaks of the several ways that capital uses subcontracting as a form of labor exploitation and the collateral effects on the fragmentation of class consciousness, the story of the janitors at Sonix speaks of the structural limitations of this labor regime. In effect, the intensification of janitorial labor at Sonix reached a limit when Bay-Clean workers reacted against the harsh working conditions they had to endure. In other words, the logic of subcontracting at Sonix ended up generating the contradictions and conflicts that prompted workers to organize, ultimately leading Sonix to shift, under public political scrutiny, to a unionized cleaning contractor. The restructuring of cleaning services in this company served as an arena in which workers could strive to unionize after the effects of this labor regime became unbearable to them. The objective contradictions in a system that sought to increase flexibility and efficiency at the cost of intensifying labor constitutes the local political context in which the immigrant workers' collective resistance first emerged. By the same token, the story of Mexican janitors at Sonix shows that the notion of labor flexibility cannot be taken as a given, but rather is a fluid and changing feature of the work process continuously constructed by management and contested by workers in the workplace (Zlolniski 2003).

In the recent past, Latino immigrants have struggled to join labor unions when motivated by a combination of traditional "bread and butter" issues—to improve wages and working conditions—and a determination to fight for dignity and respect in the workplace (Wells 2000; Zabin 2000; Milkman and Wong 2000; Cranford 2000; Delgado 1993). The motives that led janitors at Bay-Clean to unionize were the same. Particularly, the feeling of being disrespected by their Korean employers energized and mobilized the janitors at Sonix and helped fuel janitors' collective struggle. But it is important not to misinterpret the workers' goals. The Bay-Clean workers were not resisting incorporation into a disciplined proletarian workforce, as some authors believe when examining immigrants' local forms of resistance (Rouse 1992), but were instead protesting their transformation into a subclass of cheap and disposable workers at the hands of unscrupulous contractors. At both Bay-Clean and Service International, Anselmo, Luis, and their peers were reacting to the failure of these companies to incorporate them as full-time, stable janitorial service workers, as well as to the contradictions between management's official discourse on cleaning work and the harsh realities of daily practice.

But the janitors' political victory in joining a labor union cannot be explained in terms of workers' agency alone. Equally important was the local political context in which their labor resistance took place. Unlike the relocation of production outside the local community, which tends to decontextualize class relations and render workers politically vulnerable, the subcontracting of cleaning work by Sonix could not altogether ignore locality. Capitalizing on this factor, the union's political strategy consisted in highlighting the direct labor connections in Silicon Valley between the affluent capitalist corporations like Sonix and the disempowered undocumented workers to win the public's support, a central political strategy of the new unionism (Sherman and Voss 2000). While Luis and his peers at Bay-Clean mobilized around issues of respect and dignity, Local 1877 organized the campaign around broader issues of social justice and the moral responsibility of the large high-tech companies. In an era of global capitalism that tends to distance class relations through flexible employment strategies such as offshore production and outsourcing, the articulation of labor struggles with issues of social justice and ethnic equality has become a key political weapon of organized labor. This is what Paul Johnston terms "social movement unionism," a movement that uses the discourse of universalist standards of social justice to promote solidarity and mobilize sympathizers among civil, religious, and labor groups (1994: 173).

The end of the story of the janitors at Sonix reveals the important structural limits to political agency faced by undocumented immigrants and the important effects of the state's policies, carried out by agencies like the INS, on the relation between immigrant workers and organized labor. Despite the janitors' success in organizing, their status as undocumented immigrants forced many of them to find new employment, demonstrating their vulnerability and the precariousness of any leverage derived from their structural location in the Silicon Valley economy. This helps to explain why many other Mexican immigrants I met while in the field did not show much interest in becoming involved with union political activities, despite the union's success in organizing workers in the janitorial industry.[17] Instead, they looked for other work alternatives to escape the financial insecurity, rigid discipline, and poor conditions of low-paid jobs in the building-cleaning and similar industries.

CHAPTER 3

Working in the Informal Economy

Santech is one of the favorite sites of dozens of street vendors, who daily come to sell a large variety of products, including fresh fruits and vegetables, tortillas, beauty products, kitchen cookware, jewelry, pirated CDs, and others. Many residents of the barrio are themselves also directly involved in the informal economy. Some sell homemade food, candies, and sodas at home, often leaving the doors of their apartments open when the weather allows it in order to invite their clients to stop by. A few women run informal child-care centers in their homes, and others work as seamstresses repairing clothes for local residents and clients. Still others sell daily meals to single males who live in bachelor households in the neighborhood. The diversity, dynamism, and pervasiveness of the informal economy characterize much of everyday life in Santech, and evidence of this economy is one of the first aspects that grab the attention of an outsider.

The growth of informal economic activities—those income-generating occupations that escape the control of the state and local government authorities—is indeed a common feature of Latino immigrant neighborhoods (Staudt 1998; Moore and Pinderhughes 1993; Dohan 2003). Scholars interested in the study of the informal economy have proposed different theories to explain its growth in minority and immigrant neighborhoods. As Caroline Moser and Tamar Wilson argue, those influenced by modernization theory contend that the informal economy can be reduced to a set of survival strategies by workers with little education and poor occupational skills who cannot find employment elsewhere in the formal sector.[1]

A second approach, influenced by a neo-Marxist perspective, maintains that the informal economy is the outcome of structural changes in today's capitalist economy. These changes cause old forms of exploitation to reemerge: sweatshops, industrial homework, and subcontracting. Because exploitative employers escape the vigilance of the state and the labor unions, they are able to reduce labor and production costs.[2] Saskia Sassen, one of the leading scholars of this theoretical approach, distinguishes two components in the informal economy in immigrant neighborhoods. The first consists of hidden industrial activities in which immigrants are employed as a source of cheap labor to reduce production costs, as in, for example, the garment, footwear, and construction industries (1989: 71). The second component is the "neighborhood subeconomy," which consists of goods and services that satisfy the consumption needs of low-income immigrants whenever these goods are not produced in the formal sector, or when they are sold at a price beyond their reach (e.g., low-cost furniture or family day care) (1989: 71; 1994: 2296). While this approach captures well the structural forces behind the growth of the informal economy in the so-called postindustrial economy, it says little about the immigrants who are behind these activities—or the rationale behind their actions—and it tends to portray them as passive victims at the mercy of mechanical capitalist forces.

A third and more recent approach combines the neo-Marxist model with an actor-oriented perspective that underscores the role of agency to explain the diversity of activities in the informal economy (Wilson 2005; Cross 1998; Zlolniski 2000; Dohan 2003). This approach seeks to explain not only the factors that fuel the growth of the informal economy but also how workers themselves respond to these factors and develop their own informal income-generating activities as self-employed workers and petty informal entrepreneurs, in the process shaping the contours of the informal sector.[3] For example, in a recent study of a Mexican immigrant neighborhood in San Jose similar to Santech, Daniel Dohan maintains that informal work in this community represents a complementary income-generating strategy commonly used by many families with low-paying jobs in the formal sector (2003: 108). Rather than emphasizing politico-economic factors, Dohan argues that working long hours in low-paid formal and informal jobs—what he calls a strategy of "overwork"—is not just an automatic response to the structure of economic opportunities but also a meaningful response in Mexican immigrant culture, where hard work is viewed as the appropriate avenue for economic mobility (2003: 82).

Following this third approach, in this chapter I examine some of the informal income-generating activities I encountered in Santech and elsewhere in San Jose to capture the perspective of immigrant workers involved in these activities, the rationale behind their choosing informal jobs over occupations in the formal sector, and the creative ways in which they combined formal and informal occupations. What are some of the common occupations in which Mexican workers are employed in the informal economy in this neighborhood? What structural and personal factors led individuals to choose these occupations? What was the economic rationale behind the decision to work in the informal sector? What was the role of these jobs in their economic well-being? And what do these jobs tell us about the opportunities and constraints that undocumented immigrants find in the formal economy in Silicon Valley?

Informal economic activities are not merely a set of survival strategies undertaken by unskilled immigrants disconnected from Silicon Valley's formal economy, as modernization theory scholars contend. Many immigrants use them to supplement the wages they earn in low-skilled jobs in the formal sector. In other cases, informal activities represent an employment alternative to the low-paid and harsh jobs in the formal economy that they have held before. In most cases, from the immigrant workers' perspective, the differences between informal activities and low-skilled jobs in the formal sector are minimal. Immigrants often combine both kinds of occupations in a flexible, creative, and dynamic manner. The case studies in this chapter illustrate the interactions between structural opportunities and constraints, on the one hand, and personal and family circumstances, on the other, that led many Mexican immigrants in Santech to choose informal economic activities. They also highlight the connections between these informal occupations and the mechanisms that contribute to the subsistence and reproduction of cheap flexible immigrant labor in Silicon Valley's formal economy.[4]

Laura: A Self-Employed Street Vendor

Laura, a young, robust, and energetic woman, worked as a street vendor in Santech and the adjacent housing projects. She lived in an apartment in Santech with her husband and two daughters, the first one born in Mexico and the second in the United States. Laura, born in Acapulco in the Mexican state of Guerrero in 1965, married her husband, Alberto, in 1987 and enjoyed a modest life there while living with

Alberto's mother. Alberto worked as an accountant in a small business that he and a partner had started after obtaining a technical degree in accounting in Acapulco. Laura had completed the equivalent of high school in Mexico and two years of nursery education, and had occasionally worked in informal occupations to raise extra income for the family by selling beauty products, Tupperware, and jewelry to her relatives, neighbors, and acquaintances. She also worked as a part-time aerobics instructor in her neighborhood, combining these occupations with raising her first daughter, born in 1991.

In the early 1990s, Laura and Alberto started seriously thinking about migrating to the United States. A few years into their marriage, and despite making enough money to get by, they were not satisfied with their lifestyle. Living with Alberto's mother at her house, they wanted to buy their own home and enjoy a more comfortable material life but could not afford it on their income. They also wanted to have more children and send them to a good private school. But the economic crisis and currency devaluations of the 1980s hit them hard, as it did millions of other middle- and working-class families in Mexico, putting their dreams beyond immediate reach. Meanwhile, two of Alberto's siblings (one brother and one sister), who had been working in San Jose since 1987, encouraged him and Laura to come with them when they returned to California. Laura and Alberto decided to close their businesses in Acapulco in 1991 and migrate with his siblings to San Jose. To prepare, they started to save money for the trip and for the first expenses they would have upon arriving in San Jose, and also enrolled in English classes in a private institute in Acapulco to facilitate their new life in the United States.

In April 1993, after obtaining tourist visas from the U.S. consulate, according to what they told me, Laura, Alberto, and their daughter migrated to the United States in the company of Alberto's sister, who was returning to San Jose after several months in Mexico. They arrived in Santech at an apartment rented by a family they had met in Acapulco, subletting a room that they shared with Alberto's sister and her husband for $350 a month. Soon afterward, Alberto started looking for work. His first job was at a local franchise of Taco Bell, where his sister had been employed for several years. He got a job there as a dishwasher for four hours a day at $4.25 an hour, but he soon quit and went to work for a small cleaning contractor, who offered him a full-time job with a slightly better wage. He lost this job a few weeks later, when his employer was unable to renew the cleaning contract of an office building located in downtown San Jose. During the next few months, a long series of casual and temporary manual jobs followed, in many of which he had little or no previous experience, including carpentry, construction painting, cleaning, and landscaping.

At this point Laura started to work, as she realized they could not live on the wages brought home by her husband alone. With the little savings they had brought from Mexico rapidly running out, and the couple unable to pay their share of the rent and living expenses in Santech on Alberto's income, Laura was committed to raising extra income for the family as she used to do back in Acapulco. Her first job was as a domestic worker employed by a neighbor who lived in the housing project next to Santech, a job that only lasted about a month because her employer, a low-income Mexican immigrant herself, was often late in paying her. After this brief experience, Laura decided to start working at what she knew best, selling products door-to-door on her own. An aunt who had lived in San Jose since the mid-1980s while working as a street vendor encouraged Laura to "learn the trade" and introduced her into the business. From her, Laura learned to prepare some popular Mexican food items like *elotes* (corn on the cob) and *chicharrones* (pork rinds) and sell them in San Jose's Latino immigrant neighborhoods. Her aunt also showed her local stores where she could buy the raw materials in bulk at good prices. After a few weeks, with a mixture of fear and determination, Laura went out on the streets on her own and began working as a vendor in Santech a few hours a day. It was at this point that I first met her. As she explained to me at the time, it had not been an easy decision to become a vendor. Unfamiliar with the city, and afraid of being caught by the police or other official authorities, she had never imagined when she and her husband migrated to the United States that she would end up working as a street vendor to make ends meet.

SELLING HOMEMADE FOOD

Laura's job as a street vendor in Santech illustrates the evolution from part-time self-employment, first conceived as an emergency solution to a family economic crisis, to a petty but full-fledged informal business. At first, because of her unfamiliarity with the surroundings and her fear of being detained, given that her visa had expired and she was selling without a license, Laura felt intimidated and did not venture much further than a few blocks from her apartment, spending only two hours a day on the streets. She started selling a small selection of products such as cucumbers, chips, sodas, and home-cooked elotes. At the time, she was also ashamed of being seen in the neighborhood working as a street vendor, an informal occupation with low social status even among low-income immigrants. Comparing her new job with her experience in Mexico, Laura commented, "In Acapulco I used to sell Tupperware, Avon [beauty products], and jewelry to my own girlfriends and acquaintances. Here is more difficult. I have to sell in the streets, which I have never done before. . . . I have to walk a lot, which I am not accustomed to either, and which is quite tiring. [Moreover] everybody sees me—it's quite shameful!"

With time, Laura started to feel more confident, venturing outside Santech, and her business began to pick up. Her perseverance and discipline helped her to expand her business as she established and followed a work routine. By then, I had a good rapport with Laura and her husband and visited them often at home, a point at which I started to occasionally accompany her on her route. Soon I realized that Laura's job was a labor-intensive occupation that involved careful planning and coordination with Alberto. For example, a common day for her went as follows: Around four in the afternoon, after her husband had come back from work and had had dinner, Laura would leave her daughter under his supervision and go to the kitchen to prepare food items to be sold in the evening. In a big pot she cooked the elotes, and while they boiled she prepared a sauce made of chili, tomatoes, and onions. Once the elotes and sauce were ready, she assembled other goodies, including Fritos, *pepinos* (cucumbers), cherries, popcorn, chicharrones, Doritos, and sliced mangos with lemon and red pepper on top. In the meantime, her husband placed the chicharrones and cucumbers into small plastic bags in the living room while watching their child. After finishing the cooking, Laura packed napkins, salt, pepper, and lemons to be offered to her customers as a courtesy, and she filled a recycled plastic bottle with water to wash her hands while at work. After two hours of labor, Laura and Alberto brought all the goods downstairs and carefully placed them in a supermarket cart that she kept hidden behind the stairs to prevent neighbors, the police, or security personnel from taking it away. At that point, she was ready to leave; Alberto went upstairs to stay with their daughters, and Laura went out into the streets.

Laura's vending routine illustrates the usual problems that unlicensed vendors encounter when working in the streets. She usually started around five in the afternoon in winter and about half past six in summer to avoid the heat. She spent the first forty-five minutes in Santech walking up and down its three most populated blocks to catch the attention of the neighbors. After this, she started the second part of her route in the low-income housing project next to Santech, where she spent the next two hours. She was careful not to arrive at these apartments before 5:30 P.M., to avoid being seen by the housing project's manager, as there were strict rules forbidding street vendors on the property. Once inside, Laura pushed her cart and began announcing her merchandise, using a refrain she repeated every time she passed in front of a building: "Elotes, tamales, pepinos, Doritos." In the evening, dozens of children who played out in the project grounds would run to her cart to order their favorite goody, or would go home to beg their parents for spare change to buy something from her. Handling dozens of children at the same time while watching out for the police or security guards was not an easy task. Moreover, while some products were easy to handle, like those wrapped in plastic bags, others required more work. For example, every time someone ordered an elote, Laura opened the pot in which she carried them, picked one up, inserted a small thin plastic stick into it, grated cheese on top of it, added salt, lemon, and chili sauce according to her customer's taste, handed out a napkin, and at the end, collected the money. In addition, because any single customer is important in the competitive business of street vending, Laura continuously kept watch for potential clients who did not want to go outside and who called or signaled to her from their apartments to bring the cart close.

The final part of Laura's daily routine also involved some help from her husband. After dusk, when most of the housing project residents had gone inside, Laura started pushing her cart back to Santech. After three hours of work, visibly tired, she arrived home and put the cart back behind the stairs. With the help of Alberto, she unloaded the leftovers and brought them upstairs and then carefully stored them in the refrigerator, the kitchen cabinets, and a small balcony next to the apartment's entrance. She then washed the pot used to carry the elotes, and all the utensils she had taken to handle her merchandise, while Alberto cleaned the cart downstairs. Finally, around 10:45, Laura sat down to eat the dinner that Alberto warmed up for her after putting the children to bed. Shortly afterward, she went to bed, at the end of a long day that started around six in the morning, when she got up to make her husband's lunch and get her daughter ready for school.

EXPANDING A HOME-OPERATED BUSINESS

With time, Laura's street-vending job evolved into a well-established, full-fledged, though small, informal business that provided important income to her family. Several factors contributed to this transformation. First, her entrepreneurial skills and previous experience as a door-to-door vendor in Mexico allowed her to recognize business opportunities in the local community, an important asset in the highly competitive environment of street vending in immigrant neighborhoods. While at first Laura timidly sold only a few products, once she became familiar with the area and its residents she began introducing new goods tailored to her customers' demands. For example, after seeing that other vendors in Santech were selling tamales, she decided to cook and sell them too, and they soon became one of her most popular items. In 1995, two years after she first started working as a street vendor, she began preparing and selling dinners at home because she had realized that many young male workers in Santech who lived by themselves were willing to pay for a prepared meal after coming home from work. She then began cooking and selling enchiladas, *tortas* (a stuffed Mexican-style grilled sandwich often made on soft *bolillo* bread), tacos, and other courses at home an hour before starting her usual vending routine. By 1997, these meals had become the source of close to 50 percent of the income realized from her business.

Expanding her network of friends and acquaintances in the area and cultivating their loyalty as clients were central to Laura's successful venture as a street vendor. At first, she knew only a handful of people in the neighborhood, but with time she became a fixture in the local community. In addition, Laura's active involvement in community-organizing activities in Santech helped raise her visibility. She was one of the most active members of an informal neighborhood group organized by her former employer to deal with problems that affected residents. She regularly attended parents' meetings at Santech's elementary school, where her own children were enrolled, and became a popular figure among the most vocal people and leaders in the community. Capitalizing on her social network allowed her not only to expand her business clientele but also to win the trust of many people in Santech, a key ingredient in the informal economy, where business transactions are often based on trust. Thus she often sold her products on credit, but doing so involved a significant risk, especially when her customers were children. As she told me, "I often sell on credit, especially to children, because they often don't have money at hand. But often what happens is that the children who owe me money hide when they see me coming, and I do not want to go after them. Nevertheless, I don't want to keep selling to children who owe me money; I am going to be firm on that."

The flexibility to set a work schedule that accommodates the family and household chores is often considered to be one of the reasons women choose to work in the informal economy (Benería and Roldán 1987). But instead, Laura's informal work brought important changes in the division of domestic labor between her husband and her. She started delegating some household responsibilities to her husband, which allowed her to run and expand her business. At first, the implicit understanding was that Laura would work as a street vendor "to help the family" for a few hours a day while still attending to their children and the household chores. Little by little, however, Alberto started helping her more with both the housework and the business. He began spending more time with their children as her working hours expanded and the business grew. He occasionally fixed dinner and put the children to bed before Laura arrived back home. He also became more involved in her working routine, helping her to prepare or package the merchandise and warming her dinner by the time she was back from work. While the increasing importance of the income generated by Laura's business played a significant role in the gradual change in the division of labor in her family, her ability to represent and legitimize her work as a natural extension of her domestic activities helped reconcile her husband to the change.

Four years after she first started her business, Laura decided to apply for a license as a street vendor in order to expand into places outside Santech and the housing project next door. She had begun selling on Sundays in one of the most popular Catholic parishes in San Jose, one that attracted hundreds of Latinos for every mass. She was asked to obtain licenses from the city's health department and the police in order to continue selling there. When she did so, her application was denied because, as an undocumented immigrant, she did not have a valid Social Security number. While a setback, this did not prevent Laura from continuing sales, despite the risks of being caught operating without a license. Instead, she convinced her husband to help her while there on the weekends by keeping an eye out for the police. In the meantime, Alberto started working in a better-paid job installing Internet cable for a small firm subcontracted by Pacific Bell to wire the whole Silicon Valley. After that, because of the higher income he was bringing home, Laura was able to reduce her street-vending job to three days a week—Fridays to Sundays—when business was best. Despite this change, what at first started as a temporary solution to her husband's unstable employment and meager income with time had evolved into a permanent income-generating strategy in Laura's family.

INCOME, RISKS, AND SUBJECTIVE EVALUATION

Street vending is a tough way to raise an income, especially in poor immigrant neighborhoods, where vendors compete with each other for limited business opportunities and clients with modest budgets (Dohan 2003; Moore and Pinderhughes 1993). To deal with these limitations, Laura priced her products low, providing herself only a small profit margin. Prices for most of her products ranged from $.50 (chips, sodas, and cucumbers) to $1.00 apiece (elotes and mangos). Prepared dinners (homemade tacos and enchiladas) were $2.00. Despite such low prices, at the beginning she usually made between $40.00 and $60.00 in an average day, of which between $30.00 and $40.00 came from street vending, and the rest from selling prepared dinners at home. She usually worked six or seven days a week, depending on the weather, bringing home about $300.00 a week, more than what some of her friends in Santech earned while working in low-wage factory or service jobs in Silicon Valley. But the income generated by her business varied considerably. During the rainy months, for example, business was slow and she made only $25.00 a day. During the warm season, especially in summer, sales went up considerably, and she could bring home $60.00 a day or more. Laura's business was also sensitive to the ups and downs of her clients' budgets. The middle and end of the month were most profitable, as this was when many wage workers in Santech got paid and had more money to spare.

While not high by any standard, Laura's earnings as an informal street vendor soon became an important source of income for her family, demonstrating the importance of this type of work for low-income immigrant families in Santech. For several years after they first arrived in San Jose, Alberto was unable to find a job that paid more than $6.00 an hour; thus he brought home about $250.00 a week when he was employed full-time. In contrast, Laura's street-vending job, while requiring a high degree of self-exploitation and her husband's help, often generated a comparable income, especially during the summer. Not surprisingly, with time both Laura and Alberto started to appreciate the money she brought home as a modest, yet important, source of income to pay for basic family expenses, especially food and rent. Laura herself often expressed pride in her business because it made her feel confident she could raise at least the amount needed to put food on her table. As she proudly told me once, "Look, I work fewer hours than my husband and still can earn as much or even more than him! [Besides] my clients are people who live here. Like these days, I can make $20.00 or $30.00

a day [selling homemade food] and $25.00 or $30.00 selling out, and in the summer I can get as much as $50.00 just selling."

Though at first Laura had found her work both intimidating and degrading, with time she felt more comfortable and started to enjoy its advantages. While they might be interpreted as rationalization, some of the factors she identified explain the logic behind her assessment. First, she valued the autonomy of her job—not having to adapt to the rigid schedule and discipline common in regular low-paid jobs in the formal sector, where many of her women friends in Santech were employed. She also liked working close to home. The flexible hours allowed her to combine her work with caring for her children and her home. She was particularly fond of being able to prepare meals at home for sale, not only because of the good revenues it generated but also because, as she proudly commented, "Now my clients come home and I don't have to spend as much time out." On top of this, she also appreciated the social aspect of her work, which kept her in daily contact with friends and neighbors, giving her the opportunity to meet new people and expand her social network, an important economic and social asset for low-income immigrants.

To Alberto, however, it was more difficult to accept and adapt to the changes brought by Laura's work and what they implied. Resigning himself to the fact that he could no longer be the sole provider for his family made him feel humbled. Even more difficult for him was having to accept the low-paid manual labor he had performed since arriving in San Jose. Accustomed to being a self-employed accountant in his Mexican hometown, an occupation that, while modest, carried greater social prestige than blue-collar jobs, he felt degraded and humiliated by the harsh Silicon Valley jobs in which he had little experience and which paid little. As he commented,

> Back there [in Acapulco] I was somebody, I was respected, but here I am nobody. . . . Yes, I come here to work, but not to break my back or lose a finger in a lousy job. . . . I often feel anguished about the decision I made to close down my business to come here. I thought it was going to be much easier. Maybe I just needed some time off from my office, and then I could have gone back. Not having a stable job here made my ulcer get worse. . . . Yes, I feel bad because I can find only harsh and dirty jobs. I feel humiliated because I used to work in my office, and now I have to take those jobs at $5 an hour. I never imagined it was going to be like this.

In contrast, Laura adapted better to her new life and seldom spoke about going back to Mexico. She enjoyed the fact that, even with a modest income, she and her family could make ends meet. Her circle of friends and the community-related activities in which she participated were also a source of satisfaction to her, as she felt she had something to contribute to the community. Most important to her, however, was the future of her children. She believed they could have a better education in the United States than in Mexico, even if this required her husband and her to work hard in jobs not of their liking. After several years of working and living in San Jose, she felt at ease with her new life and looked forward to a better future for her family. As she explained to me when I asked about her plans, "I feel good here in San Jose, and I would be afraid to go back to Mexico, because the economic situation there is bad. Yes, I would like to go back sometime, but first I want to stay here and save money we could take with us. . . . Besides, I do not know what I could work on in Mexico. I am too fat now to teach aerobics any longer! And my children are doing very well in school; my [older] daughter was elected best student of the year!"

Laura's business illustrates a creative type of entrepreneurship in the informal economy in immigrant neighborhoods that, by capitalizing on particular consumption niches not exploited by formal businesses, offers low-income families an opportunity to earn a supplementary income. These niches represent opportunities for immigrants like Laura, who have the initiative and skills needed to seize them, and who for a variety of reasons prefer these jobs to low-paid occupations in the formal sector. Although Laura had to learn the trade from her aunt and adapt to the peculiarities of the market in her community, her previous experience as an informal sales person in Mexico played an important role in her ability to successfully exploit a particular market niche in the neighborhood. While we cannot explain the growth of the informal economy in immigrant neighborhoods as the result of immigrants importing such activities with them, as Sassen points out (1994: 2289–90), this does not mean we can altogether disregard immigrants' cultural capital and agency in the informal economy, especially when referring to self-employment occupations with no direct links to employers in the formal economy.

It would also be a mistake to interpret Laura as an example of an immigrant worker with no employment alternatives in the formal economy. To Laura, working as a street vendor was a better option than being employed in a low-wage job with strict schedules and discipline in Silicon Valley's formal sector. Her ability to establish her own schedule, and the absence of direct control and supervision, allowed her to combine work and family and earn a modest income similar to what she would have earned in a formal low-paid job. Her entrance into the informal economy was a response to her husband's low and unpredictable income and the need to take care of her children. Her income served to supplement, rather than to substitute for, Alberto's wages and, in so doing, subsidized the maintenance cost of his low-paying jobs in Silicon Valley's formal sector. And even though Laura's was not formal wage work, the income she raised increased her role in making decisions about family budget issues and altered the balance of gender power in her marriage. This illustrates a common experience of working-class Mexican immigrant women in the United States. They gain autonomy and power, while their husbands, because of their low-paid jobs and undocumented status, lose status in society and authority in their families (Hondagneu-Sotelo 1994; Torres Sarmiento 2002).

Arturo's Street-Vending Job: Self-Employment or Disguised Wage Work?

Arturo, a thin, talkative man in his late twenties, worked peddling *paletas* (frozen fruit pops) in San Jose. Unlike Laura and other self-employed workers who ran their own businesses, Arturo sold paletas made by a frozen-fruit-bar firm that operated in the formal sector. This company depended on Mexican immigrants acting as self-employed workers to market its products in the city. Arturo's "self-employment" as a street vendor can best be interpreted as a form of disguised proletarian work in which employers rather than workers own and control the means of production as well as the conditions under which work is performed.

Born in 1965 in Santa Clara Huitziltepec, a small town of about two thousand people in the Mexican state of Puebla, Arturo was the youngest of six children (four brothers and two sisters) whose father, a handicraft merchant, abandoned them when Arturo was a child. Because of this, Arturo never finished school, and he began working as a helper on a farm before reaching ten years of age. In his late teens, Arturo quit working in agriculture and tried different unskilled urban jobs, including working as a helper in a slaughterhouse, as a bricklayer's mate, and, in his final job before migrating to the United States, as an employee in a hardware store. In Mexico, he told me, he always dreamed of working in the United States because, as he often heard from his friends, "by working and earning dollars one could progress and get out of a tough life." With this purpose in mind, in March 1986 Arturo crossed the U.S.-Mexican border in Tijuana with an older brother and went to San Jose, where a friend from his hometown had offered to help them.

Shortly after arriving in town, Arturo rented an apartment in Santech, which he shared with his brother and a family, and where he lived for the next four years. In the meantime, he went back to Puebla to marry Isabel, after which they returned to San Jose, where they had two daughters, born in the early 1990s. Arturo was responsible for bringing money home, and his wife was in charge of raising their children and tending the household. Later on, when Arturo's brother left, Arturo and his family moved out of Santech to another Mexican neighborhood in East San Jose, subletting a room for $350 a month in an apartment they shared with an aunt, her husband, and six children.

SELLING PALETAS FOR A LOCAL COMPANY IN THE FORMAL SECTOR

Arturo's initiation into the informal economy resembles the experience of many young Mexican immigrants I met in San Jose, who, after having worked in low-paid formal jobs in Silicon Valley's service sector, looked for alternative employment in the informal economy. Soon after arriving in this city, he began a series of several casual jobs, the most stable of which was given to him by a local janitorial firm that paid $5.00 an hour and offered no benefits. After several months he quit the job because, he said, "I could not get used to work on a night shift, and because I had constant problems with my supervisor." At that point, his brother, who was selling oranges as a self-employed street vendor in San Jose, convinced him to look for a similar job that would give him more autonomy. Resolved to try working by himself, Arturo quit his janitorial job and became a frozen-fruit-pop vendor for Delicias de Jalisco, a company in San Jose with an established reputation. He chose this company because his brother, who had briefly worked there, introduced him to the local manager.

Arturo's business arrangement with this company illustrates the thin line that often divides self-employment from work in the informal economy. Headquartered in Northern California, Delicias de Jalisco is a large company with warehouses in several cities in the state, through which it distributes its products. From this company, vendors like Arturo obtain the fruit bars and the pushcarts they use to peddle them in the streets. Under a standard arrangement established by the company, vendors must pay a daily fee to rent the pushcarts and a predetermined amount for each frozen fruit pop they sell. When I first met Arturo in 1993, he was paying $2.00 per day for the pushcart rental and the ice and $.42 for each frozen fruit pop he sold. While workers were free to establish the selling price of paletas in the streets and keep the difference as profit, their standard price in the market was $.75 apiece, which gave Arturo $.33 for each paleta he sold. Because of the strong competition in this business, there is constant pressure to keep prices down. There is no formal agreement between the company and the vendors, nor do the latter pay taxes on their profits, which are collected in cash every day after work. Because of this, there is little control over who works for the company, vendors are free to go to work when they wish, and there is a continuous turnover of workers. At the time I met Arturo and observed his work, rules in the company were rather simple and flexible: the warehouse opened its doors at 11:00 in the morning, and from that time on *paleteros* could show up and go to work, provided carts were available. Carts had to be returned before the company closed at 9:30 at night. On any summer day, an average of thirty-five paleteros worked for Delicias de Jalisco, most of them Mexican immigrants like Arturo. Many were newcomers, young recent immigrants for whom this occupation was a first step and temporary work while they tried finding a regular wage-job in the formal sector. Others were older men in their fifties and sixties who either were retired or could not find employment elsewhere, for whom selling paletas was their only source of income.

WORKING HARD TILL DUSK

Arturo's schedule and work routine show both the flexibility and the limitations usually associated with this type of informal occupation, in which workers do not control the means and manner of their employment.[5] Arturo usually worked from noon to 8:30 in the evening, although his schedule varied depending on the season. A typical day in his job as a street vendor went as follows. At about 11:30 in the morning, he drove his old car to the paleta warehouse located in what is left of the Sal Si Puedes neighborhood in San Jose. The warehouse consisted of several industrial refrigerators containing the fruit bars, floor space with forty numbered slots on which to store the pushcarts when not in use, and a counter where the company's manager dealt with the vendors. Against one wall, many vendors stored the bikes they rode to work; Arturo was one of the few who owned a car. Upon arriving, he would first choose his cart for the day. To him, this was not a trivial matter. As he patiently explained to me, there were three main things to look at before picking one. First, the wheels had to be in good shape, otherwise it would take more physical effort to push the cart. Second, the cart's interior had to have no holes or cracks, otherwise fruit bars would not keep cold enough and would soften, after which they could not be sold to the public or returned to the warehouse. Third, the cart bells had to work well. If they did not, he had to struggle all day to make them sound while out on the streets. After choosing a pushcart, Arturo stood in line behind other vendors to load it with fruit bars. When his turn came, he ordered the fruit bars from one of the in-house employees. He usually asked for about 170 frozen fruit pops in thirteen different flavors to diversify the choices for his customers. The flavors included strawberry and coconut—the most popular on the streets—of which he would buy the largest quantities. Then he put two big ice blocks inside the cart to keep the bars cold and walked to the counter to sign a form filled out by the company's manager indicating the number and type of paletas he had, after which he handed him two dollars for the pushcart. Finally, when he was ready to leave, he filled the pushcart tires with air, if necessary, to make it easy to push and stepped out in the street.

As in other street-vending jobs, the success of Arturo's work depended on strategy and discipline. I was surprised by how systematic he was about his job, which he took seriously, following a similar route every day that he had established after carefully trying several alternatives and assessing business sales and competition from other frozen-fruit-pop vendors. After leaving the warehouse, he usually walked first to an apartment complex inhabited mostly by Mexican, Cambodian, and Vietnamese families. The high population density in this area and the large number of children and young people made it a favorite target for paleta and other street vendors. After about forty-five minutes, Arturo left this area and walked toward a bridge over a major freeway that divided the east side, stopping to work in two apartment complexes and a subdivision of single-family homes populated by Latino families. At about 3 P.M., he arrived in Santech, his favorite place to work. Having once lived in the neighborhood for several years, Arturo felt at ease working in this area where he still had many friends and acquaintances, who constituted the core of his clientele, and where many people recognized him among the dozens of paleta vendors that came to Santech everyday. Zigzagging from one building to the next, he spent the next three and half hours walking up and down each of the barrio's streets, pushing his cart while jingling the small bells that hung from the cart's handle to attract the attention of children and adults. Following a methodic routine he had developed over the years, he entered through the front of each building and then moved to the backyard, doing this maneuver twice in each building to "give people time to make up their minds and get the money to buy what they want." Whenever he grew tired, he stopped for a few minutes in the courtyard of a building to take a break in the shadow of a tree, wiping the sweat from his face, forehead, and neck with a handkerchief and, if possible, drinking a glass of water given to him by one of his clients or friends. To my surprise, Arturo did not eat anything during the long hours he spent at work because, as he explained, "I cannot store food in the cart, because it gets too cold, and if I leave it outside it goes bad with the heat." Instead, he had a good breakfast before leaving for work and a large dinner after arriving home. The need for a restroom while working, however, was a problem he could not avoid. With no fast food or commercial stores close to any of the neighborhoods he visited, Arturo relied on his friends in Santech and used their bathrooms when needed.

Around 6:30 in the evening, Arturo would leave Santech and walk back to the paleta warehouse, which was about two miles away, on the other side of the freeway. On his way, he briefly stopped by two other apartment complexes that he had visited earlier in the afternoon, trying to make a few more sales before the day was over. A few minutes past 8:00, he arrived at the warehouse, where other vendors were also coming back visibly sweaty and tired. At the store, Arturo would take all the unsold paletas out of the cart and place them in a big plastic box, which he handed over to a company employee. The latter counted them, noted the number on the form Arturo had filled out earlier in the morning, and then put them back into one of the company's refrigerators. In the meantime, Arturo patiently waited in line with his colleagues to check in with the company's manager. When his turn finally arrived, the manager, a middle-aged Mexican worker, took Arturo's form to calculate how much the latter owed him. After the manager figured out the amount by subtracting the number of paletas Arturo returned from those he had taken in the morning, he collected the money from him and moved to the next vendor in line. At that point, after a fatiguing day under the sun, Arturo was ready to leave, having spent eight hours at work, visited seven different apartment complexes, and walked about five miles pushing his cart. Hungry, he walked to his car to drive back home.

INCOME, RISKS, AND SUBJECTIVE EVALUATION

Unlike many other paleteros, for whom this was only a temporary occupation until they found a better, regular job in the formal sector, Arturo saw street-vending as an alternative to wage jobs. Because of his long experience in the business, and because he worked six days a week, he was able to generate an income similar to what he had earned while employed as a full-time janitor in a local nonunion cleaning company. On an average day during early summer, provided the weather was good, Arturo usually sold between seventy-five and a hundred fruit bars. For example, when he sold ninety at $.75 each, after subtracting $.42 for each one, which he paid to Delicias de Jalisco, he earned $29.70 (44 percent of the total) and the company made $37.80 (56 percent). Weekends were best in this business, and on a good weekend-day, Arturo could sell as many as 150 paletas. In a week's time, he often made about $220, slightly more than the $5.00 an hour he earned while employed in his former janitorial job in the early 1990s.

It would be incorrect, however, to see Arturo's informal occupation as a stable, alternative source of income. Even with several years of experience in this job, he confronted numerous risks beyond his control. For example, the single most important factor that determines sales of frozen fruit pops in the streets is the weather. The paleta season in the region usually runs from March to October, with May to August being the peak time. During these months, Arturo redoubled his efforts, often working more than ten hours per day, starting earlier in the morning and not stopping until just before the warehouse closed, in order to maximize his profits. If the day was rainy or even cloudy, sales invariably went down, bringing his daily earnings to about $15. Because of this, Arturo carefully watched the weather report every night to plan the next day, and when heavy rain or cold temperature was predicted, he did not go to work because he considered it not worthwhile. Taking into consideration these and other elements of uncertainty, Arturo distinguished between good, regular, and bad workdays: "A good day is one in which I sell 125 paletas or more; [then] I make about $40.00. In a normal day I sell about 100 paletas and make $35.00 profit. If the day is bad, I sell less than 60 paletas and only get $20.00 or less—very little!"

Like many other street vendors, Arturo had to look for alternative sources of income in the winter. Between November and March, he quit selling fruit bars and took casual and short-term jobs in construction, landscaping, and cleaning, often for independent contractors who hired him for a specific job and paid him in cash. Not surprisingly, the most regular winter job he had for several years was selling Christmas cards door-to-door for an informal business operated by the local manager of Delicias de Jalisco, who used the company's warehouse as headquarters for this business. Many of the workers were the same vendors employed in the summer to sell fruit bars, and the business arrangements were similar: vendors were paid a commission based on a percentage of the cards they sold each day.[6] To sell the cards, Arturo capitalized on his social network and the same clients who bought his paletas during the warm season, following a similar vending route and visiting the same family neighborhoods, including Santech. The time between the end of the Christmas season and March, when he started selling fruit bars, was the most difficult for him, especially January and February. During these months, Arturo usually sold flowers in the streets and in nightclubs, combining this occupation with occasional day jobs such as cleaning, gardening, truck loading, and unskilled construction work. Because of his limited income and the fact that both of his daughters were U.S. citizens, his wife collected government food stamps, which were essential during the winter season.

Seasonal changes were not the only risks Arturo confronted in his vending job. The possibility of being caught by the police while working without a license presented a more important danger. According to local regulations, all street peddlers had to be licensed by the city government. Most street vendors, however, were immigrants, like Arturo, who did not speak English and were either unaware of the permit process or afraid of dealing with government officers. To minimize the danger of being stopped, Arturo concentrated on Latino neighborhoods on the east side, where the police harassed vendors less than in the city's downtown. The risk of being caught by INS officers was even more frightening, and Arturo had firsthand experience with this. On one occasion, shortly after he started working as a frozen-fruit-pop vendor in San Jose, a friend employed at Delicias de Jalisco told him that Salinas, a nearby rural town largely inhabited by Mexican farmworkers, was an ideal place to sell paletas because there was less competition. One week Arturo went to Salinas to try it, and on his fourth day an INS officer stopped him on the street and asked for his authorization to work in the United States. Being an undocumented worker, Arturo was deported the following day to Tijuana, Mexico. Shortly thereafter, he came back to San Jose, the whole adventure having cost him time, money, the anguish of being separated from his family, and the distress of not knowing for sure that he would be able to cross the border again on his return.

Despite the seasonal nature of his paleta-selling job, the ups and downs in the income it generated, and the risk of being detained by the police or the INS, Arturo preferred this job over the badly paid jobs in the formal sector that he had held in the past. He valued the relative freedom he enjoyed in his job, especially not being subject to a rigid work schedule. He appreciated not being controlled by supervisors, an aspect he emphasized repeatedly when I asked him about the advantages and disadvantages of his work. He also appreciated not having to use a fake green card to work, not paying taxes on his income, and having access to cash every day that he worked, which he could use to buy food or any other necessity for his family without waiting for biweekly paychecks, as he had in his former cleaning job. Explaining what kept him working as a vendor despite all the difficulties he had to endure, Arturo commented,

> Those [wage] jobs pay very little, and besides they ask you for a *mica* [green card]. In my work I don't need it, nor do I have to file an income tax [form], so that all the money I make is for me. . . . Moreover, I work at my own pace and I am not under the orders of a supervisor. . . . But like in any other job, in this job one has to work hard [in Spanish, *esforzarse*] and to walk a lot because sales don't fall from the sky. . . . Yes, I prefer this job because I have more freedom, I can take a break when I want, and I am not under the constant orders of a supervisor. And if the weather is good, I can make as much money as if I was working in a full-time job [in Spanish, *trabajo de planta*] like a janitor or any of those other jobs that pay so little.

Arturo's assertiveness, however, cannot be taken at face value or as an indication of his definitive commitment to work in the informal economy. He often complained about how difficult it was to earn a decent income by selling paletas. He identified the high housing costs in San Jose and the strong competition from rival vendors selling frozen fruit pops and other goods as major considerations that made him doubtful about his future in this job. For example, he explained that, when he first started working as a paleta vendor in San Jose, there was only one fruit bar firm in town; only a few years later, there were already four big companies employing many vendors, as well as many other vendors working on their own. The increasing competition in the business, he complained, had negatively affected his earnings. If the situation worsened, it would be time to look for a regular job, maybe as an assembler in an electronics firm or, preferably, as a self-employed vendor selling ice cream from a truck. To do this, however, he would first have to become a legal resident (or as he put it in Spanish, *arreglar mis papeles*) to work in the streets without fear of being stopped by the police or deported by the INS, a dream beyond his reach at the time.

Not surprisingly, after several years of working in the United States, Arturo was disillusioned about his economic progress. At first he had believed that if he worked hard his economic status would improve, even if at a slow pace. Instead, after years of hard work in San Jose, he was still in a difficult financial position, only barely able to support himself.[7] Despite this, like many other poor immigrants I met in San Jose, Arturo seemed to prefer living in poverty in the United States than in Mexico. "Yes, you can earn more here, but you are still poor. Here one is also poor, but it is better to be poor here than there, because the little money one earns here stretches further; here money buys you more things," he explained.

Arturo is an example of several people I met in Santech and elsewhere in San Jose who preferred to work in the informal sector rather than in low-paid, exploitative jobs in the formal economy. He was willing to risk irregular earnings in exchange for being able to control his work schedule and be free from direct supervision. From this perspective, street vending is not just a response to the demand for cheap goods and services by low-income immigrant workers and families (Sassen 1994) but also a response to the low-paid jobs in the formal sector. To these workers, the differences between low-skilled jobs in the formal and informal sectors are negligible. These workers often switch between the two kinds of jobs, depending both on their incentives and opportunities and on their personal and family circumstances. Understanding the logic behind immigrants' decision to work in the informal economy is thus a necessary step in explaining the growth of these activities beyond the structural forces that fuel the growth of the informal sector.

Arturo's vending job was not, however, a long-term and stable alternative to low-wage formal jobs. What allowed him to subsist year round was a high level of self-exploitation in his work, and financial aid in the form of food stamps, which his family received for his U.S.-born children. Moreover, unlike in true self-employment, Arturo had little control over his job and working conditions, which were determined mainly by the frozen fruit pop company. This illustrates the thin line that often divides self-employment from disguised formal-sector work.[8] By the same token, his job was also different from subcontracting. In subcontracting, the client company shifts the risks to the independent contractor. In disguised employment, such risks are shifted completely to workers themselves. Like the rest of vendors at Delicias de Jalisco, Arturo absorbed most of the risks associated with this business, from weather changes and the ups and downs in sales to the legal responsibility of obtaining a license and work permit. Moreover, Delicias de Jalisco also depended on the contacts and social networks of Arturo and other vendors not only to recruit workers but also to market its products in immigrant communities like Santech. Arturo's job illustrates the structural links between the formal and informal sectors that neo-Marxist authors like to underscore. His job is part of Sassen's first component of the informal economy in immigrant neighborhoods: namely, the economic activities in which immigrants are employed as a source of cheap labor to reduce the production and distribution costs of companies that otherwise are part of the formal sector (1989).

Gustavo: Being a Dentist in the Informal Sector

The informal economy in Latino immigrant communities often evokes images of unskilled workers employed as street vendors, day laborers, construction peons, nannies, housekeepers, and the like. Yet this picture is simplistic, as there is more to the informal economy in neighborhoods like Santech than meets the eye of the casual observer. Some immigrants with professional degrees also work in the informal economy. Gustavo, a young Mexican immigrant with a dentistry degree from Mexico who worked as an informal dentist in San Jose, is an example of this point. There is a demand for skilled medical and dental services among working-poor immigrants in communities like Santech. Their lack of access to these services in the formal sector creates a draw for physicians and dentists in the informal economy. Although small, this is an important segment of the informal economy often overlooked by scholars informed by both modernization and neo-Marxist theories, who tend to solely focus on low-skilled occupations in this sector.

Gustavo was born in Aguililla, Michoacán, in 1963. The transnational nature of his family influenced his migration and work story. His father, a former schoolteacher in Mexico, first migrated in the late 1950s to San Jose, where he worked as a laborer in a tank-building factory at the time the defense industry was growing in the region. In the mid-1960s, his wife and four of their children joined him, and Gustavo's mother found a job as an assembly worker in Silicon Valley's expanding electronics industry. In the meantime, Gustavo and an older brother remained in Mexico and were raised by their grandparents with the remittances their parents sent home. In the summer, they came to San Jose to visit them, where they learned English and became familiar with life in the United States. Upon finishing school, Gustavo decided to continue his studies and pursue a degree in general dentistry in a public university in Morelia, Michoacán state's capital. In 1986, he graduated, and the next year he married Antonieta, a classmate who had graduated with him.

While studying at the university, Gustavo and his wife had planned to open a dental clinic in Morelia upon graduation. But when the time finally came, they realized they did not have the resources, especially not for the expensive equipment and instruments needed for opening a new practice. Aware of their plans and difficulties, Gustavo's parents suggested they move temporarily to San Jose, where they could work and save money to buy the equipment they needed. In 1987, Gustavo convinced his reluctant wife to leave Morelia, and they moved to San Jose to live with his parents, where they planned to stay for three or four years. The following year, they had their first child and decided Antonieta would take care of him while Gustavo worked to pay the family bills and start their savings.

PROVIDING DENTAL CARE TO IMMIGRANTS

I first met Gustavo through one of his brothers, who had been a good friend of mine for several years. At that point I had already established a close relationship with his family, which greatly facilitated my access to Gustavo and his work.[9] As he explained to me, his initiation as an informal dentist in the United States was the outcome of fortuitous events rather than of a preconceived plan. During his first year in San Jose, he worked mostly in low-skilled jobs with no relation with his professional training, the most stable of which was his job as a painter in home-remodeling projects, work that he obtained through one of his brothers, who had been in the trade for several years. Soon afterward he realized that, while he could not work as a dentist in California, he could obtain a license to work as a dental assistant and make more money than he received from manual labor. In his second year in the United States, while he continued working as a painter, he started taking courses in a private school to prepare for his certification as a dental assistant; he passed his exam at the end of that year. Shortly after, he quit his construction job and started work as a dental assistant in a private clinic in San Jose for $8.50 an hour, a job that was better paid and less strenuous than his previous job.

In the meantime, when they learned he was a dentist, a number of Gustavo's family friends, acquaintances, and neighbors started asking him to do, as he put it, "simple dental jobs" such as cleanings, fillings, and tooth extractions. Reluctant at first, he gradually started to do them in his spare time at home for free or a small fee. Soon afterward more people started calling or coming to see him at home for dental work. At this point, he realized that he could work on his own if he chose to. After discussing it with his wife, who offered to help him, he decided to set up his own clinic at home and started working part-time in the evenings to earn extra income after coming home from his formal job as a dental assistant. In 1990, with some money he had saved and an additional three thousand dollars borrowed from his father, Gustavo bought the minimal equipment and tools he needed and opened his own clinic at home. The business prospered so rapidly, with new clients contacting him, that within a few months he was able to repay his father and buy new equipment.

Because his was an informal business, Gustavo maintained only a modest dental office, reflecting the need to prevent detection by government authorities. His office was located in what used to be the garage of his parents' house, which he remodeled with the help of his brother. There was no external sign that would indicate the existence of this clinic. The office consisted of three small rooms divided by curtains that hung from the ceiling. The first room was Gustavo's laboratory, where he kept instruments and materials such as false teeth, crowns, paste for fillings, and so on. Next to it was the main room, where he treated patients. Occupying only about forty-three square feet, it had a dentist's chair in the middle, a mobile lamp attached to a wall, a tray with dental instruments, a recycled spittoon, and a crucifix hanging on the wall (see Figure 6). The third room was what Gustavo called his office, which contained a filing cabinet with patient files, a bookcase with dentistry books and magazines, and a phone and answering machine. In each of his patients' files, he recorded personal and medical

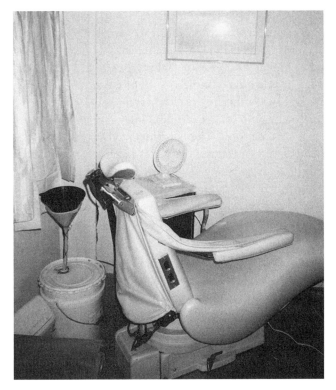

FIGURE 6. A dentist's chair in Gustavo's informal dental clinic.

information, including name, dates of visits, diagnoses, estimated costs, payments made, and other details. On the walls, he had posted a few flyers for his clients: "Call if you cannot come to your appointment," "Please be punctual," "Down payment required for all jobs." None of the three rooms had windows, and the office was ventilated by fans and protected by an alarm at the entrance of the office, which, if activated, could easily be heard at his parents' home. To avoid health and legal risks, Gustavo usually did relatively simple dental work, such as fillings, extractions, cleanings, crowns, and simple orthodontic treatment. His wife, Antonieta, cleaned the office and helped him keep it organized. She also assisted him with administrative tasks such as scheduling appointments with his patients and updating their files and occasionally helped prepare dental materials in the laboratory.

Most of Gustavo's patients were low-income immigrants employed in San Jose as electronics assemblers, gardeners, janitors, construction workers, domestic workers, and the like. The majority did not have dental insurance; others could not afford to pay the fee increases in their dental insurance, and still others were workers who had lost their insurance after changing jobs or being laid off. Regardless of why they could not go to a licensed dental office, most of Gustavo's patients came to him for emergencies such as toothaches, broken teeth, or tooth infections. Others came for longer term treatments, such as light orthodontics, crowns, or false teeth. The heavy demand for his work was evident in the fact that, less than three years after he first started working on his own, he had to stop taking new patients because he was constantly booked solid with his 175 regular patients. Usually, about 45 of these patients came to him on a regular basis, and he treated about 10 other people a month for emergencies.

Gustavo's fees were considerably lower than those charged in regular dental clinics, which explains the attraction of his underground clinic. On average, he charged about a third of what licensed dentists charged for the same treatments. He remained well informed about fees for different dental services in the formal sector, which he used as the basis for his own fees. He also offered a flexible payment policy, extending credit to his patients without demanding big down payments or regular monthly installments, a strategy that suited his low-income patients. To protect himself and leave no record of their financial transactions, he would ask his patients to pay him in cash. Occasionally a patient who was short of money would pay him in kind. For example, a janitor once paid for his treatment with discarded sterilization equipment he had recycled from the dental clinic he cleaned. This flexibility allowed Gustavo to keep many of his clients who otherwise could not afford to pay for his services, which shows that barter is a common means of exchange in the informal economy.

Despite having an informal practice, Gustavo made every effort to update his knowledge and practical training. Every year, he took several technical courses offered by private institutions in the city to learn new techniques that he could use in his clinic or that would help him get promoted in his formal job, such as X-ray techniques. He also subscribed to several professional dental publications to stay abreast of the most recent developments and technologies in his field. He often would speak to me with pride about taking and passing these technical courses, which he considered a form of *superarse* (getting ahead) and an asset in his competition with other dentists like him who also worked in the informal sector.

INCOME, RISKS, AND SUBJECTIVE EVALUATION

Gustavo's under-the-table earnings were considerably lower than what dentists earned in the formal sector, but considerably higher than what Mexican immigrants earned in low-skilled occupations in the formal or informal sectors. By 1993, working in his office in the evenings and weekends, he was making an average of fifteen hundred dollars a month, although there were months when he made close to two thousand dollars, especially if he took new patients. Out of these earnings, he had to pay the expenses generated by his business, including materials used for dental work and disposable instruments as well as phone and utility bills. He reinvested much of the profit generated by his business, buying new dental equipment, which he planned to take back to Mexico upon his return. In addition, Gustavo earned about thirteen hundred dollars a month working full-time as a dental assistant in a licensed clinic. While less profitable than his business, he preferred to keep this formal job because it provided him with a steady income each month, something he could not always count on in his informal clinic. Commenting on the comparative advantages of both jobs and the economic rationale behind combining the two, he explained,

> When I was only working full-time [as a dental assistant], I was making a thousand dollars [per month] for eight hours a day, but working at home in my own practice I made the same amount [per month] in just two hours [per day]! By working only fifteen hours [per week] here, I make the same as working forty hours in my regular job, and without anybody telling me what to do or yelling at me. If only people would pay on time, I could easily make two thousand dollars or three thousand dollars, but the real problem is that people do not pay on time. . . . But still it's a good business; it generates a good profit. . . . I use the money I earn here to pay all my bills, food, rent, and clothes for the kids. Also from here comes the money I use to buy my instruments, so I keep my paychecks [from his formal job] to send to Mexico to pay for the house we are building there.

Like most other informal occupations, however, Gustavo's underground business involved important financial and legal risks. First, the flexible payment policy that allowed him to keep his low-income clients was often one of his principal problems. Because he had no written contracts with his patients, many of them, after completing their treatment, failed to fully pay for it. Gustavo had no legal recourse to recover the loss. He estimated that, at any given point, about 50 percent of his patients either were behind in the payment schedule they verbally agreed on, or simply avoided paying him and did not come back after he completed his work. Reflecting on this issue, he commented,

> A big problem is that people are not punctual. They see this is not a regular dental clinic, and they see me wearing comfortable clothes rather than a dentist's uniform, and they take things lightly. Others never come back, so I have to call them on the phone to find out whether they are going to continue their treatment. . . . I do not have a way to press people to pay, and everybody seems to have an excuse for not paying on time: that they are unemployed, have been laid off, have a family emergency, debts, and so on.

A more serious risk that Gustavo took was that he could be denounced to government authorities, an important reason he often cited in our conversations for not pursuing his debtors with more determination. To make malpractice suits and other legal problems less likely, he provided only a limited range of dental services, even though he had the training and skill to do more complicated and financially rewarding work. He carefully checked the personal backgrounds of his clients, found out who referred them and, if he sensed a potential risk, turned them down, giving some credible excuse. Trust and personal relationships were critical ingredients in his business, just as they are in less skilled occupations in the informal sector. They both helped to protect him from legal troubles and connected him to the needs and expectations of his patients, a contrast with the more impersonal relationship between doctors and patients in the formal sector. Aware of the importance Latino immigrants usually place on trusting their family physicians and dentists, Gustavo always tried to establish a good rapport with his patients:

> I only treat Latinos because we are used to doing business under the table, and we are not afraid of it. All my patients are Latinos, except for an Irish man from San Francisco who came here recommended by my brother Samuel. . . . Besides, we Latinos look for a doctor we can trust and we can relate to. Here, American doctors only care about the technical aspect, [and] they do not offer the human touch that Latino patients look for. But not all Latino patients are trustworthy, so I have to be very careful and avoid those that look untrustworthy, who might cause me trouble.

In 1995, five years after he started working as an informal dentist in San Jose, the legal risks and consequences Gustavo faced by working in the informal sector became openly evident to him. At this point, one of his worst fears materialized when he received an official letter from state authorities declaring that they had been informed he was operating "an illegal dental practice." The letter stated that, if he continued, he would be fined, have his dental assistant's license suspended, and face criminal prosecution. To avoid further problems, Gustavo decided to dismantle his office immediately. He sold off dental equipment that could not be taken back to Mexico, discontinued receiving patients at home, and informed all his clients that he could no longer treat them.

But this solution posed unanticipated problems. Many of his patients insisted on continuing to see him, especially those who were in the middle of treatment. Some continued calling or visiting him at home. Caught between his desire for self-protection, on the one hand, and the obligation he felt to his patients, on the other, he decided to keep seeing only his most regular and loyal patients at their homes until he completed their treatment. After shutting his clinic, Gustavo lost more than 70 percent of his patients; he regularly visited about thirty of them at their homes for several months. In short, an official measure intended to diminish the health risks created by an underground dental clinic ended up producing the opposite effect, as Gustavo began performing his work at his patients' homes in an environment less hygienic and riskier than his informal clinic.

Despite the setback, Gustavo was not surprised by what happened, as he had always been aware of the potential risk of working underground. Yet in his view, shutting down his office accomplished little because it left low-income immigrants without access to basic dental treatment, worsening their problems rather than helping them. When I asked him about possible alternatives, he replied, "They [government authorities] should change the law so that I could register my clinic; and all dentists like me [working informally] would agree to only treat low-income clients who do not have insurance, so we would not be stealing clients from regular dentists." His comments reflected his perception of a dual health system in Silicon Valley, where low-income Latino immigrants had to look for alternative sources for health care to meet some of their basic needs. He used this perception to justify his proposal instead of questioning this dual system itself. Indeed, Gustavo often spoke of himself as somebody who provided much-needed dental services to the underserved Latino population. When I asked him whether he would rather work as a licensed dentist to avoid all these legal problems, he responded,

> Well, yes, because I could make more money, because here dentists make lots of money. On the other hand, I would not like to practice here, because there are too many regulations and laws, and that puts a lot of pressure on you. You have to have insurance for everything—against lawsuits, fire, robbery, and so many things—because otherwise they don't

authorize you to work. Besides, you have to pay taxes, which I do not have to pay in my work. All this is an financial burden and a source of constant pressure and preoccupation, so I'd rather work in my home underground.

In spite of the financial setback, Gustavo continued with his plans to go back to Mexico. He estimated that by 1996, with the income generated by his job as a dental assistant and his own dental practice, he had invested about twenty-five thousand dollars in building the new house in Mexico where he and his wife planned to set up their own dental clinic when they returned. In addition, he had spent a considerable amount of money on medical equipment and instruments to take back home. With the lower cost of living in Mexico, he and his wife expected to raise their living standard to a level they regarded as commensurate with their professional status, a scenario he preferred over living as an undocumented immigrant in the United States, where his professional degree was not recognized.

In 1998, after more than ten years in Silicon Valley, Gustavo, Antonieta, and their two children returned to Mexico. Their departure came as a surprise to me. I had believed that, like many other immigrants who first come with the intention of staying temporarily and who end up settling down, they would stay longer. In the end, Gustavo's choice was to practice his profession as a licensed dentist in Mexico rather than in the informal sector in the United States. For all the years he worked in secret, his goal had remained the same, as his identity was closely tied to his profession. He preferred to openly develop his career in the formal sector in Mexico, which would not require him to renounce his hard-won degree. To him, working in the informal sector was a means to accomplish this dream. As he explained to me in San Jose,

> Yes, I prefer working as a licensed dentist in Mexico than under the table here. . . . Look, I have seen how dentists work here; it's a very competitive profession. Yes, you make a lot of money, but you have to work very hard and many hours. I am not after the money, we just want to have a good and quiet life so we [can] live well and have free time to enjoy our family and children. I do not want to live working on a profession that gives me a lot of money, but where I am a slave of my clients and the phone.

Gustavo represents a small but important group of professional immigrants who work in the informal sector because their formal degrees are not recognized in the United States. While many of these professional workers are employed in unskilled jobs with no relation to their training, the informal economy offered Gustavo an opportunity to put his skills to work and a better option than working in the sort of low-paid jobs that most undocumented immigrants in Silicon Valley accept. With little access to credit and capital markets in Mexico, Gustavo found that the informal economy also offered an avenue for building savings at a rate he could not have duplicated by working solely in the formal sector as a dental assistant. Rather than merely supplementing low wages earned in the formal sector, Gustavo's self-employment as an informal dentist helped him to accumulate capital to open his own dental office in Mexico's formal sector.[10] And as in the cases discussed earlier, Gustavo's active mobilization of his human and social capital was a central factor behind the rise and growth of his informal dental business.[11]

But Gustavo's informal dental office was not merely the result of these factors and his personal determination to accumulate savings. The working-poor Latino immigrants in Silicon Valley had a strong need for affordable dental services. The fact that they could not afford basic dental care because of their low wages and lack of insurance was an equal if not more relevant factor. This was the structural context that allowed him to work as a dentist in the informal sector in the first place: the situation of an important segment of the local population, whose access to licensed professional services is limited by poor wages and lack of social benefits. Given the high cost of medical and dental insurance, and the increasing barriers to basic health services that undocumented immigrants face, it is unlikely that informal practices like Gustavo's will disappear despite government efforts to eradicate them. They are part of an important but less visible segment of the informal economy in immigrant communities like Santech that is often neglected by structural approaches like Sassen's "neighborhood subeconomy" (1994), which tend to focus on low-skilled goods and services produced to satisfy the consumption needs of low-income immigrants.

Like other Mexican barrios in San Jose, Santech is a hub for a large variety of informal economic activities in which residents are either producers or consumers. The variety of activities found in this sector belies the assumption that the informal economy in these immigrant neighborhoods can be reduced to a set of unskilled survival occupations held by poorly educated workers with no access to employment opportunities in the formal sector. More often, in Santech, Mexican immigrants I spoke to used income generated by work in the informal economy to supplement wages from low-paid jobs in the formal sector. For others, like Laura or Arturo, the informal economy represented an alternative to unstable, unpleasant, and poorly paid jobs in the formal economy. They had greater independence and were less subject to control than in some of the low-skilled jobs available to them in the formal sector, and at the same time they earned a similar income. The apparent paradox of petty informal economic activities in Santech in the midst of Silicon Valley cannot be explained, then, as the result of the lack of integration of Latino immigrants into the local economy. Rather, the fact that immigrants are paid below-subsistence wages while employed as janitors, gardeners, construction workers, domestic workers, and so on is a central force behind the proliferation of informal activities in this barrio. In fact, most of the households of the immigrant workers I met in Santech were involved in some sort of informal income-generating activity to make ends meet. Apparently disconnected from the reality of the industrial parks in the region, these informal activities subsidize the workers employed in the low-skilled sector of Silicon Valley's labor market.

The three cases presented here also reveal the importance of considering immigrants' agency and motivations when examining informal economic activities in Santech. As authors like Sassen (1994) point out when criticizing the assumptions of the modernization theory, the informal economy in immigrant communities cannot be explained as the product of cultural practices immigrants bring with them. Yet we cannot ignore the skills and experience that people like Laura, Arturo, and Gustavo bring with them, including their previous involvement in the informal economy in their home communities, which reflects a common subsistence strategy employed by a large segment of working-class families to make ends meet in Mexico (González de la Rocha 1994). The cultural capital of each of these workers is essential in explaining how they started their respective informal businesses in the first place and the creative strategies they developed to confront the numerous legal and financial risks involved in their jobs. These factors play an important role in explaining their initiative and creativity and their ability to seize business and market opportunities in the informal economy that structural forces alone cannot explain.

We should be careful, however, not to interpret these informal occupations as stable, long-term employment alternatives to low-skilled jobs in the formal sector. The main purpose of self-employment for people like Laura is to complement the poor wages brought home by family members employed in the formal sector. Moreover, as the cases of Laura and Arturo illustrate, work in the informal economy is often labor-intensive, involves the collaboration of family members, and entails a high degree of self-exploitation. In addition, unlike those who work in formal wage jobs, workers self-employed in the informal economy often bear all the financial and legal risks associated with their businesses. This is true of Arturo, who, like many immigrants, is not actually self-employed but instead functions as a disguised employee. For many, the line that separates the formal and informal sectors is thin. As a result, they often move between formal and informal jobs in a highly dynamic manner or combine both types of occupations simultaneously while constantly assessing the advantages and disadvantages that the jobs offer them.

In sum, the growth of informal economic activities in immigrant neighborhoods like Santech responds to the same forces that have propelled the growth of low-paid service jobs in Silicon Valley's formal sector. The informal economy in this barrio cannot be understood as a self-contained reality, but is the inevitable outcome when low-skilled occupations provide immigrant workers with only limited avenues for economic stability and mobility. Combining formal and informal jobs, organizing informal economic activities in a flexible manner around other work and household activities, and distributing the work among several family members are all part of what Dohan calls the strategy of "overwork" (2003: 81–82, 89–98), the only option available to first-generation immigrants who seek to make ends meet and, if lucky, achieve some degree of economic mobility.

CHAPTER 4

Mexican Families in Santech

When I first arrived in Santech, I was shocked by the large number of residents crowded together in the barrio's small, two-bedroom apartments. Whether employed in formal or informal occupations, most Mexican immigrants in Santech lived with relatives and boarders in extended family households, sharing rent, utilities, and other living expenses.[1] Rather than being stable, many of these households seemed to be in permanent flux, with constant changes in size and composition. It seemed that every time I visited a family, new people had joined their household and former members had left. In addition, households did not always coincide with families: often households included more than one nuclear family, and in other cases members of the same family lived in different households. Because of that, I had trouble at first keeping track of who and how many people lived in each household at any given point and how they were related.

I soon noticed that there were important differences in financial status among the members of these households as well, and that, along with cooperation and mutual help, there were also clear signs of economic stratification and conflict. And I was surprised by the number of immigrant women living without their husbands as single mothers in extended family households. For example, fourteen out of twenty-five families in the Santech households I surveyed included single mothers.[2] How did Mexican families in Santech make ends meet in one of the most expensive regions in the country? What effects did the structural forces that define flexible employment in this region have on the lives of low-income families in this barrio? How did these families preserve their unity and stability despite their frequent changes in size and composition? What explained the internal differences I observed among the members of these families? And how did working mothers who were undocumented immigrants maintain the financial integrity of their families without the support of their husbands?

As stated earlier, the concept of "family economy" that focuses on income-pooling and other cooperative strategies has been widely used to explain how immigrants and other low-income workers cope with poverty and social exclusion from the welfare state.[3] Leo Chávez, for example, maintains that the diverse domestic arrangements of undocumented Mexican and Central American immigrants in Southern California are examples of immigrants' adjustment to specific conditions of their lives as undocumented residents, including the high cost of housing, low income, child-care demands, and social responsibility for the care of other family members (1990: 57). Along similar lines, Carlos Vélez-Ibáñez (1993) and Javier Tapia (1995, 1996) propose the concept of "clustered households"—a dense network of households organized around a nuclear or extended family that serves to distribute scarce resources within the cluster—to explain how Mexican families subsist in the midst of poverty in urban barrios in Tucson and Los Angeles.

But scholars using a feminist perspective have criticized the family economy model for depicting the immigrant household as a monolithic unit. In her influential study of a Mexican undocumented immigrant community in Northern California, for example, Pierrette Hondagneu-Sotelo (1994) criticizes the "household strategies model" because it ignores important internal differences along gender and generational lines and does not pay attention to the problems within their families that undocumented immigrant women face. Sarah Mahler has also questioned the assumption of generalized reciprocity and solidarity in Latino immigrant families, arguing that one of the most important consequences of migration and proletarianization is the "suspension" of balanced reciprocity within immigrant families and communities (1995: 216–26). On similar grounds, Patricia Zavella (1995) has criticized what she identifies as the romantic portrayal of the Latino family, arguing that what might appear to be intact nuclear or extended families are often fictitious marriages in which women are the main economic providers or are trapped in exploitative relationships with their husbands.[4] More recently, Socorro Torres Sarmiento (2002), writing about flexible employment and exclusionary policies for Latino immigrants in Southern California, has shown that Mexican women's jobs in the formal and informal economies play a critical role in balancing the budgets of their families.

During my fieldwork in Santech, I realized that, along with clear forms of cooperation, there were visible indications of inequality, conflict, and even internal exploitation in several of the families I met, which I could not ignore without distorting my field observations and the way in which members of these families themselves described and interpreted their own experiences. Because of that, while aware that the household is a crucial unit of analysis in determining how many low-paid Mexican immigrants in Santech made a living, I paid close attention to signs of inequality and conflict within households. In order to understand how low-income workers in Santech are able to make ends meet and preserve the unity of their families in the context of Silicon Valley's flexible labor regime, I focused on three major areas: family background and immigration history; income-generating activities, including wage work and informal occupations; and internal domestic arrangements, including the specific challenges that working mothers confront while trying to keep their families together. My decision to present the case studies of three extended families through the lens of working mothers was not a random choice. Behind what at first glance appeared to be homogeneous families, I often discovered that women were central figures who kept these families together.

The flexible employment regime in Silicon Valley penetrates the households of Mexican immigrants, who absorb much of the cost associated with the economic and social production of low-skilled immigrant labor in this region. The constant change in size and composition of these households mirrors the dramatic and destabilizing effects of the flexible-employment pattern on immigrant workers in both formal and informal jobs. Extended-family domestic arrangements are crucial to the subsistence of these workers and to the advancement of their own interests and plans, as the household strategies model states. But rather than being organized according to the principle of generalized reciprocity, these households often are segmented along gender, age, and immigrant-status lines, with undocumented working mothers occupying the most vulnerable position, as feminist critics of the model contend. The dynamic interaction between politico-economic forces that define the position of undocumented immigrant labor in Silicon Valley, on the one hand, and gender and generational relations at the family level, on the other, shapes the opportunities of and constraints on low-income Mexican residents in Santech.[5]

Silvia: An Income-Pooling Household

Silvia was a short, quiet woman with gentle manners whose wrinkled face revealed years of hard work. She first arrived in San Jose in 1986, when she was in her early forties. She became the oldest person in an extended family household composed of ten members sharing a two-bedroom apartment in Santech. I first met Silvia in 1992, shortly after she moved to Santech, at a public talk sponsored by a nonprofit organization in the barrio about the Immigration Reform and Control Act's amnesty program. Hospitable by nature, she and her family opened their home to me, and from then on we developed a good relationship and mutual trust. Silvia's case illustrates what many other families I met in Santech experienced, as members pooled income for housing and other living expenses. At the same time, her case also reveals the tribulations of undocumented working mothers who raise their children without help from their husbands. The closest to the household strategies model, Silvia's case reveals that, rather than being a cultural ideal, living in an extended household often represents a pragmatic compromise between achieving the goal of nuclear-family autonomy and accepting the limitations encountered by working mothers in Silicon Valley who are undocumented immigrants, as they attempt to provide for their children and protect the unity of their families (Pessar 1999).

SILVIA'S MIGRATION TO THE UNITED STATES

Born in 1945 in the small rural town of El Español in the state of Guanajuato, Silvia was the fourth of five children, three daughters and two sons. As her father worked on his *ejido* parcel (agricultural land under communal ownership), she attended elementary school for six years and helped her mother at home with household chores. Later on, when her mother fell seriously ill, Silvia abandoned school and started working as a domestic servant. In 1963, she migrated to Mexico City with one of her brothers and met Gabriel, a farmworker who had also moved to this city in the early 1960s. They married in 1965. In 1970, soon after their first baby was born, Gabriel started migrating every year to the United States, following the crops in Texas, California, Oregon, and Washington, and returning home for a few months during the winter. As the years passed, however, his visits to Mexico became more sporadic and his remittances smaller and less frequent. By 1984, he stopped coming back home and sending money to Silvia. Not knowing his whereabouts, but suspecting her husband had formed another family in the United States, Silvia was left with the responsibility of sustaining herself and her four children on her own. At first, she worked as a laborer for various *ejidatarios* in her hometown, raising pigs, selling secondhand clothes, and running a small food store she had opened in the early 1980s with the money her husband sent her. Despite her efforts, she was unable to sustain her children and depended heavily on the sporadic help of two brothers who were seasonal migrants to the United States and who sent her money after they found out Gabriel had deserted her.

In 1984, with grim prospects for improving her situation in Mexico, and encouraged by her brothers, Silvia decided to migrate to California. After selling her small home business and a few personal possessions, she headed north, leaving her children in the care of one of her sisters. Crossing undetected through the mountains of the Tijuana–San Diego border region, she headed to a small rural town in Northern California, where one of her brothers had found a job for her in a local sawmill. After working as a manual laborer for two years, she brought her two youngest children to California with the money she had saved. In 1991, the sawmill closed down and Silvia moved to San Jose to join her other brother and her two oldest children who, following her path, had also migrated to California, in 1987 and 1991, respectively. Five years after leaving Mexico, Silvia was able to reunite with her four children. By that time she had become a grandmother, as her oldest daughter had recently married a young Mexican immigrant and had borne her first child.

A FLEXIBLE HOUSEHOLD

In San Jose, Silvia and her family lived in a household composed of relatives and friends, a domestic arrangement common among Mexican immigrants in the United States (Chávez 1990, 1992). But far from being stable, Silvia's household experienced frequent changes in size and composition. For several years, she lived in an extended household composed of a permanent core made up of members related by kinship and a provisional periphery made up of fictive kin, *paisanos* (fellow countryfolk), and friends from her hometown in Guanajuato. The core of the household was formed by two nuclear families: one composed of Silvia and three of her children—Gabriel (eighteen years old), Alfonso (twelve years old), and Lorena (ten years old)—and a second one made up of her oldest daughter, Luisa, her husband, Ismael, and their daughter. The periphery of the household was composed of relatives, often nephews, and fellow countryfolk, usually recently arrived migrant workers who stayed only temporarily in the household. The migrant workers lived there for short periods of time that lasted from days to several months, until they could find employment or some other place to live. While Silvia, her children, and grandchildren formed a stable family unit, the periphery experienced continuous changes as different persons moved in and out. Between 1992 and 1995, for example, eight different people not related by kin lived with them, none remaining for more than two years. Adding boarders to the household helped Silvia and her family to preserve their own financial stability during their first years in San Jose, especially in harsh economic times.

Despite the frequent changes in the household's size and composition, the principles around which it was organized remained fairly stable. Within its core, all members participated in a system of generalized reciprocity in which income was pooled to cover rent, food, household utilities, and other living expenses. When any of the family members were out of work, the others covered their share of the expenses. For example, when Silvia was out of work or did not have enough to pay her share of the rent, her married daughter and son-in-law would cover her part and buy food for her and her children. The members of the periphery were only partially included in this system of income pooling. They were expected to pay rent according to their individual abilities, which generally depended on whether they were employed or not at any given point in time. However, they did not share food with the family and, in fact, many used the apartment only as a place to sleep at night. In short, financial cooperation occurred only within the core group, while peripheral household members, who remained only on a temporal basis, contributed to the financial stability of the household as a whole.

COMBINING FORMAL AND INFORMAL JOBS

Silvia's household participated in a large variety of formal and informal economic activities to generate income. The principal source of income for all the adults, including Silvia, was janitorial work at Building Service System. In this cleaning company, Silvia, together with Elva, Ismael, Luisa, and her oldest son, Gabriel, formed a family crew in charge of cleaning several office buildings nightly in Fremont, a city located about thirty minutes away from San Jose. In a common pattern of chain employment, a pioneer immigrant is used by an employer to locate more employees through his or her social network, Silvia's son-in-law was the first person in the family to be employed at Building Service System. After being promoted to supervisor, he helped to hire all the adult members of his family one by one, the last one being Silvia, who up until then had encountered serious problems finding a full-time job because of her age.

In addition to wage work as janitors, all the members of Silvia's family were engaged in supplementary informal economic activities. Most of these activities depended on two or more family members pooling their labor and were generally organized along gender lines. The family's most common informal occupation was baby-sitting, a job nominally carried out by Silvia but with the help of her relatives at home. Silvia was known in Santech as a baby-sitter, and she had two or three children under her care on most days, usually from neighboring Chicano and Mexican working-class parents who could not afford to pay a day-care center. While the verbal agreement to care for the children was made between the children's parents and Silvia, her baby-sitting depended on help from family members, including that of her oldest daughter, her daughter in-law, and Silvia's two youngest children. Another informal occupation that engaged several family members was recycling. Luisa organized and coordinated this activity each morning, assembling the aluminum cans, cardboard boxes, and paper that she and her relatives collected from the offices they cleaned at night, which she then took to the recycling center for cash. Although this recycling generated only about twenty dollars every two weeks, the extra income helped Luisa to cover the expenses of her own nuclear family. Both baby-sitting and recycling were considered "women's work" even though they involved the collaboration of the adult male members of the household.

A third informal source of income was the small family janitorial company run by Silvia's oldest son and her son-in-law in their spare time. Ismael and Gabriel were occasionally hired as self-employed workers to clean private homes and small offices. To do these jobs, they used recycled cleaning equipment cast off by janitorial companies that had previously employed them. Most of Ismael and Gabriel's clients were friends, neighbors, or acquaintances met while they lived in Santech. The two men printed a bilingual business card picturing a smiling woman holding a mop, offering "Family Cleaning Services" for residential and commercial establishments, which they distributed in the community. Working weekends, they could earn as much as a hundred dollars, which they split in half. This type of informal work was considered a "man's job," not because of the nature of the work (in fact, they chose the image of a woman for the company's card), but perhaps because, unlike child care and recycling, it involved the manipulation of heavy cleaning equipment outside the home.

The children in Silvia's household also engaged in petty informal income-generating activities. Alfonso and Lorena—Silvia's two youngest children (twelve and ten years old, respectively)—occasionally helped her raise extra income. On weekends and during school vacations, for example, they worked in a big Latino supermarket carrying groceries to customers' cars in exchange for tips, which often amounted to fifteen dollars per day each. Moreover, during the weekends and occasionally on weekdays, Alfonso helped his mother at her nighttime janitorial job, especially when Silvia was sick or too tired to do the work by herself. Although Silvia did not refer to her children's activities as "work," the income they generated made a significant contribution to the family's supplemental income, which shows the importance of these occupations for Mexican and other Latino immigrant families.[6]

CHARITIES AND INFORMAL CREDIT ASSOCIATIONS

While living in an extended family household based on mutual reciprocity was central to ensuring Silvia's financial stability, her ability to mobilize material and social resources beyond her family was also crucial, especially in times of need. Having lived in San Jose for several years, Silvia was familiar with churches and charities that helped poor families in San Jose by providing food, used clothes, and secondhand furniture, and which offered job placement assistance, legal counseling, and other services. On several occasions, especially when she was out of work or short of money, Silvia sought assistance from these organizations, usually to obtain food and clothes for her children. For example, she would go to Sacred Heart Church, located in a popular Latino neighborhood, which offered free food once a month to people in need. She also visited a shelter downtown that gave away bags of secondhand clothes, and a Christian chapel that once a month gave away clothes and food. Silvia's knowledge of these and other nonprofit organizations in the region provided her and her family an important safety cushion.

Silvia and her family were also members of a *tanda,* an informal rotating savings and credit association common among Latino and other immigrants and generally used to raise and save money. This system allows low-income immigrants—who have no access to bank loans and few opportunities to save—to obtain small, interest-free loans, usually through their kin (Vélez-Ibáñez 1988). Four of Silvia's household members participated in a *tanda*, which was composed of ten people, including neighbors in Santech and *paisanos* from her hometown in Mexico who lived in San Jose. It was organized on an occasional basis whenever its members agreed to it. While the tanda was active, every week all but one of its members deposited fifty dollars into a common fund, which in its entirety was given to one person on a rotating basis according to a prearranged schedule. Members of the tanda generally used the money to deal with an emergency or as a down payment to buy something on credit. Silvia, for example, first joined the tanda to collect part of the fifteen hundred dollars she needed to pay a person who, claiming to be a lawyer, had promised to legalize her immigrant status and that of her children, but who turned out to be a scam artist.[7] Over the years, the wealth of social connections developed by Silvia and her relatives, and their acquaintance with charitable organizations in town, helped to ensure the survival of the family in times of need.

THE STRUGGLES OF AN UNDOCUMENTED IMMIGRANT MOTHER

Living in an extended family household made it possible for Silvia to provide for herself and her children despite a meager income from wage work, but it was not a panacea. Even though loved and respected by all her children and in-laws, Silvia still occupied the most vulnerable position in the household. As a middle-aged, undocumented woman, she was relegated to the bottom of the job market, her work opportunities limited to low-wage and highly exploitative jobs, often in the informal economy. Some of her first jobs in San Jose consisted of working for distant relatives in ambiguous and rather exploitative conditions. She first started working as a janitor for the father of her nephew's wife, a self-employed worker who had cleaning contracts with restaurants, small offices, and other small businesses in San Jose. He informally employed Silvia under a verbal agreement without any stipulated wage, which was left to his discretion. For more than two years, Silvia worked for him with little stability in her job, as he continually won some contracts and lost others. During this time, she often worked six hours a night, three days a week, cleaning a restaurant and a combination office and shops for $140.00 a month, or $2.30 an hour. Like many other undocumented immigrants exploited by more seasoned immigrants (Mahler 1995; Malkin 1998), Silvia put up with the situation not only because she needed the income but also because her employer was a relative to whom she felt certain moral obligations. With a tone of resignation, she talked about her sense of being exploited in this job:

> One kills oneself at work to do a good job and [make a good] impression on the patron, but it's useless. I would lie down on the floor to clean the grease in the kitchen, but my efforts were worthless—he didn't appreciate my effort. . . . It doesn't make a difference that you work hard. . . . When I started working for him when he got contracts with several restaurants, I worked hard with good will because I expected to get about $350 for two weeks of work or at least $600 a month. But I got discouraged when the first month he barely paid me $140! . . . In the first month, I worked seven hours a night and I only rested three days, but he only counted five hours a day, so the first time he paid me $140 and the second time $100. . . . He thinks one is a fool and works just for pleasure!

Then, reflecting on the dilemma of working for an unfair employer related to her by kin ties, Silvia added, "I feel bad about complaining to him because he is the father of my niece. . . . [But] he hasn't paid me in two months; he owes me [for] fifty-four hours of work. . . . I don't want to talk to him directly, because I feel bad about his daughter, because she is a relative of mine and I appreciate her; that is what holds me back."

To complement her meager income, Silvia worked in a variety of part-time informal occupations, including baby-sitting, domestic work, housecleaning, and others. As in her first janitorial job, some of her employers and clients were distant relatives. For example, among the several children she baby-sat was her nephew's child (the grandson of her janitorial employer), whom she took care of five days a week, nine hours a day, for $35 a week (that is, $7 a day). Frustrated by how the baby's mother treated her, Silvia complained, "I take care of him from 6 in the morning to 2 in the afternoon. That is the agreement, but she often doesn't come to pick him up until 4 P.M. And she doesn't even bring enough food for her baby, only a milk gallon once in a while. . . . I don't say anything because it's my nephew's child."

To escape the exploitation in low-paid informal jobs by unscrupulous employers and her own relatives, Silvia put all her effort into finding a full-time job that would give her financial autonomy. This was not an easy task. Because of her age and her status as an undocumented immigrant who did not speak English, she was turned down repeatedly when she applied for hotel, cleaning, electronics assembly, restaurant, and other jobs in Silicon Valley. Seeking an alternative, she began volunteering as a kitchen helper in Santech's elementary school, where her children were enrolled, with the hope that this could turn into a more permanent job. A year later, after winning the confidence of the school principal, she was officially hired to work ten hours a week as a school aid during lunchtime, earning $7.50 an hour, the highest wage she had received since arriving in California. At this point, she quit her part-time janitorial job with her nephew's father in-law. Her decision was not welcome to her employer, who allegedly asked his daughter to stop taking his granddaughter to Silvia for child care unless she returned to work for him. This was the end of the relationship between Silvia and this part of her family; after she quit the janitorial job, they had no communication with her for several years.

Silvia achieved some financial stability only several years later, when she was hired as a janitor by Building Service System. By combining the incomes from her full-time job and several part-time informal occupations, she was finally able to pay her share of housing and living costs and sustain her children who were attending school. But this financial stability came at a high price. As her financial situation improved, her physical health progressively declined because of extended hours of work. She slept only five hours a night between her night-shift janitorial job and her part-time work in Santech's public school, and she started to feel sick more often as time went by. Not surprisingly, one year after she took the full-time janitorial job, her health had deteriorated so much that she was forced to quit her job in Santech's school, a hard decision that threatened her financial autonomy. Worried about her health, her children and in-laws helped Silvia pay her share of rent and other household expenses when needed. Reflecting on her financial hardships, Silvia commented,

> I cannot save any money. The first check I receive in the month is about $200, which I use for rent and other expenses, and the second check is for lunch and *el mandado* [food and basic expenses]. . . . So you see, I cannot save any money. . . . When I work in the school, I don't sleep much and I feel tired all day long. That is why I sometimes bring Lorena and Alfonso to help me at work. I finish earlier and the *patrones* pay $5 per day per child. . . . I keep my work at Santech [school] because, as a janitor, I don't make enough to pay all the expenses. . . . When my son Alfonso is on vacation, I take him to help me at work so I can finish my shift at ten thirty rather than at one in the morning, while Lorena [thir-

teen years old at the time] stays home taking care of Gabriel's and Luisa's children.

While happy about having her family around, and resigned to accepting financial help from her relatives at home, Silvia believed that, even in an extended household like hers, each nuclear family should be able to provide for their own. To her, living in an extended household was the product of financial necessity rather than her own preferences or cultural values. Indeed, she often stated that her dream was to live only with her single children and to be able to raise and educate them without the interference of her married children and other household members. Living in an extended household was a compromise between achieving this ideal and accepting the reality of her unstable financial situation. Commenting on her disadvantaged financial status and her preference for living on her own, Silvia explained,

> Although we share rent among all of us, everybody keeps their own money. They [her oldest daughter and son-in-law] have more money because both of them work. But my children and I barely have any money. . . . I don't even have money to buy them shoes. . . . Alfonso has been wearing the same pair of shoes since I bought them for him last year, and they are falling apart. . . . [But] I would like to live alone with my [single] children because then I can better educate them. Also, having my grandchildren at home means more work for me. . . . We don't have problems at home—we all get along—but I'd rather live on my own, it's more quiet and independent.

MOVING OUT OF SANTECH

Extended family households help recent immigrants cope with problems of housing, jobs, and poverty (Chávez 1990). These domestic arrangements do not always transform into nuclear family households with time as immigrants settle down, but may instead continue playing an instrumental role in helping members experience some degree of financial mobility and escape poor barrios like Santech. This was the case of Silvia's family, who, in 1996, four years after first arriving in Santech, moved out of their small, run-down two-bedroom apartment to a more spacious and comfortable three-bedroom rented house in a less crowded neighborhood in San Jose. Leaving Santech was not easy for Silvia. She missed her friends and the wealth of social relations she had built throughout the years, which had given her some sense of material and emotional support. But she believed the change would be good for her children, because they could attend a better public school and live in a neighborhood quieter and safer than Santech, which she viewed as being plagued by poor housing and drugs.

In 1999, Silvia's extended family facilitated another move forward, this time by buying a home in Pittsburg in Contra Costa County. Silvia's son in-law purchased the house with the help of all the working members of the family, who contributed to the down payment. This was a major change for the whole family. Given that they could not afford to buy a home in San Jose because of the skyrocketing housing prices, they bought one located about fifty miles away. Because all members of Silvia's family continued working as janitors for Building Service System, they had a long commute to work every night. In Silvia's case, the increasing time she spent working, including transportation time, put an additional strain on her health, and she started feeling sick again, often needing the help of her youngest son to complete her janitorial work. The move, however, did not considerably alter the composition and internal financial arrangements in her household. The core of the extended family remained essentially intact; one of her sons remained in San Jose when the family moved. The household continued to take in boarders, this time to help pay the mortgage, but fewer boarders were needed as the financial stability of Silvia's family improved.

Silvia's was one of the most cohesive and harmonious extended families I knew in Santech. While low-skilled service jobs available in Silicon Valley offered her and her relatives employment opportunities, the low wages, employment instability, and high cost of living forced them to work in multiple formal and informal jobs to make ends meet. Silvia experienced a high degree of social, financial, and emotional solidarity, and her family serves as an example of a well-integrated extended family. The financial stability and improvement that the family experienced over the years were largely the result of mutual reciprocity within the domestic group. And the frequent changes in the size and composition of Silvia's household, including the temporary incorporation of relatives, friends, and countryfolk as boarders, illustrates the unrelenting flux that many Mexican immigrant families experience as they try to accommodate the needs of their members (Torres Sarmiento 2002; Palerm 2002; Chávez 1990). Embedded in a large transnational migrant network, Silvia's extended household helped her meet the family's social obligations to newly arrived immigrants from her hometown in

Mexico. The dynamic combination of wage work and secondary informal occupations was also crucial to the financial stability of the family,
although the boundary between formal and informal jobs was a faint
line. And obtaining help from charitable organizations was an important part of how Silvia was able to make ends meet in times of crisis, and
a central strategy commonly used by Mexican immigrant women to
cope with poverty, preserve the integrity of their families, and develop
roots (Hondagneu-Sotelo 1994).

Even though Silvia had a cohesive household, she still experienced
the same predicaments endured by other undocumented immigrant
women in San José. Her difficult financial position, along with her status as abandoned wife and undocumented worker, made her especially
vulnerable to exploitative employers, which included her own relatives.
Her struggle to gain some degree of financial autonomy can be interpreted as an effort to pull away from this milieu of family-related jobs
where exploitation is often masked. As other authors have pointed out,
it is often within immigrants' own social networks that some of the most
exploitative relations take place, which reveals that kin and family relations can be commodified as a result of migration (Mahler 1995; Mení-
var 2000; Malkin 1998). At the same time, living with her extended
family offered Silvia some protection from a hostile labor market by
providing economic and emotional support, and she was still able to
retain some control over her own life and that of her youngest children.
To Silvia, rather than a cultural ideal, the extended household represented a compromise between reaching her goal of autonomy and being
overwhelmed by the limitations she encountered in Silicon Valley as an
undocumented immigrant and middle-aged working mother. The
household strategies model helps us to understand how Silvia and her
family were able to make ends meet with low-paid jobs in Silicon Valley. But it says little about the predicament of the many immigrant
women like her who are made invisible by that model, because, as
Malkin (1998) argues, it explains their behavior in terms of household
reproduction while ignoring their own voices and interpretations.

Margarita: A Household in Flux

It is 7 P.M. on a summer day in Santech. As I arrive at Margarita's apartment she, her parents, and several siblings are sitting in the living room
watching a soap opera on an old black-and-white TV. Her youngest children run back and forth across the apartment as she yells at them to be

quiet and not to go outside. A few minutes later, the phone rings. It is her *comadre* [godmother], Teresa, to whom Margarita relates her latest problems. Her old car parked downstairs was towed the day before because it had not been moved in seventy-two hours. When she called the company storing it, she found that she would have to pay the police ticket, a fee to the company that towed the vehicle, and an additional charge for each day the car was in storage. Upset, Margarita explains she does not have the money to pay all those fees, so she will give it up. To make things worse, she continues, two days ago her supervisor at work told her she might be laid off temporarily, because work orders at Muzok—a subcontractor that assembles CDs and music tapes—were slowing down. Without her job, Margarita tells her *comadre,* she will not be able to pay her rent by the end of the month, a scary outlook given that she still owes last month's rent.

After about twenty minutes, she hangs up the phone and goes to the kitchen to fix dinner for the family with her mother and youngest sister. Tonight, they will have beans, rice, and cheese because, as she explains, "I did not have money to buy meat." She bought the cheese from an vendor who comes to Santech once a week, and they prepared the tortillas at home, using corn flour they buy in bulk, because "they taste better and are cheaper than in the store." As we talk, Margarita struggles to turn on one of the kitchen burners, but the stove is out of order and does not respond. She curses her landlord, complaining that he never fixes anything in the apartment and that many things are falling apart. In fact, only two of the four burners work, and the igniter cannot be used because it gives a light electric shock. Moreover, the wall next to one of the stoves is burned, the kitchen linoleum is full of holes, and one of the walls has a big hole that mice run through at night.

Despite these and many other problems with the apartment, Margarita feels she cannot sue her landlord, because she owes him money. Indeed, she explains to me, this is not the first time she has been late with the rent, which is $640 a month: on at least three other occasions, she has fallen behind, either because she was out of work, her kids were sick and she had to take them to the doctor, or some other family emergency occurred. With a worried expression on her face, she comments that if she is laid off from work she will need to find another job soon to pay her bills, especially now that her husband is in jail and cannot help her. And if she does not find the money for the rent this time, the landlord might try to evict them. On top of that, she adds, she owes two months' worth of electricity bills, and if she does not pay them by the end of this month, the company will cut off the power. In an angry tone, she complains to her mother about her brothers' lack of help: "They are working, [and they] often eat and sleep here, but when I ask them for money to help me with the household bills, they always give excuses, saying they are short of cash and cannot help."

After finishing dinner, Margarita and her sisters wash the dishes and she puts her children to bed. Usually, ten people sleep in the apartment. In one bedroom, Margarita sleeps with her husband when he is home and her youngest boy and girl. Margarita's parents and their two youngest daughters occupy the second bedroom. Her two youngest brothers sleep on two sofas in the living room, and her three oldest children sleep on the floor. Around 11 P.M., everybody but Margarita and her father have gone to bed, and the silence in the apartment sharply contrasts with the noise, loud voices, and general agitation that prevailed earlier in the evening. A few minutes later, Margarita goes to bed, as she has to wake up early and be at work by 7 A.M. Only her father stays up, watching the end of a movie in the living room after turning down the volume.

Margarita's was one of the poorest and most troubled families I met in Santech. With a large household composed of five children, her parents, and a fluctuating number of siblings, Margarita lived continuously on the edge of poverty and had a history of constant marriage and family problems. Her husband, Alfredo—a drug addict and occasional street-drug seller—was often in jail, and Margarita was the de facto head of the family. Relying on her own income and the financial contributions of her parents and siblings, she was constantly worried about being able to buy food for her children, pay her bills, and otherwise keep her family afloat. With a mixture of courage, resignation, and pragmatism, she navigated troubled waters.[8]

Margarita's case vividly illustrates how the flexible employment of Mexican immigrants in low-skilled jobs in Silicon Valley affects the stability of their families. It also shows that, behind apparently intact nuclear or extended families, women are often the principal providers, which points to the need to move beyond the household strategies model that portrays households as undifferentiated units (Zavella 1995).

FAMILY MIGRATION TO CALIFORNIA

Born in 1966 in Arroyo Seco, an isolated rural ranch in the *municipio* of Aguililla in the northwest corner of the state of Michoacán, Margarita was the fourth child of nine. Her father was an itinerant farm laborer who traveled with his family to rural ranches throughout the region in search for work. As the oldest girl in the family, Margarita was responsible for helping her mother raise her younger siblings and cook, clean, do laundry, and attend to other household chores. As a result, she was able to attend elementary school for only four years. In 1967, her father started migrating periodically to the United States to work in agricultural harvests in California, Texas, and Washington. Ten years later, with the savings from his work, he bought a parcel of land in a small rural town in Aguililla, where he built a house and operated a ranch and butcher shop. When Margarita was fifteen years old, she met Alfredo, an itinerant farm laborer like her father; she lived in common-law marriage with him until they got married in 1985. They and their children shared her parents' household at her father's ranch.

In the mid-1980s, following her brothers' path, Margarita and Alfredo decided to migrate with their children to California, after which her parents and the rest of the family followed, a migration pattern usually known as "family stage migration" (Hondagneu-Sotelo 1994: 39, 56–75). The first person in the family to migrate and settle down in the United States was her oldest brother, who went to Chicago to join a cousin in 1977. In the early 1980s, a second brother migrated to San Jose with a cousin whose family had been living in the region since the mid-1950s. Then, in 1986, landless and with a growing family, Margarita and her husband joined her two oldest brothers in California, both of whom had settled in San Jose. Three years later, Margarita's parents and her four youngest siblings joined the rest of the family in San Jose; no family members remained on the ranch in Mexico. The family had severed most links with their hometown and committed themselves to starting a new life in California.

A CLUSTER OF FAMILY HOUSEHOLDS

After reuniting in San Jose, Margarita and her relatives formed an extended, tight family group that included three generations and twenty-three people, as shown in Figure 7. But rather than living under the same roof, they formed a family household cluster, in which independent households of an extended family are interconnected by intense financial cooperation, exchange of labor, frequent family visits, and participation in common social activities (Vélez-Ibáñez 1988). The members of Margarita's extended family lived in three different but highly interdependent households. The first and largest one was composed of Margarita's nuclear family, her parents, and her siblings, all sharing a two-bedroom apartment in Santech. The second household was smaller and composed of the nuclear family of Margarita's oldest brother, which occupied a separate house in East San Jose. The third household was made up of Margarita's second-oldest brother and his

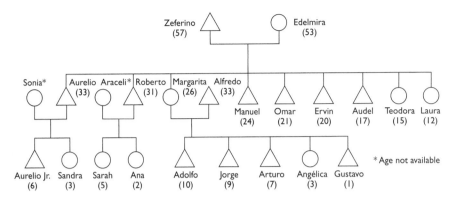

FIGURE 7. Margarita's extended family; ages of family members are in parentheses.

family in a home also located in East San Jose, and it occasionally included some of his siblings.

Despite living in three different households, Margarita and her relatives maintained strong ties of financial cooperation and reciprocity as they helped each other find employment, cooperated in times of financial stress, and maintained close contact with daily visits and telephone calls. In fact, the boundaries between these three households were rather flexible. For example, several of Margarita's siblings alternated sleeping at her apartment and the home of Margarita's oldest brother, often coming to Margarita's for dinner. Kin ties played a central role in finding jobs for most adult members of her extended family, as most of Margarita's siblings were employed as janitors by the same cleaning company. Aurelio, Margarita's oldest sibling, was employed as a supervisor in this company, and in this position he helped most of his younger siblings, including Margarita, find employment. Others worked as informal employees in a small, family-run landscaping firm. Roberto, Margarita's second-oldest brother, had started this business in association with a relative of his brother's wife, and he often employed several of his siblings and other relatives, including his father, especially when they were otherwise out of work. Manuel, Margarita's third-oldest brother, worked as an informal employee at his brother's landscaping firm during the day and as a janitor at the cleaning company where his brother was a supervisor at night.

In San Jose, Margarita's extended family maintained a traditional sexual division of labor, a common pattern among Mexican families who migrated to the United States after the mid-1960s (Hondagneu-Sotelo 1994: 117–18). Women in the family spent most of their time doing household-related chores. Margarita's mother helped her at home, taking care of her children when she was at work and doing other household chores such as cooking, cleaning, and laundry and occasionally ironing clothes for neighbors for a fee. Margarita's two youngest sisters, who were attending school, were also expected to help Margarita and her mother with the household chores. The only exception was Margarita, who, in addition to doing household work, was also employed as a janitorial worker.

As noted earlier, many Mexican immigrant families are composed of a combination of legal immigrants, undocumented immigrants, and U.S. citizens (Chávez 1992). Margarita, her husband, and two of her siblings were legal residents who had adjusted their immigrant status by means of the Immigration Reform and Control Act's amnesty program in the late 1980s. Margarita's parents and six of her siblings were undocumented immigrants; they had arrived in the United States after the deadline to qualify for the amnesty program. Six other family members were U.S. citizens, all of them children born in this country after their parents migrated from Mexico. The legal status of the members of her family had important effects on Margarita's ability to secure financial aid for her children, as I will show later.

FAMILY LIFE AS A ROLLER COASTER

Margarita's household was subject to continual financial crises, instability, and frequent changes in size and composition. The following developments illustrate the ups and downs in Margarita's life. In winter 1992, going through a difficult time after she had been fired from her janitorial job, and while her husband was in jail charged with the use and sale of drugs, Margarita was barely making it. She and her children survived on the welfare aid ($550 a month) allotted to her and her two youngest children and financial help from two of her brothers, with whom she shared rent and other household expenses.

Her situation improved temporarily when she found a full-time job in a small company assembling CDs and cassette tapes at one of Silicon Valley's industrial parks, where she earned $5 an hour. Shortly afterward, her husband returned home after spending ten months in jail. At that point, her parents and siblings moved out of her apartment to allow Margarita and her nuclear family to live on their own. However, after

Alfredo came back home, Margarita's welfare aid was sharply reduced, throwing her precarious financial situation out of balance. After a while, unable to make up for the lost welfare income by working, she fell into debt with her landlord, a point at which she decided to sublet one room to a boarder for $250 a month. Several months later things got better again, when her husband found a part-time job in a janitorial company in San Jose for $5 an hour. But her financial situation soon deteriorated again when the boarder moved out and she was unable to find a substitute. Finding themselves in a tough spot, Margarita and Alfredo decided to ask for temporary welfare relief. To their distress, the local welfare office rejected the petition. Although a family of seven, they were regarded as a family of four for official purposes, because three of their five children were undocumented immigrants and the $1,600 monthly income they reported was above the $1,512 that a family of four could earn and still qualify. Several months before, Margarita and her husband—both of them legal immigrants—had started the process of legalizing the status of their children born in Mexico, but had decided to discontinue it because, having more urgent needs, they could not afford the $350 in fees required at the time ($225 for the INS, and $125 for the nonprofit agency handling the case).

Unable to pay the rent and preserve the independence of their nuclear family, Margarita and Alfredo gave up the apartment in Santech and moved, along with her parents and several of her siblings, to a rented house in a different San Jose neighborhood. The new household was composed of sixteen persons sharing a house with two bedrooms, a living room, a basement, and a garage. As the composition and structure of the household changed, so did the internal budget arrangements. Only housing expenses were now shared. Margarita and her husband contributed $600 a month, and her father and one of her brothers $300 each. Each family, however, provided their own food and other basic expenses separately.

Margarita's troubles soon started again, when she and her husband unexpectedly lost their jobs. Margarita was laid off along with several of her coworkers when orders in the assembly company where she was employed slowed down. Alfredo was laid off when his janitorial employer lost a cleaning contract.[9] In a matter of a few weeks, their family income dropped to $175 a week in unemployment benefits that she and her husband collected ($100 and $75, respectively). The new crisis increased the tension in her marriage as Alfredo complained about the lack of support they received from her siblings at such a difficult time. Anguished by her critical financial situation, Margarita felt trapped between the demands of her husband and her siblings. With limited welfare aid, unable to pay her share of the rent and family expenses and receiving little support from her siblings, Margarita reached for help beyond her family circle to several charity organizations that donated food to poor families in San Jose and other Silicon Valley cities. She told me,

> I don't feel supported by my brothers. I told my mother today that I helped them for two years when they first arrived here, and now that I need their help they are not cooperating. My brother Manuel only puts down $300 for rent and doesn't want to cooperate with food and bills. . . . Ervin just cashed two checks on Friday, and today he didn't have any money left—he spent it all on the weekend in the disco. Manuel doesn't want to give money for the bills . . . [and] he left the job he had with his brother [Roberto] cleaning yards because they had a fight, and now he only has one job. They fought instead of treating each other as brothers. Now my brother Omar is going to work with him [Roberto] in the yards, but he doesn't want to give any money for anything; he doesn't give money for food, rent, or bills. . . . My husband complains because I don't say anything to my brothers, but I do and they just don't listen to me; so I have told him I don't want to listen to more of his sermons and complaints.

As had happened several times in the past, Margarita's family situation improved temporarily: Alfredo's former janitorial employer hired him when he got a new cleaning contract. This recovered stability did not last long, however: Alfredo was sent back to jail for using drugs and failing to complete his drug rehabilitation program. To add to her anguish, Margarita realized she was pregnant. This time it was an unplanned pregnancy that, in her view, came at a rather difficult moment. With $585 a month from public aid as her only income ($278 from the Aid to Families with Dependent Children program and $307 in food stamps), Margarita was unable to pay her share of the rent and provide for her children, a point at which one of her siblings came to the rescue by paying half her rent. To make things worse, after several warnings the local electric company cut off the power for failure to pay the bill. For several weeks, all members of her large family lived without electricity, cooking on a grill in the backyard until the Salvation Army agreed to pay half the outstanding bill and Margarita borrowed the second half from her *comadre*, Teresa.

Several months later, after delivering her baby, Margarita found a new job as a house cleaner for an independent contractor, earning about

$800 a month for an average of seven hours of work a day. Unlike in the past, when she reported her full wages to the local welfare office, this time Margarita decided to report only half to prevent her benefits from being cut. Losing her full benefits could have jeopardized her already delicate financial situation, especially since her husband was in jail.[10] Later on, Margarita's situation improved considerably when she and her children moved to a subsidized apartment for low-income families in a housing project close to Santech.[11] Months later, Alfredo was released from jail and returned home. For Margarita, the change was a big relief, especially because her nuclear family had regained the independence and privacy lost when they moved out of Santech; they could now afford to pay the rent on their own. Nonetheless, her family's financial situation continued to be highly unstable. Shortly after they moved to the housing project, Margarita and her husband started working full-time for a large janitorial company that had employed him in the past. Later that year, they were laid off when the cleaning company lost the contract for cleaning the building in which they were employed. As neither Margarita nor Alfredo qualified for unemployment benefits, given the short time they had been employed by that company, they found themselves again in a harsh financial position. A few months later, Alfredo began taking drugs again and stopped contributing to the family budget. Confronted by all these troubles, and to avoid being evicted from the subsidized apartment for which she had waited so long, Margarita started working part-time as a house cleaner. She did not report her income, because she wanted to avoid a rent increase (the rent varied according to their reported monthly income). Margarita's roller-coaster experience during this time closely mirrored the ups and downs in her employment status, as she continuously moved from one unstable job to another as an assembly worker, house cleaner, and so on.

BALANCING WORK AND WELFARE

The welfare aid Margarita received was an important source of income that helped her to keep her nuclear family together. Relying on this aid is a common strategy among poor immigrant families whose adult members experience frequent periods of unemployment and underemployment (Torres Sarmiento 2002; Dohan 2003; Briody 1986; García 1992). For the several years I knew her family, Margarita was on and off welfare repeatedly, in a pattern that directly correlated to the times she was temporarily unemployed. Her own feelings about her use of welfare aid were ambiguous. On the one hand, her ideal was to be self-sufficient, both because of the social stigma she perceived was attached to people on welfare and because she profoundly disliked having her family life scrutinized by public officials every time she asked for financial aid. On the other hand, she acknowledged it was very difficult to achieve financial autonomy and stability solely on the basis of income from their work, because the instability of their jobs and her husband's erratic behavior. With time, she came to view work and welfare not as exclusionary options but as complementary sources of income. Welfare aid—in the form of cash assistance, food stamps, or subsidized housing—became one of the most reliable sources of support in an unstable employment market. One of her major goals, after several years of struggling to keep her family together, was to find a stable regular job without jeopardizing the welfare income that had helped in the past to overcome important financial crises in the family.

Margarita's feelings about welfare aid became clear to me once I accompanied her to the welfare office. At the time, unable to cover all the family expenses with the income from their two jobs, Margarita and Alfredo decided to ask for temporary aid while they regained some financial stability. The eligibility worker at the local Social Services Agency office—a young, jovial Latino man in his thirties—listened to her and offered his sympathy but, as I mentioned earlier, denied their petition because of the immigration status of three of her children. Margarita decided that, from then on, she would not report all the income from her work, including that generated by part-time informal jobs for which she was paid in cash. The advantages of working in informal occupations on the side became clear to her. After leaving the office, upset and worried because she could not obtain the help she needed, Margarita commented, "From now on I am going to lie so they help me. There are many women I know who live quite well and have money, and who are getting welfare aid because they know how to manipulate their cases and lie. But people who really need help don't get any aid. Next time I might give a different name and Social Security [number to my employer] so they [the welfare office] give me money, then I will fuck them." She elaborated with an alternative idea: "My plan is to look for a job cleaning houses or taking care of an elderly woman where they pay me in cash, so I don't need to report it and I receive unemployment and welfare aid. Only then I can get ahead."

Unable to sustain her family on the income she and her husband received from work, Margarita found that moving to subsidized housing gave her and her family more stability and security. Living with her children alone in a subsidized apartment was an important step toward her coveted goal of autonomy, and it made her feel calmer and more optimistic about the future. Her partial independence, together with the occasional support she received from her parents and siblings, represented a good compromise between achieving her ideal of financial autonomy and accepting the harsh reality she confronted as a low-skilled immigrant. Despite this improvement, Margarita's life was still marked by periods of financial stability followed by sudden relapses and crises, most of them related to the instability of her jobs and her husband's drug relapses.

In 1997, a tragic event transformed Margarita's life. A few months after Alfredo was last released from jail (where he had spent the previous two years), as he was returning from a janitorial job he had recently started, he was killed in a car accident on a busy freeway in Silicon Valley. This tragedy was the last step that finally transformed Margarita from the de facto head of the family to its official head. In the meantime, her parents had moved to a subsidized apartment in the project where she lived. Although the members of this extended family lived in two different homes, their cooperation and mutual support continued as in the past, this time reinforced by the fact that Margarita had became a widow with dependent children.

Margarita's case illustrates the highly volatile environment in which many immigrant families in Santech lived. The combination of employment insecurity and Alfredo's drug addiction put her and her children in a vulnerable position. The different types of household arrangements that she tried, including living in nuclear and extended family households, represented alternative approaches through which she tried to cope. The periodic extensions and contractions of her household mirrored the employment instability that she and her husband experienced, the family's inconstant welfare benefits, and her husband's periodical withdrawal from the family. And as in Silvia's case, financial aid from both public institutions and private organizations was an additional source of support in times of need. Together these economic strategies helped to subsidize the subsistence costs of Margarita, who was employed in an array of low-income formal and informal occupations—as a janitor, assembly worker, and house cleaner, among others—since arriving in Silicon Valley.

At the same time, Margarita's case illustrates the role of the family as a bastion of resistance to poverty and exploitation often experienced by poor immigrant women (Pessar 1999). It was hard for her to adjust to the loss of family autonomy after migrating to San Jose. First, being periodically hired and laid off prevented her from reaching the financial autonomy she wanted for her family. Her precarious position made her dependent on the sporadic aid of public institutions, whose scrutiny she felt was both invasive and insensitive to the needs of her family. She resented a judiciary system that, from her perspective, did not hesitate to send her husband to jail without considering the high cost of his punishment for his family. She could not understand a system of rigid and contradictory bureaucratic rules that prevented her family from qualifying for welfare because of her Mexican-born children's status as undocumented immigrants and, at the same time, prevented her from changing their status because she had received welfare aid. Confronted with immediate and pressing needs, Margarita saw the rules of such bureaucratic institutions as both arbitrary and unfair. In the midst of such a hostile world, her extended family represented a source of material and emotional support, and her household was the only private domain where she could preserve her life on her own terms.

Carmen: A Home Divided?

Carmen lives on Shortride Drive, the most dilapidated street in Santech. As I knock on the front door of her apartment on a sunny spring day, a young teenager wearing a white undershirt and a blue handkerchief around his head politely invites me in.[12] Inside, the living room is dark and filled with a pungent smell that seems to come from the worn carpet. Sitting on a chair in one corner is Don Francisco—Carmen's father-in-law—an old man wearing a ranchero hat who listens to Mexican music on an old battery-powered radio. Around a small round wooden table next to the kitchen, Felipe, the teenager who opened the door, his brother Joel, and a cousin sit drinking soda while chatting about work. After a couple of minutes, Isabel—a young woman in her early twenties and the oldest of Carmen's two daughters—comes out and invites me to her mother's room. As I walk in, Carmen—a short, round, fifty-two-year-old woman with gray hair, a wrinkled face, and violet eye shadow—receives me warmly and apologizes for the disorder inside. The small room is shared by five people and crowded with furniture, which hardly leaves any room to move around. Carmen and her youngest daughter sleep on a double bed placed at the center of the room. Isabel and her husband sleep on an old twin-size mattress on the floor in one corner of the room, and Carmen's youngest son uses a small mattress aligned along one wall. On the opposite wall, there is a small table crowded with clothes, home tools, cosmetics, a phone, and a small TV.

After I sit down on Carmen's bed, she lowers her voice and says, "I asked you to come to the room because I want to talk to you and I do not want them to listen," referring to her common-law husband and her sons, who are also in the apartment. She then starts complaining about her husband: "He came home yesterday night completely drunk again because the woman with whom he now lives threw him out. I do not want to see or talk to him. . . . Let's wait until he is gone, and I will fix something to eat." Then she explains to me the problems she has been having while trying to legalize her immigrant status: Raúl—the man with whom she has been living in common-law marriage for more than twenty years, who was once an undocumented immigrant—legalized his status several years ago, and now she hoped to convince him to marry her so that she and their two daughters can also become legal immigrants under his sponsorship. The problem, she adds with a sad tone, is that she is not on good terms with him because of his relation to "the other woman." But she does not want to do anything in relation to him that could jeopardize her plan.

As we continue our conversation, somebody knocks on the door. It is Raúl. Standing in the doorway, he asks his daughter whether she could lend him money to fix his car, promising to pay her back as soon as he gets his next check from work. When he is about to leave, Carmen, who until then has not looked at him, asks Raúl whether he is going to pay his share of the phone bill, adding that she has only a few days to pay before the line is disconnected. In a vague tone, he replies that he will give her the money soon, after which he quickly leaves, closing the door after him. Upset, Carmen starts complaining that he always promises to pay his share of the bill, which is under her name, but never does so despite the fact that he often makes long-distance calls to his relatives in Mexico. And her sons, she adds, follow his bad example and do not help her either, so in the end she has to pick up the phone bill for all the people who live in the apartment.

After a few minutes, when Raúl leaves the apartment to go to work, Carmen gets up and asks her daughters to go to the kitchen to fix dinner. As in most apartments in Santech, the kitchen presents a dismaying scene: the linoleum is full of holes, several of the cabinet doors are missing, and only two of the four stove burners work. Yet, surprisingly, there are four refrigerators in this small apartment. Three of them are lined up next to each other along a kitchen wall, and the other one is in the living room. When I ask Carmen why there are so many refrigerators, she responds in a matter-of-fact tone that each of the four families who live there has a refrigerator: one is for herself and her two youngest children, the second is for her husband's oldest son and his family, the third is for her son and his wife, and the fourth is for her married daughter and her husband. The second refrigerator has a door lock, and when I ask Carmen about it, she responds that only her daughter-in-law has the key. When dinner is ready, Carmen, her daughter Isabel, and I sit around a table in the living room to eat. Tonight's dinner consists of beans, rice, and tortillas. After about twenty minutes, the phone rings. It is Ray, Carmen's janitorial employer, who tells her to get ready because he is on his way to pick her up. After hanging up the phone, Carmen complains that he always calls her at his convenience and wants her to be ready at once. Trying to help her mother, Isabel says she will take care of the dishes, and Carmen goes to her room to quickly dress for work. A few minutes later, her boss honks, and after apologizing for not being able to stay, she leaves the apartment to start her six-hour night shift as janitor in San Jose, where she cleans a large office building owned by a nonprofit agency, and a law office located across the street.

Carmen's extended family, composed of seventeen people, was one of the largest I knew of in Santech. She and her relatives had lived crowded into a two-bedroom apartment for several years, until they could move to a larger apartment in a different neighborhood. Carmen's also was one of the most divided and stratified families I met in San Jose. Although they practiced several forms of cooperation and mutual help, her household was constantly permeated by an atmosphere of distrust and tension, which reflected an internal division among its members. Carmen's case reveals the danger of reducing the extended household to a unit of income pooling and solidarity, a romantic image often associated with Mexican immigrant families. In fact, Carmen experienced the inequality, internal stratification, and exploitation that often trap undocumented working mothers who have been deserted by their husbands (Zavella 1995; Hondagneu-Sotelo 1994).

I first met Carmen when she and Raúl still shared an apartment in Santech but were no longer together. Because my initial contact with this family was through her, my relationship with Raúl was cordial but distant, as he saw me as her friend. Carmen at first seemed to believe that I was some kind of social worker who could help her solve her most pressing problems, despite my explanations to the contrary. Her little understanding of immigration law and regulations, her goal to become a legal immigrant and obtain authorization to work, and her bad experience with fake lawyers who had taken advantage of her situation had all led her to hope I could help her to navigate those complicated legal waters. As time went by, and as we developed a stronger rapport, she also confided to me her problems in the family, especially with her husband, and her sense of isolation. Carmen experienced many difficulties as an undocumented working mother living in an extended family that was sharply segmented along gender and immigrant status lines.

CARMEN'S MIGRATION TO SAN JOSE

Born in 1940 in Teocuitlán de Corona in the Mexican state of Jalisco, Carmen was the third of eight siblings, four sons and four daughters. Her father was a landless peasant, an agricultural worker employed in the reedbed in western Jalisco. Her mother sold fruits and flowers from a small orchard and garden she had inherited from her parents. As a child, Carmen completed only six years of primary school, after which she quit to help her mother raise her siblings and do other household chores. In 1955, when she was fifteen, she married Ramón, the son of a peasant who labored in his own *ejido* in the same town. With Ramón she had three daughters and two sons. They lived at Ramón's family ranch until he died in 1962 from complications of alcohol addiction. A widow at the age of twenty-two, Carmen went to live with her parents in Guadalajara and worked in a children's-shoe factory for the next six years. In 1968, she left her parents' home again, this time to live with Raúl, whom she had met the year before in Guadalajara. Born in 1943 in a small village in Zacatecas, Raúl was the son of a poor, landless field laborer who worked in *rancherias* in his hometown to support himself and his family. Like Carmen, he had been married before, and he had two children of his own, a son and a daughter. With the children of their previous marriages, they formed a new family living in an extended household in Guadalajara composed of Raúl's parents and several of their married siblings with their respective families. After getting together, Carmen and Raúl had eight more children, only four of whom survived. While Raúl worked in construction as an unskilled laborer, Carmen raised their four children and performed domestic chores along with her mother- and sister-in-law.

In 1987, Carmen's family began migrating to San Jose, following the pattern of family stage migration noted earlier in this chapter. Raúl was the first member to arrive in this city, following a relative who offered him a job as a janitorial worker. A few months later he arranged for three of his sons, including one from his previous marriage, to join him in the apartment where he was living in Santech. Finally, about a year and a half later, Carmen and their two daughters headed north to join the rest

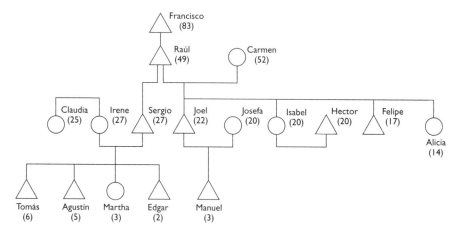

FIGURE 8. Carmen's household; ages of family members are in parentheses.

of the family in San Jose. Carmen's five children from her first marriage, most of whom were already married and had their own families, remained in Mexico.

A STRATIFIED HOUSEHOLD

Once in San Jose, Carmen lived in an extended family household composed of three generations and seventeen people, as shown in Figure 8. But this household was not a domestic unit that engaged in income pooling and generalized reciprocity. Instead it was made up of several family groups, each of which maintained independent budgets except for basic common expenses. The household was composed of three distinctive units, each with a high degree of independence. The first unit consisted of Sergio—Carmen's stepson—and his nuclear family, which also included a sister of Carmen's daughter-in-law. A second group was made up of Raúl, Joel (Carmen and Raúl's oldest son), Joel's nuclear family, and Don Francisco, Raúl's father. The third distinctive unit within the household was composed of Carmen, Felipe and Alicia (her youngest children), and her daughter Isabel.

The three groups of Carmen's household were divided according to the financial and legal status of their members. Thus the members of the three units shared rent and electricity, but each group was responsible for their own expenses, including food, clothes, and other expenses according to their own needs. Carmen's stepson Sergio and his nuclear family had the highest status in the household and enjoyed the most comfortable lifestyle. Several factors explain this. First, Sergio was a supervisor in a unionized janitorial company, and his wife and sister-in-law also worked in the same company, providing a relatively stable income. Moreover, as legal immigrants, he and his family had access to several social services unavailable to undocumented immigrants, including financial aid when needed, because his children were born in the United States. Joel and his nuclear family lived more modestly. For a time he was employed as a janitor in the same company as Sergio, and, like Sergio, he was a legal immigrant. Unlike Sergio, however, Joel liked to drink, and he was fired from his job because of repeated absences. He was often unemployed or underemployed because of the instability of his jobs and because of his problems with alcohol. Carmen and her youngest children occupied the most vulnerable position in the household. After Raúl left Carmen for a younger woman, he spent little time at home and only sporadically contributed to the household budget and the support of their children. The apartment, which was in Raúl's name, cost $650 per month. He contributed $150 and charged Isabel—his oldest daughter—$110 a month for the bed she had in Carmen's room. Carmen had to support herself and her youngest children, paying her share of the rent and other living expenses. As an undocumented immigrant, Carmen was ineligible to collect welfare and other types of aid. When Isabel married Hector in 1992, the newly formed couple lived with Carmen and shared expenses.

The economic stratification in Carmen's household was mirrored in the distribution of space. Both in Santech, where they first lived upon arriving in San Jose, and in the larger apartment to which they moved a few years later, Sergio contributed the largest share of the rent and his family occupied the master bedroom. This bedroom contained a TV, a VCR, and their own telephone line and remained locked whenever they were not home. They also owned the largest refrigerator in the house, which, like the room, was locked. Joel's family occupied a smaller room with only a mattress on the floor and a small TV. Carmen, her two youngest children, Isabel, and Hector were confined to the smallest room in the house (see Figure 9). Francisco—Raúl's father—slept on a couch in the living room, as did Raúl when he was at home. Common areas like the kitchen and the living room were used for functional purposes such as cooking and eating, but each woman cooked separately for her own family. Household maintenance chores were also carried

FIGURE 9. Carmen poses in the room she shares with several relatives in Santech.

out separately according to a prearranged schedule. Whenever I visited this family, I sensed an atmosphere of distrust. Carmen seemed particularly distrustful: she was suspicious of her stepson, with whom she had a distant relationship. Because of this, when at home, she spent most of the time in her own room, the only place where she felt at ease.

THE DILEMMAS OF AN ABANDONED IMMIGRANT MOTHER

Life had been uphill for Carmen ever since she had first arrived in San Jose. The lack of financial support from her husband, her age and undocumented status, and her limitation to poorly paid jobs all helped to put her in a vulnerable financial position. Upon arrival, she had been completely dependent on Raúl, a situation experienced by many other Mexican women who migrated to the United States through the social networks of their husbands (Hondagneu-Sotelo 1994). Her first job was as a janitor for her husband. At the time, Raúl had several years of experience as a janitor and was able to secure a few contracts on his own as an informal, self-employed worker cleaning small business offices in town. He also had a regular, full-time janitorial job with a large cleaning company. To operate his own cleaning service, he employed the members of his family, including Carmen, their two sons, and Sergio. This arrangement was particularly difficult for Carmen. Unlike the others, whom Raúl paid in cash for their work, Carmen received no payment. Instead, he paid her share of the rent and other expenses, an arrangement Carmen did not like but could not reject. Later on, when Raúl's sons quit working for him after finding better-paid jobs in formal janitorial companies, Carmen, unable to find a better job, was the only member of the family who remained tied to this informal occupation. Her financial dependence on Raúl increasingly frustrated Carmen. "Because I do not pay rent, Raúl humiliates me badly. . . . He tells me I have to follow him where he goes because I am not paying rent. . . . Raúl pays rent for his children and father, but I [earn] the money for food because he does not give me anything. I am the one sustaining them, and Don Francisco because sometimes he goes without eating."

Raúl had assumed responsibility for paying the housing, food, and other maintenance expenses for Carmen and their daughters when they first arrived in San Jose. Shortly afterward, however, he got involved with a young woman, and when she became pregnant, he started to spend less time with his family in Santech and sharply reduced his financial contribution to the household. As a result, Carmen was left with the responsibility of covering most of the household expenses and sustaining her daughters on her own. At that point, her major goal was to gain independence from her husband and sustain her youngest children. She realized that to do so she had to develop social connections independently from her husband and her relatives, a common strategy among Mexican women who want to free themselves from oppressive patriarchal control (Hondagneu-Sotelo 1994). Overcoming her fear of being deported, she began looking for jobs outside her family circle. The first job she found was through her social contacts at a Christian church she started attending on Sundays. An African American cleaning contractor who, like her husband, was self-employed, offered her a job (see Figure 10). Realizing she could make more money this way than in her other job, Carmen quit working for Raúl. Her new job was far from a blessing, however. Aware that Carmen was an undocumented immigrant, her new employer offered to pay her in cash under the table, determining her wages on the basis of the number of hours worked every month. Her schedule was rather erratic and her earnings meager and unpredictable. Some nights, for example, she worked from 7 P.M. until midnight. Others she worked from 10 P.M. to 5 A.M., and still others she did not work at all, depending

FIGURE 10. On the night shift, Carmen cleans an office building while working as a subcontracted janitor in the informal sector.

on the changing needs of her employer. Because of this, her earnings varied considerably. Sometimes she earned as little as $275 a month, and others as much as $850, and her employer charged her a monthly fee for giving her a ride to work (usually $25). To supplement her income, Carmen started working in the mornings in other informal jobs—as a baby-sitter and as a caregiver for elderly people—that she found through her own social contacts. It was evident to her that, to escape her dependence on her husband, she had to develop even more social connections outside her family circle. As she proudly told me, "Although I do not have a family, I have many friends. . . . I have many female friends, so I don't care if my family helps me or not, because I have my own *hilos* [influence]. . . . And most of my friends are Americans [Anglos]. Yes, I do my own groundwork in silence [*me muevo por lo bajito*]."

However, Carmen depended on Raúl to change her status to that of a legal immigrant, and this contributed to her vulnerability. Like many other undocumented immigrant women at the time, Carmen could legalize her status only if her husband applied on her behalf. The two of them were not officially married but lived in a common-law union, which, even if legally recognized by many official institutions in Mexico, did not have legal standing according to U.S. immigration authorities. This placed Carmen in an odd position because, just as she was trying to pull away from Raúl, she needed to marry him as a prerequisite to becoming a legal immigrant. Putting her feelings aside, she decided it was in her best interest and that of her children to persuade Raúl to marry her despite his involvement with another woman. Using the influence her two daughters had on Raúl, she started pressing him to get married. After several months, and with hesitation, Raúl reluctantly agreed, in the summer of 1992, to marry Carmen if she covered the costs of the wedding and the immigration proceedings. Seizing the opportunity, Carmen organized a civil wedding in San Jose and invited me to serve as a witness. To Carmen this was an important victory and a step toward her goal of becoming a legal immigrant, after which she planned to obtain a good job that would give her complete financial independence from Raúl.

After her wedding, and seven years after arriving in San Jose, and more than three years after first applying for legal status, Carmen was still anxiously waiting for her case to be decided by the INS. To avoid jeopardizing her legal case, she quit the only formal job she had at the time, as a caregiver contracted by Santa Clara County to tend elderly people, fearing that, if she were caught working illegally, her application would be rejected. Instead, she started working as an informal house cleaner. After some time in the business, and after having expanded her network of clients, she earned more money than in her former job, about $200 a week. With time, and by working several jobs, she gradually became financially independent from Raúl, which made her proud after her years of struggle. Meanwhile, Raúl formed a new family and moved in with his girlfriend, with whom he had two children. After he moved out of Carmen's house, tensions in the household seemed to diminish, and her relations with her relatives improved. Commenting on these changes, she said, "When he [Raúl] was at home, I felt nobody took me into account. They did not consult my opinion for anything, even when we moved here [from Santech] they did not ask me. I felt very bad and ignored. . . . Now, as my [oldest] stepson told me the other day, I am the woman of the house. Yes, I am now *la jefa* [the boss] of the family."

PLANNING FOR THE FUTURE

Despite her difficult and uncertain future, Carmen did not intend to return to Mexico any time soon. She believed she was better off in the

United States because of the greater employment opportunities and financial support for women like her, a perspective commonly shared by other Mexican and Latina immigrant women in similar positions (Hondagneu-Sotelo 1994; Pessar 1999). Explaining her rationale, she commented, "In Mexico if you don't work, you don't eat. Here if you work, you eat; and if you don't, you also eat, because there are always places that give food to the needy. You go to the Sacred Heart [a local Catholic parish with a program to assist low-income immigrants] or call to many places where they help you. In Mexico, nobody gives you a piece of bread."

Carmen thus continued her life in San Jose, trying to consolidate her roots in this city while waiting for the decision on her petition to legalize her status. At the same time, uncertain about her future, she saved money and send it to Mexico to build a room in the house of an older daughter from her first marriage in case she could not make it on her own in the United States. Afraid that her husband would find out about her plan and try to take advantage of her savings, she concealed it from him, telling only her daughters about it. Her fallback plan was also a plan for her future: she hoped to retire someday in Mexico, after working a few more years in the United States and after her youngest children got married. In a tone of confidence and pride, she said,

> I intend to return to Mexico when I retire [and] to live with my daughter [from her first marriage]. . . . I send money to one of my daughters in Guadalajara, and she deposits it in an account she opened there for me. . . . I save money to prepare for the future because I feel very tired and I cannot count on this man [Raúl]; and my children keep growing and they will get married and then I will be alone. . . . Raúl doesn't know I am saving money, and I don't tell him. If he finds out, he would ask to borrow it from me. Only my daughters know.

Carmen's family is an example of extended immigrant households in which, along with cooperation and mutual help, there is also inequality, conflict, and exploitation along gender and legal status lines, a common experience among poor immigrant families (Malkin 1998; Mahler 1995; Pessar 1999). Carmen's membership in an extended household obscured the fact that her husband's economic role was only peripheral, and that she took financial responsibility for herself and her children. Her household was not a domestic group that practiced the principle of income pooling, but instead better resembled a "house divided"—an alternative to the income-pooling household described by some anthropologists—generally associated with internal financial and power inequalities (Dwyer and Bruce 1988).

Carmen's case also illustrates the common predicaments of other undocumented working mothers I knew in Santech. On the one hand, taking advantage of the large supply of low-skilled formal and informal jobs for Mexican women allowed her to gain some financial independence after having arrived in San Jose. On the other hand, the fact that she depended on her husband to legalize her immigrant status pressed her to stay in a relationship that she wanted to escape. Not surprisingly, Carmen's strategy for dealing with this predicament was to engage in wage labor, often in low-paid jobs in the informal sector to avoid detection by government authorities. To her, the extended family was not a bastion of resistance to labor exploitation and social segregation in low-paid and harsh jobs (Pessar 1999). Instead, wage work, even in exploitative circumstances, was a way to reduce her disadvantage while trapped in an exploitative marriage and a patriarchal family. Her situation was the result of not only the opportunities and limitations she found as an undocumented immigrant in Silicon Valley but also the constraints she faced as a deserted wife in a patriarchal family household. Carmen's choices and behavior reflected her effort to achieve financial independence in order to ensure the well-being of her children, as well as her effort to maintain a sense of dignity within her extended family, a common endeavor among Mexican immigrant women (Malkin 1998: 221).

Rather than residing in fixed, stable domestic groups, many of the Mexican immigrant families in Santech lived in extended households that experienced continuous changes in size and composition and constantly adjusted their internal financial arrangements. Inserted into a regional labor market defined by employment flexibility and insecurity, extended and flexible households helped immigrants in Santech cope with the instability and the low, unpredictable incomes from their jobs. Extended households cannot be simply interpreted as the result of cultural ideals that immigrants bring with them to the United States, as the romanticized version of the extended Mexican family seems to imply. Rather, they are largely the result of the pattern of flexible employment to which immigrants are restricted in the low-wage service sector of Silicon Valley's economy, and they help subsidize the subsistence costs of workers employed in these jobs. As in the case of income-generating activities in the informal economy, Mexican immigrants' familiarity with extended family households in their home communities provides them with cultural capital they can use to adapt to their new reality when they migrate to the United States.

Extended households in Santech also facilitated a dynamic articulation between formal and informal income-generating activities. The three families portrayed in this chapter pooled incomes from a variety of occupations, including formal wage jobs, disguised wage-employment, and petty informal activities. In these families, the boundaries between formal wage-labor and informal work were thin. Women frequently viewed informal income-generating activities as an extension of the household domestic chores, as Silvia's child-care job at home illustrates. As Torres Sarmiento argues, these "secondary jobs," even though not considered to be "work" by immigrant women like Silvia, constitute an important source of income that complements the low wages they and their husbands earn in the formal sector (Torres Sarmiento 2002: 158). In addition, welfare aid, usually in the form of food stamps, was also a source of some income during harsh economic times for many families like Margarita's and Carmen's.[13] This shows the role of the state in indirectly subsidizing employers who pay their workers below-subsistence wages.

Finally, reaching out to churches, charities, and nonprofit organizations was another strategy used by immigrant families in Santech to cope with financial hardship. Silvia's, Margarita's, and Carmen's families used assistance from any of these sources at times of unemployment, underemployment, or an unexpected crisis or family emergency. This confirms the findings of other studies that, to undocumented immigrants like Silvia who are excluded from most welfare programs because of their status, charities and nongovernment agencies provide critical resources to ensure the financial stability of their families (Torres Sarmiento 2002; Hondagneu-Sotelo 1994).

I found that extended family households were common among immigrants in Santech, but they were far from harmonious and egalitarian domestic groups. Internal inequality, stratification, and even exploitation were not uncommon among them and often went hand in hand with income pooling. This stratification and the social tensions that prevailed in households like Carmen's must be placed in the larger context of the social transformations experienced by immigrants. Legal status has an important influence on immigrants' economic opportunities: those who become legal residents gain access to certain rights and benefits, and those who remain undocumented are excluded from most of these rights and benefits, which often introduces an element of differentiation and exploitation within families (Chávez 1992; Heyman 1998). In addition, rather than a single model of income pooling based on the principle of generalized reciprocity, a large variation of budgetary arrangements can be found among extended families in Santech, each of which has different implications for the internal structure and the well-being of family members.

Silvia's was the most egalitarian of the three families presented here. As an abandoned wife, she had to work hard to provide for her children and cover her share of household expenses, but she could always count on the support of her relatives in times of need. In contrast, Margarita's family was heavily structured along gender lines, and although she received help from her siblings when confronted with an financial crisis, her role as wage earner did not translate into a more egalitarian division of labor in the family. Finally, Carmen's family was also shaped by hierarchies of power along gender, occupational, and legal status lines, which placed her in an extremely vulnerable position within her extended domestic group. A desegregated study of extended immigrant families that does not view the household as a unit but instead pays attention to how members cope with low-paid jobs, and to variations in the budget arrangements and power relationships within the household, helps us to move beyond the monolithic model of the income-pooling Mexican immigrant family (Zavella 1987; Hondagneu-Sotelo 1994).

The three cases discussed here show that, despite women's subordinate position in immigrant families in Santech, working mothers played a crucial role in maintaining the integrity of their families. These women's numerous formal and informal income-earning activities, their central role in organizing and coordinating household maintenance tasks, and their active participation in social networks of friends, neighbors, and acquaintances in Santech and the larger local community were all critical to the stability of their families. For working mothers like Silvia, Margarita, and Carmen, extended family households represented both an arena for gender subordination and a bastion of resistance to financial exploitation in the larger labor market. To Margarita, who had a long and harsh experience dealing with employers, landlords, and officers of public institutions, the family was a refuge from a hostile world. In contrast, Carmen, who was trapped in an exploitative patriarchal relationship, saw wage labor and proletarianiza-tion as an avenue to escape this exploitative relationship at home. Unlike middle-class immigrant women who perceive full-time employ-ment as a loss of social status (Pessar 1999), Mexican women who, like Carmen, come from a working-class background and who experience oppressive patriarchal relations may prefer exploitation outside the fam-ily rather than within it, because earning a living gives them a sense of self-control and dignity.

CHAPTER 5

Community Politics in the Barrio

It is 4:15 in the afternoon on a Tuesday in October 1992. A group of women, including Laura and Silvia, start arriving at the library of a public school half a mile from Santech. They have come to attend a neighborhood meeting, called by Elena, a well-known Santech woman who is the informal leader of many social and community political affairs in the barrio. Most women come accompanied by their children. As they arrive, they cheerfully greet each other and start chatting. Some complain that they could not find anybody to look after their children and so had to bring them along. After a few minutes, they sit down around an oval table at the entrance of the library and send their children to play to a corner of the room, asking them not to make noise. In all, there are eleven women at the table and fifteen children playing in the room.

Elena—a large, affable, thirty-nine-year-old woman with a chubby, rounded face that shines every time she smiles—presides over the meeting. She loves to talk, and a stream of creative, funny expressions mixed with profanities and traditional Mexican proverbs punctuates her conversation. She starts the meeting by explaining to her friends that they are here to discuss their major problems, complaints, and needs, especially at a time when they are having serious difficulties with the barrio's school and its principal. Also, she adds in an animated tone, they should use meetings like this to pass on information among themselves about opportunities available for their youngsters and families. To illustrate her point, she tells her colleagues about a number of churches and charitable organizations that give away free clothes, food, and used furniture to low-income families. Other women then start talking about similar organizations they personally know or have heard about, giving names and directions for finding them. One woman comments, "The Vietnamese are very united, and we should also learn to be united," to which a friend sitting next to her nods her head in agreement and replies, "Yes, the Chinese are always well informed about places that help poor people, and we Mexicans should do the same," referring, in fact, to the Vietnamese families who live in the neighborhood.

After this discussion, Elena takes the lead again and explains to her friends that her idea is to hold a series of weekly meetings to identify their major needs and discuss how to organize to address them. She says, "As we all know, we cannot expect much help from the school or the community center, referring to Santech's public elementary school and a neighborhood community center run by city employees in the barrio. "If we get together and organize, we can find solutions to our problems. . . . Sí se puede; la unión hace la fuerza" (Yes, it can be done; together we are stronger), she adds.

At this point, she asks her colleagues to start spelling out their major concerns, one person at a time. Monica, a middle-age woman who sits to the right of Elena, begins by complaining bitterly about Santech's elementary school, criticizing the education the children are getting there: "I have a son who is in fourth grade who still does not even know how to read, either English or Spanish! How can this be?" Several women in the room agree with her and start talking about the their own children, expressing similar complaints. Elena says that what they need are bilingual teachers, but that the school's principal "does not want to listen to us." The conversation gets increasingly lively as the women in the room air their complaints. Cecilia, a vocal young mother, harshly criticizes the community center, explaining that she is tired of attending its monthly community meetings: "They are completely useless. They [city workers] are always promising us much, but we never see any results." Another major problem in the barrio, she adds, is the lack of child-care centers. She explains that, because she does not have a place to leave her three-year-old daughter, she cannot take jobs outside her home, which makes it very hard for her and her husband to pay the monthly rent. Following her, other women also comment on how difficult it is for them to find child-care centers for their children. Later on, Alejandra, a middle-aged woman who came to the meeting with her two kids, complains about the "ugliness" of Santech: "Our barrio looks very ugly; there is only earth and dust and no grass, and there is always a lot of garbage in the streets and the parking lots, so our children do not have any place to play."

After an hour and a half of spirited discussion, in which the women talk about various problems, the children in the room start getting visibly tired and anxious to go outside. At this point, their mothers decide it is time to end the meeting. Following Elena's suggestion, they commit to meeting again the following week to discuss what to do about the problems they have brought up today. As they leave the room, Elena and her colleagues look relieved at having had the opportunity to share some of their concerns, but also worried and overwhelmed by the numerous and severe problems they confront.

In retrospect, the meeting held by Elena and her friends was a seminal one. It marked the beginning of a grassroots community campaign organized by these and other local residents to address some of what they expected to be their central needs in the years to come. Indeed, shortly after I first arrived in Santech, I noted the energy, commitment, and perseverance of many residents, especially women, actively involved in a variety of local political efforts to improve education and housing and address discrimination and other problems in the community. Often they engaged in these activities in direct opposition to school authorities, local officials, and government authorities, as well as despite the objections of their husbands. As I familiarized myself with this neighborhood, I realized such activities were an integral part of the lives of many of its residents, particularly working mothers. I felt I could not ignore them without distorting the reality that shaped the experience of Santech's residents. While they were not part of my original research plan, I decided to document these political activities as an important part of community life in Santech, although at the time I was uncertain about their significance.

In the academic literature, the study of Latina women's community politics has attracted considerable attention. In a study of Latina immigrant politics in Boston, for example, Carol Hardy-Fanta (1993) maintains that what at first glance might appear to be domestic, nonpolitical activities are in fact a major expression of political demands by disempowered minority women. And, in her study of an immigrant community in Northern California, Pierrette Hondagneu-Sotelo contends that Mexican women's participation in a variety of civic and educational associations is crucial for advancing their social and political incorporation and establishing roots in the local community (1994: 175–78). Similarly, Cecilia Menjívar has shown that the social networks constructed by Salvadoran immigrant women in San Francisco provide valuable information about job opportunities and about health, social, and other community services and programs, as well as aid in different forms of community building (2000: 172–78). More recently, in the case of a Mexican immigrant community in the small California town of Carpinteria, near Santa Barbara, Concha Delgado-Gaitán (2001) argues that parents' concerns about education often inspire the critical first step toward collective action, politicization, and the development of community leadership among low-income immigrants, especially women.

These and similar studies portray immigrant women at the forefront of community activities through which they forge a sense of community, transform their political identity, and advance new forms of political citizenship (Pardo 1998a; Jones-Correa 1998). While these studies illuminate the political agency of immigrant women, the challenges these women confront in integrating politics with work and family have received comparatively little attention. Also, how community politics in immigrant communities change over time, and how these changes affect women's political consciousness, has been neglected under the assumption that community organizing develops as a natural extension of women's social networks and community activities.

I considered these issues after observing the grassroots political activities of Elena and a group of other Mexican immigrant women in Santech. What moved this group to come together in the first place and take collective action to address their concerns? What goals did they pursue and what political strategies did they use? How did they manage to combine community politics with their work and family responsibilities? And what do community politics in Santech reveal about the political agency of low-income Mexican immigrants in Silicon Valley? Along with labor organizing, grassroots community politics constitute a central avenue through which undocumented immigrants in Santech, especially women, otherwise excluded from electoral politics, channel some of their basic political demands. Grassroots community politics represent an important but generally overlooked dimension of political agency by low-income immigrants in Silicon Valley. Like union organizing among Mexican workers, grassroots politics in Santech heavily rely on immigrant kinship and social networks, through which they mobilize from the bottom up. Unlike union organizing, however, community politics in Santech form a gendered space dominated by women who, as they become engaged in these mobilizing activities, develop a strong political and ethnic consciousness. To do so, women activists in Santech struggle to overcome a cultural ideology that restricts them to the spheres of the household and work and away from the public arena of politics.[1]

Government Programs in Santech

Often newcomers in low-income immigrant communities experience life in the United States through key mediating local institutions such as workplaces, schools, rental housing, and community organizations (Lamphere 1992: 2). Mexican immigrants in Santech are no exception. Residents' gradual politicization in the barrio occurred in a context of direct interaction between them and several local government institutions and programs. This process entailed several progressive stages. The first stage started in the late 1980s, when the San Jose city government announced an ambitious rehabilitation program to address drugs, gangs, crime, and substandard housing in several low-income minority neighborhoods in San Jose. At this point, Santech, long neglected by the city government, suddenly became the target of an aggressive "neighborhood rehabilitation" plan. Project Crackdown, a multimillion-dollar program designed to attack drug dealing and improve housing conditions in this and other poor barrios in San Jose, was the central piece in this plan.[2] From the city government's perspective, the problems in Santech resulted from the arrival of poor immigrants, weak community ties in the neighborhood, unscrupulous landlords who profited from local residents, and drug dealers who used this barrio as a home base for their illegal businesses.[3] Because of this, one of the principal components of Project Crackdown—launched in Santech in the early 1990s—was community organizing. The main purpose of this component was to encourage residents in Santech to develop a sense of community and support the efforts of the police and other city departments. To accomplish this goal, the city included in the project a neighborhood community center, which was housed in a portable building next to Santech Elementary School. The plan was to provide information and referral services to local residents, promote community organizing, and foster a sense of community action and pride. "Activity community workers" employed by the city were in charge of organizing monthly community meetings with Santech residents to gain their support and collect ideas about how to address the numerous problems that affected this neighborhood. These community workers were also responsible for establishing a "community action team" made up of local residents willing to work with city officials to improve living conditions in Santech. One of Project Crackdown's principal coordinators explained its purpose to me several years after the program was first launched in the barrio:

> One of our central goals is to get the community involved so residents participate in the community meetings, give their input, and, eventually, form their own community group, so that when we leave the area they can take over and fill the vacuum. . . . We do not want to come with preconceived ideas about what the community problems and solutions are. We want to get [residents'] input and ideas about what their concerns are. . . . We need to develop trust with the community so residents get involved. This is one of our principal goals.

In practice, however, the monthly community meetings organized by Project Crackdown allowed little room for input from Santech residents and mainly served to implement government programs administered in a top-down approach. Most of the numerous evening meetings, for example, which I regularly attended, followed a similar script. First, the neighborhood center's coordinator announced the projects that the city government planned to implement in the following weeks. These included, among others, the installation of traffic signs and streetlights, the introduction of parking restrictions, and the banning of ice-cream trucks and street vendors in parts of the neighborhood, all of which were justified in the name of enhancing public safety in the community while facilitating police work against drugs and crime. In an additional attempt to reduce crime in the barrio, police officers tried to talk Santech residents into participating in neighborhood watch, block parent, and crime prevention programs, among others.

In the second half of the meetings, invited speakers usually talked to local residents about topics of public interest. Most often these speakers were public officials from the police department who came to talk about drugs and gangs. These presentations were intended to raise public awareness about the issues and to exhort parents in Santech to keep an eye on their children to prevent them from getting in trouble. Finally, in the third part of the meeting, a representative from a nonprofit organization would talk about the programs the organization sponsored. These nonprofit organizations consisted of groups that worked with Latinos and other ethnic groups in San Jose and that sponsored a variety of programs, including those related to drug and gang prevention. The Mexican American Community Service Agency, one of the largest and most well-established Mexican American community organizations in San Jose, was one such nonprofit group. Having won a major grant from the Santa Clara County government, the agency developed a variety of antigang and drug-awareness programs, as well as job-training and elder-care programs, which it offered to the residents of Santech and which fit well with the goals of Project Crackdown.

RESIDENTS' RESPONSES TO CITY PROGRAMS

Santech residents welcomed Project Crackdown and the accompanying government programs when they were first launched. Concerned about the bad housing conditions in the barrio, abusive landlords, and the presence of drug dealers and gangs in the streets, many neighbors hoped that city officials would help them to solve these problems. Some residents, for example, hoped that police presence in the streets would deter people from coming to sell drugs and deter rival gangs from fighting. The high expectations generated by Project Crackdown were evident during the first community meetings organized by city workers, which were packed with people eager to learn about the new plans for the community.

After this warm reception, the interest of many residents began to fade. Many were upset about how the police handled the searches of suspected drug dealers and gang members in the neighborhood. Parents of teenage children complained about police abuse and argued that, in their zeal to detain suspected gang members, police officers often harassed their children who were not involved with drugs or gangs. I was unable to verify the accuracy of these allegations; however, they helped to generate an atmosphere of distrust. Residents also complained that the meetings focused on a narrow range of topics, such as drugs, gangs, and crime, while ignoring other issues important to the community, like poor housing and the need for child-care centers and after-school activities for children.

Among the critics was Rafael, Elena's husband. Employed for many years in Silicon Valley as a landscape worker, Rafael was an outspoken person well known in the community who had been involved in local affairs for a long time. When Project Crackdown first started, he was one of the most active participants in the community meetings. After a while, however, he grew tired of these meetings, as he considered them to be of little value to the people of Santech. "This month is about this [drugs], and two months later they again talk about the same thing. It is always the same, and yet they say in the meetings, 'What do parents want?' But then, they come back to the same issues again. . . . It is the same thing they talk about, nothing changes, maybe one, two, or three words, that's all." On a different occasion, he talked about his distrust of most of the community workers who ran the programs: "Many people manipulate us. First they cultivate our sympathy, they win us over, and later they do not support us. . . . I do not like to go to those meetings, because they [city workers] use us to get what they want, but then we do not see the benefits. . . . They only mobilize when they are interested in something. . . . They [neighborhood center staff] do not care whether the community suffers or not. . . . This is not working with the community; they work for the city, not for the community."

Elena, the most visible and charismatic community leader in Santech, also had harsh words to describe these meetings. "I am fed up with all that talk, all the promises they do not keep. I am fed up from hearing all this foolish talk. Instead of trusting the community, talking with us. . . . That is why parents do not go any more, if they do, they only go for the raffles; and not even that motivates them any longer." Cecilia, one of the most active women in Santech community affairs, expressed the growing feeling of alienation shared by many local residents: "They do not take our opinions seriously. Everybody knows that the [neighborhood] center does nothing, but nobody says what he or she thinks in those meetings."

With time, public reaction to the government project ranged from passive resistance to open contestation. Class and cultural differences between city workers in the neighborhood center and Mexican immigrants aggravated the sense of alienation among many Santech residents. For example, while city officials were proud of employing bilingual community organizers in Project Crackdown and the neighborhood center, Santech residents, especially women, felt that the people hired to work in these programs did not have the social and cultural sensitivity necessary to understand their real needs and win their trust. On this point Elena commented, "We need leaders who demonstrate that they really want to help us, because those people [city staff] only work for their own benefit so they can keep their jobs—that's it. Whether they truly help people or not, they do not care—they do not care whether people take advantage of their services or not. . . . What we need is people of our own race, our own level, our own culture."

In truth, many felt that things had improved considerably in Santech after the arrival of Project Crackdown. There were fewer drug dealers in the streets, the barrio was safer than before, and code enforcement officials had started to crack down on landlords whose buildings were falling apart. At the same time, however, the results produced by the government programs did not meet the high expectations they had generated. Neighbors complained about the little input they had had in the programs and the way that the needs of the community were identified. Tired of the monthly meetings, residents gradually but consistently withdrew, forcing city workers to come up with strategies to attract them back, including raffles and food and clothing giveaways.

The fact that city officials publicly stigmatized the community by identifying it as a site of drugs, gangs, and crime also contributed to residents' alienation. This is what Daniel Dohan calls the "infection metaphor," according to which the lack of internal community strength is identified as the reason for criminal activities instigated from the outside, and thus residents are called upon to partner with the police to resist such an external invasion (2003: 152–53). By emphasizing the representation of Santech as an immigrant slum rife with poverty, ignorance, and crime, government officials undermined the very trust they hoped to cultivate among the residents. In fact, Project Crackdown sent a contradictory message to the people of Santech. It asked for their cooperation and involvement in order to restore the neighborhood and build community pride, but it also presented a negative, stereotypical image of the barrio as a site of crime, drugs, and gangs.

Becoming Political: The Struggle for Bilingual Education in Santech

As Delgado-Gaitán (2001) maintains, education often galvanizes political consciousness and mobilizes parents in low-income Latino immigrant communities. Residents' interactions with Santech Elementary School over educational issues was another central experience that helped politicize them. Questions about what they viewed as the deficient quality of the education their children were receiving had commanded the attention of Mexican parents in the barrio for a long time. They were especially anguished about the fact that many of the children did not speak, read, or write English even after several years of schooling. Thus, while in Santech, I often heard parents ask critically, "What are our children being taught? How can the school let our children move on when they are not even able to read or write English? What kind of teachers are educating our children?"

Mexican parents' concern in Santech occurred in a context of dramatic demographic changes that had taken place in the community since the early 1990s. After Santech had been transformed into a low-income neighborhood for Mexican immigrants, the number of children in the school who did not speak English skyrocketed. The number who possessed what was officially classified as "limited English proficiency" (LEP) increased tenfold between 1976 and 1992—from 54 to 559—and in the school district the number increased almost twentyfold, from 244 to 4,051 (Franklin-McKinley School District 1993: 2). The arrival of Mexican immigrant families in the barrio also placed increasing pressure on the school's facilities. Badly prepared for such demographic growth, at a time when public funds to build new schools were drying up, district officials decided to add portable buildings to house the newcomers. By the early 1990s, Santech Elementary School already had seven such tem-

porary buildings. At the same time, the school district started to dismantle the few bilingual programs designed to meet the needs of immigrant children. Between 1984 and 1993, the number of bilingual teachers in Santech declined from seventeen to only two, and in the district
the number fell from fifty-five to twenty-four. The principal of Santech
Elementary School, a middle-aged Anglo woman who had been on the
job for seven years, was opposed to bilingual education because she considered it counterproductive for immigrant children. As she explained
when I interviewed her,

> We encourage parents to speak their own language with their kids at
> home, so that the kids learn their language at home and English at
> school. . . . We do not have the capacity to provide a full bilingual pro-
> gram in the school, and even if we had, it would not work unless the pro-
> gram is continued throughout middle school as well. . . . By the time I
> arrived in Santech, there was a bilingual program because it was manda-
> tory by law, and there was bilingual education in all grades, and there
> were many teachers involved. Yet teachers told me that [the program]
> was not successful, and that a much better strategy was to mix native and
> non-English[-speaking] kids in the classroom, because in the old system
> children did not have role models in class, and that is a key to
> improve[ment]. . . . Moreover, research shows that, for kids who are not
> proficient in their own language, the best strategy is to educate them in
> English. . . . I am willing to hire bilingual teachers if they are good, but I
> am very careful not to hire a teacher just because he or she is bilingual,
> because I prefer a good English teacher over a poor bilingual teacher.

A dramatic decline in students' performance in this school took place
in the context of a rapid increase in non-English-speaking children and
a drastic reduction in bilingual programs. By the mid-1990s, the Santech school had some of the lowest scores in reading, writing, and
mathematics in the whole district, and the district ranked near the bottom among all school districts in the Santa Clara Valley. Mexican parents in Santech became increasingly worried about the education of
their children, and about the fact that the children were moving on to
the next grade level despite being badly prepared and seriously limited
in their basic language skills.

POWER STRUGGLES
AT THE SCHOOL SITE COUNCIL

The next stage in the experience of parents in Santech was critical for
the development of their political consciousness. They perceived them-

selves as a group with shared interests who rejected the official rationale for their children's situation and recognized the need for collective action, a key ingredient in grassroots political activism (Pardo 1998b). A group of Mexican parents led by Elena decided to take action and demand that more bilingual teachers be hired at Santech Elementary School. As the first step, they planned to win influence over the School Site Council, an official organization, whose main function was to serve as a bridge between the school and the community. In Santech, the School Site Council had ten members, including the school's principal, four schoolteachers, and five parents elected by their peers to represent the community. Previously, Mexican parents had been skeptical of the council, which they considered to be a puppet institution manipulated by the school principal that ignored the voice of the community. Francisca, a forty-two-year-old woman who was the first Mexican elected to the council, expressed this view in one of our conversations about her experience:

> When I was in the council, I felt I was just a puppet of the [school's] administration, that they were not interested in my opinion. They just do things carefully so they do not violate the law, but that does not mean they are doing things right; they only do that to cover their backs. For example, in the council meetings when I was the president, they never explained anything to me about what they were talking about, and they only called me to be part of the meetings to fulfill the requirements. I was physically there, but without saying, understanding, or doing anything.

With a mixture of sadness and anger, she explained why she felt ignored by the school administrators:

> Whenever I went to the council meetings, the agenda had already been set up, so my presence there was only part of the requirements. Once they gave me a little present as a symbol to acknowledge my work. I did not know why they were giving me anything, because I was not doing anything and I did not understand what my role there was. Later I realized that they just wanted to keep me happy, so that I could keep playing my role. . . . [But] whenever one tries to change things, you get into trouble. . . . Since I am not the president any more, I do not go to the council meetings. I am not interested. I feel depressed and let down by this school.

Seeking to end the passivity of Mexican parents in the school council, a group of them elected Rafael, one of the most vocal critics of the school's principal, as a member and the chair of the council. Rafael was determined to use his position to turn things around in the school and convey the concerns of barrio parents about the quality of education. The new activist, militant approach that Rafael brought to the council was not well received by the school's principal, who perceived him as a troublemaker representing the view of only a small group of parents. With time, confrontations between Rafael and the principal escalated, with the former complaining that the principal systematically blocked the discussion of the issues that interested Mexican parents at the council meetings. With anger and a sense of disempowerment, he explained, "When she [the principal] does not want to talk about something, then she just keeps postponing it from one meeting to the next so it never gets discussed. I am tired of her tactics. She wants to win one's confidence by saying there are several Latina workers in the school. But they are not teachers, but people who work in the cafeteria, and so, I am not interested in what she says but in what she does."

In the next council elections, a rumor spread in Santech that the school principal was determined to remove Rafael as council chair and replace him with Sophie, a person she trusted and who worked as a volunteer in the school cafeteria. The events that followed further undermined many Mexican residents' trust in the school as a public institution. Angered by what they perceived as manipulative tactics used by the principal to silence them, the group of parents headed by Elena decided to organize and ensure that Rafael kept his post. Relying on the large network of friends, neighbors, and acquaintances developed by Elena and about ten Mexican women in Santech, they mobilized a large number of Mexican parents, many of whom had never participated in council elections before, to cast their votes for either Rafael or Elena, who was also running at the time. This campaign reached its climax during the week when parents were scheduled to mark their ballots and send them to the school. During the intense weeks that preceded that deadline, Rafael and Elena, as well as the most active women in their group, were busy visiting or calling their neighbors to make sure they would send their ballots in on time. By the end of the election week, recognizing the high and unprecedented number of parents who had voted, Rafael, Elena, and their supporters were confident they had scored a big win.

One week after the ballot deadline, a council meeting was scheduled to announce the results of the elections. The meeting was held on a weekday in the early afternoon, when most residents were at work, and only twelve Mexican parents were able to attend. As I sat in the meeting, invited by Elena, I noticed that they were visibly anxious to find out the results of the elections, as they expected to win at least two council seats

FIGURE 11. Santech activists throw a children's birthday party in the barrio, demonstrating the close integration between their social and political activities.

due to the high turnout. When the meeting started, the school's principal read the names of the five people who had been elected to represent the school personnel, and the five elected to represent the parents, without indicating how many votes each had received. The elected parents included Elena; Rafael; Mr. Lee, a Vietnamese resident; Mr. Yeng, a Cambodian neighbor; and Sophie, the Mexican American woman whom the principal was rumored to support as the new chair. After that, the principal asked the new council members to step up to the front of the room and cast their votes to elect a new chair. Elena nominated Rafael for the post, and a member who represented the school staff proposed Sophie. Finally, the ten council members cast their votes in secret, after which the principal read the results to the public: the newly elected council chair was Sophie, who had received five votes, followed by Rafael with three, and Elena and a member of the school staff, with one each.

The result was a blow to Mexican parents gathered in the room. They could not believe that Rafael had lost the council chair and that the principal's candidate was to replace him. They were especially disappointed after all the effort they had invested in the council elections, and after the mobilization of many parents who had voted for either him or Elena. Once more, they felt, the school's principal had deceived them. Visibly disturbed and angry about what had just happened, half the Mexican parents in the room walked out of the meeting, while the others were asked by the school interpreter to "stay calm and behave." As things calmed down, and in an effort to placate the parents, the principal thanked Rafael in public for his service while chair, a gesture that even further angered the parents still present in the meeting.

The Mexican parents' impression that they had been deceived in the council elections was not wrong. As Rafael discovered shortly afterward, the elections had in fact been conducted in violation of the council's bylaws. Several irregularities had led to his replacement by a new chair. Rather than offer an open ballot with a full slate of previously nominated candidates, in a system in which the five candidates with the most votes would win, the school administration had sent a ballot on which the candidates were arranged by the school in four groups along ethnic lines: one for "Cambodians" (with five candidates), one for "Spanish-speaking" (with six candidates), one for "Vietnamese" (with two candidates), and one for "Other" (with two candidates, including Sophie).

The official rationale for such a grouping, printed in the ballots, was "to represent the various languages spoken in the school." In each ballot, parents were instructed to vote for three candidates from the Cambodian group, three from the Spanish group, two from the Vietnamese group, and two from "Other." The five winning council members were to be selected from the candidates with the most votes within each of these groups, including two from the Spanish-speaking group, and one from each of the others. While three of these groups represented the predominant ethnic makeup of the school's population, the two candidates labeled "Other" were set apart and publicly known for their strong support of the school's principal. By requiring parents to vote for two candidates in each group, the school's principal ensured that at least one of her two loyal supporters would be among the final five council members. To select a new chair of her liking, the principal needed only to ensure that most of the members representing the school staff, all of whom were part of her inner circle, would vote for the same candidate rather than for Rafael.

Shortly after the council elections, a Latina teacher who used to work in Santech, and who was supportive of the Mexican parents' push for change, explained to me why she believed they traditionally had shown little interest in participating in the school's council: "They get discouraged because they see that, no matter how much you fight, you go to meetings, you get involved and participate, the people at the top are the ones who always run the show."

The outcome of the council elections further undermined the little trust that local residents had in the school and its administration. Two days later, when I accompanied Rafael to a meeting he had scheduled with a public official in the school district, he was told that the ballots used for the elections were in violation of the council's bylaws, after which the official advised him to file an official complaint with the State Department of Education in Sacramento. Tired after the time and effort he had already put into the council's elections, and disappointed about the results, Rafael felt overwhelmed by the prospect of embarking on yet another bureaucratic proceeding, and decided not to file the complaint. In his view, there was little that could be changed by following the rules, and the best alternative was to put this bitter experience behind him and abandon the idea of using the council to try changing things from within. Rafael's feeling of having been the target of racial discrimination by the school's principal was echoed by a local officer in charge of bilingual programs in the district. An Afro-Caribbean Latino, he was convinced that the school district's opposition to bilingual education was a disguise for racial discrimination against Latinos. The answer, he commented, was grassroots organizing:

> Organizing parents[, then,] is crucial. If they do not organize, the district will not implement the few bilingual programs that exist, because they are the ones who have the power to demand them. . . . The problem is that since many parents do not vote because they are undocumented, the administration does not worry much about them. . . . The district is not interested in empowering [Latino] parents. They just give them some power; but when parents start being effective and exercising their rights, the district isolates them and labels them as troublemakers.

The experience in the council elections marked a turning point in the history of grassroots politics in Santech. Mexican parents who up until then had tried to work within official institutions to seek a solution to their problems arrived at the conclusion that this was a long and uncertain path, which often did not pay off and was disheartening. After their negative experience with government programs like Project Crackdown, the disappointment with the school council—a legal institution especially created to give parents a voice—marked the end of residents' involvement in community politics that were based on the idea of working within the system to bring change.

The Campaign for a Homework Center:
Learning the Ropes of Political Mobilization

If ethnic and class discrimination is often the source of political consciousness for first-generation immigrants excluded from mainstream
electoral politics and institutions in the United States, their interaction
with labor unions and civil rights groups is a key ingredient of their
political mobilization and articulation of their needs in the larger public realm. Thus, the next and crucial step in the politicization of Santech
residents took place when they started to reach out to other organizations and local politicians for support. Frustrated by the little progress
made in both the School Site Council and the neighborhood center, a
group of about fifteen Mexican parents led by Elena decided to organize their own community meetings to talk about their major problems
and concerns and the best course of action to address them. As I
explained earlier, Elena had originally planned these meetings as an
opportunity to talk about their problems in their own terms in a setting
not controlled by outsiders. This time, residents agreed on the need to
come up with an alternative form of collective organizing that would
promote changes not from within local institutions but from the outside by putting pressure on them. To do so, they had to look for support from local groups and organizations eager to listen to their needs
and help them.

The new meetings marked a radical departure from how Mexican
residents in Santech mobilized to channel their demands. As a first step,
a group of about twenty residents, all of them women except for one
retired man, identified the most urgent problems and needs in the community. The issues they selected included the presence of apartments in
substandard conditions with exorbitant rents; lack of child-care centers;
poor education in Santech Elementary School; lack of recreational centers for young people in the barrio; need for classes to teach English as
a second language to adults; need for legal assistance with issues like
housing, immigration, and employment; and need for help for women
who were the victims of domestic abuse or whose husbands were alco-
holics. As a second step, Elena and her friends decided to invite the
director of a well-known and influential, church-based, interfaith civic
organization in town, People Acting in Community Together (PACT).
This person was one of the organizers she had met while attending a
meeting in a Catholic parish to protest police brutality against Latinos
in San Jose.

Founded in 1985 by Catholic clergy in San Jose, PACT was known for its "in-your-face" confrontational style and its demand that city officials spend less public money on urban redevelopment plans benefiting the rich and invest more in poor neighborhoods with substandard housing, gangs, drugs, unemployment, and a lack of public facilities and services.[4] With an ethnically diverse base of middle-aged Anglo, Latino, and Asian members, PACT has made a special effort, beginning in the early 1990s, to reach out to Mexican immigrants, who were rapidly becoming the majority in many working-class neighborhoods on the east side. When Elena contacted PACT, the director and community workers of the organization were eager to take advantage of the opportunity to work with her and other Mexican parents in Santech.[5]

PACT organizers' first message to Elena and the rest of the group was that, to be politically effective, they had to learn the techniques of community organizing. This meant that, instead of following the informal method of mobilizing they had used until then, they would have to implement a more formal, organized, and disciplined approach that could produce more tangible results. With no hesitation, Santech residents accepted this offer to teach them. This was the first time that anyone had offered to explain how the city's political system worked and the ropes of community organizing. Disappointed with their experiences at the neighborhood center and the local school, they were encouraged by the new prospects that PACT seemed to offer. As a first, short-term project, and in order to accomplish a tangible result that could win the trust of more people in Santech, PACT proposed the idea of a homework center in the neighborhood for children who lagged behind in school. The homework center would provide hired and volunteer bilingual tutors to assist children who could not read and write English. Having already identified education as one of their major concerns, Elena and her followers rapidly accepted the proposal.

After the project was launched, Elena and her friends were drawn into an intense political campaign that lasted several months, critically contributing to the building of community mobilization and leadership skills. An important part of the campaign consisted of numerous meetings to discuss the details of the project: who should fund it, where to house it, and what strategies were needed to press city politicians to support it (see Figure 12). After recruiting dozens of community residents through an intense door-to-door campaign by PACT organizers in conjunction with Elena and her group, the director and leaders of this organization started to organize public meetings with city officials in

FIGURE 12. A large meeting of People Acting in Community Together
promotes community organizing in San Jose.

order to bring them to the table along with neighbors in Santech. For
the first time, Elena and the rest of the group were able to meet face-
to-face with city officials in a setting not controlled by the latter.

The campaign reached its peak when PACT called for a meeting with
a member of the San Jose City Council, the highest-ranking official with
whom Santech neighbors had ever met. A middle-age man of Mexican-
Japanese descent, this politician was known for supporting a progressive
political agenda on behalf of Latinos in the working-class electoral district to which Santech belonged. In the meeting, held in one of the local
parishes associated with PACT and attended by about two hundred
people, Elena and her colleagues announced the problems they had had
with Santech Elementary School and criticized the poor education their
children were receiving. Presenting numerous public testimonies, Mexican parents who had been involved in the School Site Council campaign, and children who attended this school, made a clear impact on
the audience and the invited council member. At the end of the meeting, the latter endorsed the Homework Center project and committed
himself to seeking city funds to support it.

The new community organizing tactics soon started to pay off. Several months later, the campaign for the homework center reached its
goal. As a result of PACT's lobbying and the numerous meetings held

with many public officials, the people of Santech were able to collect the $68,500 needed to get the project started.[6] Equally significant, a board was formed to direct the project and represent all the groups that had participated in the project's planning and funding, including the people of Santech, PACT, the school district, and the city council. Elena and two other women of her group were elected to represent Santech neighbors on the board.

One year after Elena's group first met with PACT, the homework center was officially inaugurated in a public school near Santech whose administration was more sympathetic to Latino parents than Santech Elementary School had been. Attended by San Jose's mayor and other important city politicians and the local press, the inauguration was an important event for many Santech residents, who were proud of their accomplishment. About seventy-five neighbors, many of whom had been involved in the campaign at one time or another, showed up for the event, including most of the original members of Elena's group that had first started meeting to look for alternative and more efficient forms of collective action. The opening ceremony conducted by the mayor had a special symbolic value for Elena, who was presented with an award to acknowledge her key role in mobilizing the people of Santech for the project. To her and her friends, this was a time to rejoice after enduring all the obstacles and defeats they had met in their long and lonely fight against the administration of Santech Elementary School.

While the homework center was only a first step in addressing the problem of education for Mexican children, the community campaign renewed the hopes of Santech residents that they could achieve positive results through collective action, and it represented one of the few occasions in which they could celebrate an important victory. Equally significant, as in the case of Mexican janitors and the local union mentioned earlier, the collaboration between Santech residents and the well-established grassroots political organization PACT fueled the political socialization of this group of first-generation immigrants into civic politics in the United States. It also contributed to a politically effective articulation of their demands in the larger community of Silicon Valley.

ETHNIC POLITICS AND THE TRANSFORMATION OF COMMUNITY ORGANIZING

The political experience of the homework center campaign also helped to shape the ethnic consciousness of Mexican residents in Santech, which corroborates the claim that class, gender, and ethnic identity are dynamically interrelated in the political mobilization of immigrant parents, especially women (Pardo 1998b). Thus, as a result of this campaign, people in the barrio learned to use ethnicity as a political weapon in the struggle to improve living conditions in the community. Although the issue of ethnic identity is beyond the scope of this chapter, this grassroots campaign was a case of situational politics in which the people of Santech learned to use the term *Latino* as a pragmatic political label. While in the past Elena and her colleagues usually referred to their ethnic identity as Mexican, once they worked together with people and organizations outside the neighborhood, organizations that, like PACT, had a large Latino constituency, they started thinking of themselves as part of a larger pan-Latino ethnic community in town with similar concerns and demands.

To a political activist like Elena, involvement with grassroots community groups that used ethnicity as part of their mobilizing strategies affected how she saw and identified herself as part of a larger Latino community in Silicon Valley sharing similar problems and political interests. Like the janitors who began organizing a union, Elena and her group of activists found that articulating their needs on behalf of Latino parents as an issue of ethnic and social justice in San Jose allowed them to redefine and legitimize the issue of education on their own terms and win the sympathy and support of influential local politicians and public officials for the homework center project.

On another level, the political socialization of immigrant women in Santech, following the model of civic activism sponsored by PACT, transformed the nature and style of grassroots politics in the local community. For one thing, Elena and her friends had to accommodate PACT's model and rules of community organizing. Drawing on years of experience in mobilizing people, and on its church-based model, PACT followed a methodical, highly disciplined approach that consisted of regular meetings that Elena and her friends were asked to attend. In addition, Santech residents had to participate in numerous rehearsal meetings to prepare for key meetings with important city politicians. Busy with work, family, and household obligations, Elena's group found that attending so many meetings took a toll on residents; the meetings demanded a special effort and commitment by the group, who, in the past, had had more leeway to structure such meetings around their day-to-day activities. More important, once PACT took control of community organizing, the former flexibility of the meetings, which had allowed people to bring issues to the table that were not included in the agenda, was significantly reduced.

As a result, residents partially lost control of their own meetings and of the power to decide which goals and issues would be addressed by collective action—these decisions were now largely shaped by PACT's political agenda. In this context, residents had to accommodate an external group and its organizational style; adjust to its internal structure, rules, and priorities; and adapt to its different style and culture of community politics. In exchange for gaining political effectiveness, Elena's group learned to negotiate with PACT not only the terms of community mobilizing but also which needs and priorities could be effectively addressed through collective action. In the process, community politics became more formal. As a result, political activities that in the past had been embedded in and indistinguishable from women's everyday lives and their social relationships gradually became more structured and occupied a realm of action of their own, an aspect often overlooked by the more romantic portrayals of Latina community politics (Hardy-Fanta 1993; Pardo 1998a).

Elena and her friends were generally satisfied, however, with their collaboration with PACT, despite the time and effort it required. This collaboration proved to be a much more efficient form of channeling their demands than all their meetings with government institutions and programs in the past. Moreover, they gained access to influential leaders and public officials that they otherwise could not have reached on their own. In the process, they also helped to revitalize the core membership of grassroots community organizations like PACT, bringing young low-income immigrants to the forefront of grassroots community mobilization in San Jose.

The Case of Elena: Balancing Politics, Work, and Family

For Latina women, civic politics is often an interpersonal affair woven into the fabric of daily life (Hardy-Fanta 1993: 29). From this perspective, motherhood is not a constraint on immigrant women's political involvement, but rather an incentive to engage in political action out of concern for their children (Pardo 1998a; Hardy-Fanta 1993: 145–46). Yet, like their engagement in wage work, immigrant women's involvement in political activities in the public realm often creates dilemmas over how to combine them with their activities in the household sphere. In Santech, women active in community affairs often had to negotiate with their husbands or other male kin to participate in such activities, which took them away from home, a process not exempt from friction.

The case of Elena, Santech's most popular and effective community leader by far, illustrates some of the common difficulties and dilemmas that women involved in community politics in the barrio confronted and the solutions they developed. Elena's first limitation on her role as community leader was her work. Her husband was employed as a low-wage gardener and experienced frequent episodes of unemployment and underemployment, so Elena had to work to help sustain her family. Her favorite type of employment consisted of informal selling, because it allowed her to combine work with domestic chores and the care of her children. Capitalizing on her rich network of friends, neighbors, and acquaintances, she sold beauty products, jewelry, kitchen pots, life insurance, and other commodities. Her sociable, upbeat, and cheerful personality was the principal asset that helped her in the competitive business of selling. While important for the economy of the family, all these occupations severely limited the time and energy she could put into her political activities. With time, she learned to better combine her income-generating and political activities and to capitalize on her community-related contacts as potential clients for her businesses.

For example, public officials often expected Elena to act as an intermediary and to help them recruit people for a variety of programs in the neighborhood, a role commonly played by activist immigrant women who serve as political intermediaries between government and local immigrant populations (Jones-Correa 1998: 343–44). Thus, Elena was constantly invited to different types of training courses that government programs and nonprofit organizations alike offered in the city, centered on leadership skills, children's education, drug and alcohol prevention, and so on. She was often paid to attend, recruit for, and even teach (after proper training) such workshops, earning between four hundred and a thousand dollars depending on her responsibilities on each particular occasion. To her, this was an opportunity to develop her political skills, mobilize the community, and, at the same time, earn extra income. Over time, Elena learned to use her informal occupation as a door-to-door vendor to recruit supporters for political activities and increase her political capital. By integrating these two spheres of her life, she expanded her personal social network, associated with influential local politicians and community leaders, and consolidated her position as a political broker in Santech. In times of financial hardship, she often relied on the social networks built on her business and political activities to gain help, including borrowing money. In short, the mutual embeddedness of work and politics in her life was a pragmatic solution to the difficult problem of maintaining roles as both a working mother and a community leader.

Despite her efforts to integrate family, work, and politics, Elena's role as community leader remained a heavy burden in her life. She felt under constant pressure, especially during difficult economic times. On such occasions, she questioned the wisdom of getting involved in politics, given the effects it had on her family. During one of the numerous times when she felt frustrated about the time consumed by her political activities, she commented, "Politics is great, but you don't eat from it. . . . From now on, I want to dedicate myself to my business and spend less time going to [community] meetings. . . . Yes, I want to put more time in my business and stop attending so many meetings, because with so much activity, my home is falling apart. And now that I have serious financial troubles, who is going to help me? Community meetings are great because you learn about the resources that are out there for us. But it is too much, and because of these community activities, I am neglecting my home and my family." Feeling that family, work, and politics did not make a good mix, she added, "Ever since I got involved into politics, my home seems to be falling apart, and I have gotten into debt. If at least I could make some money out of it . . . [But] ever since I got involved in politics I neglected my business and I have financial problems. Either business or politics, one of the two . . . the damn politics does not give you enough to eat!"

For several years Elena constantly faced the dilemma of how to, on the one hand, indulge her deep passion for community politics, with its opportunities to meet public figures, and, on the other hand, still play her role as a working mother with financial responsibilities. To her, getting involved in politics was an opportunity not only to do something good for the community and its people but also to get away from tedious domestic work, which she openly disliked. Whenever she slowed down in her involvement with community affairs because she felt obliged to dedicate more time to her family and household, she became depressed and missed the excitement of politics. On one such occasion she told me, "I go from one place to the next; I get invited all the time from one meeting to another and to everything that goes on here. [And] when I am not active in something in the community, I feel depressed, disheartened. But when I go to community meetings, it is very different. I get excited and full of energy!"

Elena's role as political leader was also constrained by pressure from her husband, who wanted her to concentrate on the family and household chores. Rafael was ambivalent about Elena's political activities. On the one hand, he was supportive of his wife, having himself been involved with politics as one of the leaders in the campaign for the School Site Council. More frequently, however, he questioned Elena's involvement because it took her away from her household and family duties. He often complained that she was rarely at home and did not take care of their children. Rafael himself had gradually withdrawn from community politics because, as he explained, politics interfered with family and household duties. "When we get involved with politics, we neglect our home, so that we fail outside and we fail at home also. . . . It is better to put politics aside and concentrate on our work so that at least our home and family are fine. . . . What does politics give Elena? What does she get from going to all those meetings? . . . [Nothing.] That is why I stopped going to community meetings; they take a lot of your time and one neglects the family." Complaining that Elena's political activities obliged him to take care of domestic chores that she used to do, he said, "Elena goes from one meeting to the next and leaves [our] home unattended. Often I arrive home after work and there is nothing to eat, and she tells me, 'I am going to a meeting; fix dinner for the children when they get home.' . . . It is hard after arriving home from work to have to work at home too."

In this context, Elena's involvement with community politics required her to constantly renegotiate with her husband the domestic division of labor. When Rafael was out of work, Elena used the opportunity to get more involved with her business and political activities, leaving him in charge of household chores like cleaning, taking care of the children, and sometimes cooking. But when Rafael was employed, he would take a more passive approach to household work, and Elena felt pressured to get more involved with housework and the children. On the assumption that the father should be the main provider for the family, Rafael and Elena argued, sometimes bitterly, about how to divide work at home. Rather than questioning the assumption, Elena used it in her favor to carve out time for her business and political activities whenever Rafael was out of work.

Elena's role as community leader was thus deeply embedded in everyday life as a working mother, a common situation for many Mexican women involved in community politics (Hardy-Fanta 1993). This situation changed considerably in 1996, when, after several years' experience as an informal leader in the community, she was hired by a public school near Santech to serve as a liaison to parents and families in the neighborhood. To Elena, her new job marked a transition from her informal community leadership role to a formal, part-time paid position. Her appointment as community liaison also helped to change her work life. At that point, she was able to quit many of her informal occupations and concentrate instead on what she liked best: community politics. From then on, she channeled her energies into addressing problems that she and her followers had identified when they first began meeting in Santech. For example, shortly after the homework center project was completed, the principal of Santech Elementary was removed from her post and a new administration supportive of bilingual education was put in place, which implemented many of the changes that Elena and other Latino parents had advocated for several years.

Elena's new job as community organizer also had a dramatic impact on her family life. With a modest but secure income, she was able to sustain her family on the income from her job and supplementary income from sales. After years of a difficult marriage with Rafael, and as tensions between them escalated significantly, Elena felt more financially stable than in the past and asked him to move out, which he did after considerable resistance. This was a difficult transition for the family, especially for their youngest children, who had to adapt to not having their father with them. Despite this, Elena was proud of her newly gained independence, and her new job as community organizer made her feel more self-confident and allowed her to invest more time in community politics than in the past. At last she had found her own solution to the complicated problem of how to balance family, work, and politics, which had confronted her for years.

Grassroots politics, like labor organizing, constituted a central arena through which Mexican immigrants in Santech channeled their political demands. As in the case of union participation, legal status was not a prerequisite for political activism among the people of Santech. The campaign to take over the School Site Council, for example, shows that legal and undocumented immigrant parents alike were willing to engage in collective mobilization to address concerns about the quality of education for their children. The political efforts described in this chapter illustrate the process of political socialization in which a group of first-generation immigrants, particularly women, learn the ropes of U.S. civic politics and culture and become engaged in promoting change from the bottom up.

This portrait of undocumented residents who successfully engaged in political organization challenges the image of timid immigrants whose lack of legal status paralyzes them as political actors or leaves them unable or unwilling to assimilate. Immigrants' grassroots politics portrayed here involved only a small segment of the neighborhood population, but these events reveal the vitality and charged political nature of collective mobilizations in Santech. Community politics enabled immigrant women excluded from electoral politics to carve new spaces in which to struggle for civic and labor rights and, in the process, challenge the traditional meanings of immigrant politics and citizenship in the region. Unlike union political mobilization by immigrants, which focuses on labor issues in the sphere of production, community organizing focuses on family- and community-related issues, which occupy the sphere of social reproduction. But while labor union campaigns involving low-income workers in the region have attracted considerable attention, grassroots community movements that revolve around issues of social reproduction and political rights, such as housing, education, and civic rights, have received less attention.

The politicization of the people of Santech did not take place in a vacuum; rather, it was largely the result of interaction with government agencies, actors, and policies representing the interests of the state (Lamphere 1992). In fact, the political consciousness and mobilization of Mexican immigrants in Santech first emerged in the context of interaction with official institutions and policies. In this localized context, the political meaning of the notion of community was at stake. Residents were caught between two competing views about community organizing. The official government model—a model based on the "infection metaphor" (Dohan 2003)—identified a lack of community and social integration as the source of crime and many other problems in Santech. Moreover, the government programs sponsored an apolitical and homogeneous image of local community in which the interests of Santech neighbors and the city were one and the same.

In contrast, civic organizations like PACT located the source of the problems that affected this and similar neighborhoods in the uneven distribution of public resources and called for the political mobilization of the working poor from the bottom up to challenge those policies. As in the case of the Justice for Janitors campaign sponsored by Local 1877, PACT's model of grassroots mobilizing was based on a politically charged idea of community characterized by social and economic inequalities in Silicon Valley that needed to be challenged. It was in this context that Elena, Rafael, Luisa, Laura, Silvia, and many other residents in Santech, disappointed with the lack of results produced by local government programs in the neighborhood, and by local institutions like the school, embraced PACT's model of community organizing. In the process they developed a stronger Latino ethnic political consciousness. And, as with Elena's experience as a community leader, women's ethnic identity was transformed as they moved beyond the neighborhood boundaries into larger public arenas to engage into political issues that affected Latino families in the region (Pardo 1998a: 229).

As in the union mobilization of janitorial workers, the symbiosis between an experienced leadership trained in the model of neighborhood organizing and a large base of new immigrants eager to fight for better living conditions in the barrio, and for their local rights as residents, was a key factor in the success of community mobilizing in Santech. Likewise, grassroots community organizing in Santech used a discourse that alluded to the sharp ethnic and class inequalities among city residents to gain public support. Thus PACT helped Santech residents to cast their plight as a matter of ethnic and social justice, in the process helping to raise political and ethnic consciousness among people in the barrio, especially women. Ultimately, labor and community organizing efforts represented two sides of the political agency of residents in Santech: namely, production, as they addressed work and labor conditions of immigrants as workers; and reproduction, as they dealt with the civic and political rights of immigrants as residents that allow them to raise their families in the communities where they live. Ironically, while responding to the needs and demands of the same segment of the immigrant population, neither the leaders of the union nor the leaders of the civic organization nor the people in Santech made a connection between these two social movements at the time.

In Latino communities, grassroots politics are a gendered space heavily dominated by women (Hardy-Fanta 1993; Pardo 1998a; Jones-Correa 1998); this was true in Santech. For activists and working mothers like Elena, Luisa, Silvia, and others, the central challenge was to balance work, family, and politics. Thus, although motherhood may induce women to become political (Pardo 1998a; Hardy-Fanta 1993), working mothers like Elena confront challenges when involved in grassroots politics. In addition to combining politics with work and family duties, immigrant activists often have to struggle with their husbands or male kin to legitimate their political activities in the context of a patriarchal ideology that locates women at the core of the household, and which only reluctantly accepts their participation in politics.

Finally, community politics in Santech did not remain static but were transformed over time. Perhaps the most significant transformation was the gradual change of a set of informal, loosely structured activities deeply integrated into local residents' day-to-day activities into a more formal, structured, and autonomous sphere in the life of the community and its people. Reaching out to other political actors and organizations marked the first step in this direction. From then on, community activists in Santech learned to negotiate with outside actors and political allies and to adapt to their rules, discipline, organizational styles, and political agendas. In the process, women in Santech gained effectiveness and political power but lost the ability to integrate politics with their social and family activities, and, more important, partially lost the ability to decide their own goals and influence the decision-making process of community politics.[7]

Conclusion

Subproletarians in a Postindustrial Economy

Silicon Valley is the most successful high-technology region in the world. With a high concentration of technicians, professionals, and managerial workers, it is also one of the wealthiest metropolitan areas in the United States. Yet the rise of the high-technology industry in this California region is also associated with economic unevenness, social inequalities, and contradictory mixes of economic opportunity and exploitation. In fact, the explosion of this industry is the single most important factor behind the demand for Mexican immigrant labor in Silicon Valley since the 1970s. The new immigrants came to work in the myriad new jobs created in the low end of the manufacturing and service sectors, dramatically reconfiguring the contours of the working class in the region.

Immigrants employed in these manufacturing and service jobs represent the modern cohort of proletarian workers who came to the region after the preceding generations of Mexican American and Mexican workers employed in the agriculture and cannery industries. Just as the Santa Clara Valley's agricultural and food-processing industries previously propelled the expansion of Mexican American neighborhoods in East San Jose (Clark 1970, Matthews 2003, Pitti 2003), the rise of the modern high-tech industries in recent decades prompted the emergence of new Mexican barrios like Santech, populated mainly by subcontracted workers employed in the low end of the service sector. I see the new immigrants as being subproletarian—they are workers who, despite being fully integrated into the regional economy and local community, are denied most of the rights to which the rest of the working population is entitled. Located at the bottom of the hierarchy of the region's working class, subproletarian immigrants often receive casual rather than protected wages, do not benefit from a stable contractual relationship with employers, receive few if any working benefits, have limited access to state and welfare benefits, and are denied most of the political rights of legal citizens.

Key to the formation of a new cohort of Mexican immigrants at the heart of the working class in Silicon Valley is the capitalist logic of large high-tech corporations in the region. The case of the building-cleaning industry, one of the largest employers of new immigrants, best illustrates this point. Unlike electronics assembly jobs, which began to be relocated abroad when this industry went global in the 1970s, service maintenance jobs could not be sent overseas. This presented a challenge to the industry, given the structural trend toward decentralization and labor flexibility. The industry's response to this dilemma came in the 1980s in the form of outsourcing, a labor strategy that led to the systematic replacement of unionized custodial workers by a cadre of recent, mostly undocumented Mexican immigrants employed by independent nonunion contractors. Subcontracting was used to avoid the labor costs of full-fledged proletarian workers and was key to the consolidation of a new cohort of subproletarian Mexican workers as the backbone of the custodial labor force. Worlds apart in terms of class location and social and cultural backgrounds, the maintenance managers of companies like Sonix and the working crews made up of undocumented immigrants meet face to face, revealing the structural interdependence and power inequality that characterize this labor regime. The workplace is where these structural forces articulate and become more readily observable, and where class inequalities become apparent.

How can we conceptualize poverty in the midst of otherwise dynamic and affluent regions like Silicon Valley? Despite the notion that poverty is the result of a mismatch between the labor needs of the new economy and the poor skills that immigrants bring to the labor market (Borjas 1994, 1996), most Mexican workers in Silicon Valley are employed in full-time jobs, often holding more than one full-time job. There is no question that Mexican and other Latino immigrants have a place in the mainstream economy here. Their segmented incorporation as subcontracted workers at the bottom of Silicon Valley's labor market explains the seeming paradox of poverty in the midst of affluence, and the glaring income inequalities and class disparities that characterize this region.

How Immigrants Survive the Regime of Flexible Labor

The regime of flexible employment in Silicon Valley is at the root of the problems, opportunities, and constraints that undocumented immigrants confront in this region. Using an ethnographic perspective, throughout this book I have illustrated how this powerful structural force works itself out in the everyday lives of Mexican workers, and the varied and creative ways in which they respond to its unsettling effects. Demonstrating the interactions between the realms of work, family, and community, the ethnographic stories presented in this book speak about the complex set of opportunities and constraints that these workers face in one of the most affluent yet polarized regions in California.

The heavy presence of Mexican immigrants in the informal economy in Silicon Valley speaks about both the costs and the responses to their segregation in low-paid industries in the formal sector. While at first glance immigrants' informal economic activities appear to be marginal survival strategies disconnected from the mainstream economy, they can be seen as the by-product of the regime of flexible employment of immigrant labor in the region. The janitor in Santech who, unable to make ends meet with his or her nightshift cleaning job alone, takes a second job in the informal sector in landscaping, baby-sitting, house cleaning, or street vending demonstrates the role such activities play in subsidizing labor in the private sector. The informal economy is an integral part of the production and consumption strategies of these workers and a critical mechanism for the maintenance and reproduction of immigrant labor. In other words, it is the employment of immigrants in the formal sector through subcontracting arrangements that, by shifting the risks and costs of labor to both independent contractors and the workers themselves, drives these workers or their family members to engage in informal economic activities to supplement their meager incomes.

For some of the workers, however, the informal economy represents an alternative to employment in the formal sector. Many of the immigrants employed in informal occupations I met in Santech and elsewhere in San Jose took informal jobs not because of a lack of job opportunities in the formal sector, but because they were disenchanted by the wages, labor conditions, and lack of advancement opportunities offered to Mexican workers by jobs in the formal sector in which they had been previously employed. This resembles the findings of recent studies of informal occupations among Mexican immigrants in Northern and Southern

California cities, where workers combine income from jobs in the formal sector with that generated by diverse informal economic activities (Dohan 2003; Torres Sarmiento 2002).

Living in extended family households with multiple workers in overcrowded conditions is an additional price immigrants pay to adapt to the low wages, unstable jobs, and high housing and living costs they encounter in Silicon Valley. Extended households in Santech constitute a pragmatic response to the set of economic and legal constraints that govern the lives of these immigrants and their families, illustrating the effects of the regime of labor flexibility that penetrate as far as the immigrant worker's household. This should temper our tendency to generalize the extended Mexican family as a cultural characteristic that immigrants import with them. As in other regions that depend on Mexican immigrant labor, extended households and their continuous changes in structure, size, and composition reflect the pressures and stresses to which these families are subjected, and the ways in which these workers respond to such pressures (Palerm 2002; Torres Sarmiento 2002; Griffith and Kissam 1995).

The unsettling effect of the regime of labor flexibility is also illustrated by the high incidence of women in Santech who live without their husbands. The proliferation of female-headed families in this and similar Mexican neighborhoods tends to be obscured by the fact that they are usually integrated into larger domestic groups and thus are invisible to statistical surveys (Chávez 1992). Yet as the cases presented in this book suggest, the situation in which the husband is either absent or plays a peripheral economic role is not uncommon in working-poor immigrant communities. And even in nuclear or extended families where the husband is fully employed, women's wage work, income from informal occupations, and domestic and community political activities play a key role in keeping these families together despite the disruptive effect of external pressures, a finding that resonates with other studies (Torres Sarmiento 2002; Hondagneu-Sotelo 1994; Zavella 1995). Despite this key role that women play, the families examined here also reveal that income pooling can go hand-in-hand with inequality and stratification, revealing the risk of romanticizing the extended Mexican family as a cultural construct. This is especially relevant for undocumented immigrant women, who often have the most vulnerable position in these domestic groups, either because of their dependence on their husbands for their immigrant status, or because of the additional workload that running these large households entails (Adler 2004; Torres Sarmiento 2002). Because of this, while immigration and wage work might lead women to financial independence (Hondagneu-Sotelo 1994), we should not overlook the other powerful forces that keep working mothers in a vulnerable and subordinated position despite their engaging in paid work (Pessar 1999).

While most of the problems Mexican workers encounter in Silicon Valley are rooted in the system of contracting out and other flexible labor arrangements, some of the features associated with this employment regime have also opened new economic and political opportunities for immigrants trying to improve their working and living conditions. Thus, rather than just adapting to this employment regime, Mexican workers have learned to use the logic of subcontracting to their own advantage. Relying on their kin and social networks, they have, over time, capitalized on the opportunities provided by labor subcontracting to dominate certain parts of the low-skilled labor market in the region, such as the building-cleaning sector. For example, many of the janitors I met in the early 1990s, when they first arrived in the region, had by the end of the decade brought in many of their brothers, spouses, cousins, and other relatives and helped to introduce them to local contractors and employers. As Roger Waldinger and Michael Lichter (2003) argue, labor recruitment based on kin and ethnic networks facilitates detaching the hiring process from the open market, an opportunity that immigrants segregated into low-skilled occupations use to their advantage.[1] Because kinship is the main idiom spoken in labor recruitment in the building-cleaning industry in Silicon Valley, the realms of work and family in immigrants' lives are deeply intertwined, with kin ties and social networks penetrating the realm of work and shaping the internal organization of labor. The close relationship between the realms of work and family is illustrated by cases like Silvia's, in which members of an extended family form a working crew employed by a maintenance company to clean office buildings. This arrangement provides the employer access to the cheap and flexible labor of an extended family unit. In turn this kinship-based system of labor recruitment and organization allows flexibility inside the family—to optimize its labor power by rotating members and by replacing some members with others when needed.

At the collective level, immigrant janitors in Silicon Valley have also capitalized on their kin- and ethnic-based social connections to recruit members for the union campaign, as illustrated by the case of workers who cleaned Sonix's buildings. The importance of kinship and fictive-kinship ties based on common regional origin in Mexico is also evident in the fact that Local 1877 has taken advantage of the density of immigrants' social networks, often using them to recruit new members and organize public rallies. The effectiveness of this tool for recruitment shows the limitations of the concept of social networks in labor immigration studies that tend to focus on how employers exploit immigrants' kin and social ties as tools for labor recruitment and control, and that ignore how workers can also use such networks as tools for collective resistance and political mobilization.

Labor and Community Politics of Mexican Immigrants in Silicon Valley

As Eric Wolf states, working classes are not made in the place of work alone. The wider web of connections workers establish in their everyday lives gives them the ability to develop different forms of political responses to challenge employers and governments, organize civic and political associations, and join labor unions (1982: 360). The case of Mexican immigrants in Silicon Valley illustrates this point. One of my central arguments in this book is that the integration of recent Mexican immigrants into the working class in this region has opened new opportunities for different forms of political mobilization by this segment of the local population. More specifically, I have highlighted two forms of collective mobilization in which Mexican immigrants in Santech are actively involved: namely, union organizing and grassroots politics. Together they illustrate the main forms of labor and community politics pursued by the newcomers in the region.

The unionization of thousands of Mexican immigrants in the past decade is especially significant when we consider the strong antiunion political climate for which Silicon Valley is known (Benner 2000). The key to the political victory of low-income janitorial workers in this region is the combination of grassroots mobilization by immigrants who use their kin and social networks to organize, and the innovative and creative organizing strategies of labor unions like Local 1877. This synergy between a Chicano leadership seasoned in labor and civil rights struggles since the 1950s (Pitti 2003) and a rejuvenated union membership made up of young, recently arrived Latino immigrants has brought new energy to the labor movement in Silicon Valley, as embodied in the Justice for Janitors campaign. The unionization of Mexican janitors in Silicon Valley also provides additional evidence that corroborates the findings of studies conducted in other industries and regions in California, which challenge the common image of timid immigrants whose lack of legal status paralyzes their union political actions (Milkman 2000).

From a different angle, the mobilization of Mexican workers at Sonix and in Silicon Valley can be interpreted as a reaction to the labor commodification involved in the regime of labor subcontracting. As shown in the case of janitors cleaning Sonix's high-tech buildings, labor subcontracting treats workers as merchandise by covering only the basic production costs while shifting the costs of maintenance and reproduction of labor to workers, their families, and the state. When the janitors of Sonix mobilized in Silicon Valley, they were demanding to be treated as full-fledged proletarian workers with rights to benefits to cover their subsistence and reproduction needs. This represents a political response to the artificial separation between production and reproduction costs characteristic of the regime of labor subcontracting in the low-skilled private sector. It also helps to explain why social movement unionism frames immigrant workers' claims not in narrow economic terms but in a broader fashion, using a political discourse that also concentrates on universal labor and human rights, social justice issues, and immigrants' membership rights in local communities (Johnston 1994; López 2000). By linking labor with social and political claims, the political discourse of this type of social movement unionism brings together the spheres of production and reproduction, contesting the separation of the two realms in the capitalist logic of labor subcontracting.

Yet the union struggle of Mexican workers employed as janitors in Silicon Valley cannot be interpreted in class terms alone. Mexican immigrants who mobilized in Silicon Valley to unionize did so not only to demand better wages and labor conditions but also to rebel against ethnic discrimination. As illustrated by the Sonix case, workers' motives for organizing were critically shaped by their reaction against forms of racism and disrespect they experienced in the workplace at the hands of their supervisors and contractors. It is not surprising, then, that the political campaigns to unionize Mexican and other Latino immigrants are often articulated by workers and unions in a public discourse that combines class and ethnicity issues in an integrated whole (Cranford 2000; Johnston 1994).

The lessons learned from the labor union movement in Silicon Valley cannot be overlooked. The movement shows how economic restructuring can serve as an arena for the emergence of social movement unionism in the private sector among low-wage immigrant workers (Johnston 1994: 170–71). The unionization of cleaning workers in this region provides support for the thesis that low-skilled service workers whose jobs cannot be sent abroad can exploit their indispensability in the global city to organize new forms of resistance (Sassen 1999; Burawoy 2000: 32). In fact, the success of the Justice for Janitors in Silicon Valley demonstrates the contradictions generated by the regime of labor subcontracting that tends to increase labor intensification and exploitation over time, and the opportunities for resistance and political mobilization by the legal and undocumented immigrant workers it creates. If the capitalist logic of outsourcing jobs abroad represents a barrier to labor organization in the global economy, labor subcontracting creates the basis for new forms of labor mobilization at home.

A second realm of political activism for new immigrants in Silicon Valley is community organizing. As Mexican immigrants become incorporated into the ranks of the working population and settle down in low-income communities like Santech, they begin to engage in the local political life to improve the conditions in these neighborhoods. Unlike labor unionization, community politics focuses on issues that have to do with local living conditions, particularly housing, education, and access to public and community services. Less visible and glamorous than union politics, grassroots community organizing nonetheless represents a key avenue through which working-poor immigrants in Santech, excluded from electoral politics, channel their political demands. Although there are structural limits to what low-income immigrants as political actors can accomplish, there is political vitality in these grassroots movements, and novel forms of citizenship and political agency developed by immigrants excluded from the institutional political realm.

Unlike union organizing, in which most leaders are men, community organizing among Mexican immigrants in barrios like Santech is a political space dominated by women. Concerned with issues of education, housing, access to child care, and health and public services, working mothers actively engage in community affairs on behalf of themselves and their families. It is in the context of interaction with local public institutions and actors, and the responses this interaction elicits from local residents, that immigrant women gradually develop a political consciousness and become political activists. And while husbands and other male members of the family may oppose women's participation in community organizing activities, they seem to oppose such participa-

tion less than women's engagement in union-related activities, proba-
bly because women are able to frame community activism as an extension of their caregiver role in the family.

Yet because community activism penetrates the realm of the family,
community politics in Santech did not come without a price and was
often a source of gender tensions within the families of women activists,
as illustrated in chapter 5. Husbands often protested wives' involvement
in community activities that took them away from home, and even if
they consented to them, they still expected women to fulfill most
household tasks. These tensions were often negotiated within the family, with women pushing hard to gain some autonomy. In some cases,
like Elena's, the tension added to already strained gender relations. As
several authors have pointed out, while motherhood is often an incentive to become politically active (Pardo 1998a; Hardy-Fanta 1993), the
way in which labor and community politics affect gender power and
relations in the family cannot be taken for granted and deserves further
scrutiny.

At the same time, there are important similarities between the political discourse and strategies of immigrants' union and grassroots movements. As in the case of labor unions like Local 1877, recent Mexican
immigrants in barrios like Santech have also helped to reinvigorate
grassroots organizations in San Jose. The newcomers have benefited
from a long tradition of grassroots organizing that, after several decades
of struggle for civil and political rights, produced a favorable local political climate that has empowered Mexican and other ethnic groups in the
Santa Clara Valley (Pitti 2003; Matthews 2003). But the new immigrants
have also rejuvenated, and provided an infusion of new blood to, these
community groups, as illustrated by the case of Latino immigrants in
PACT examined earlier.

Moreover, kin and ethnic ties have served as the basis for recruitment
for community organizing in Santech. Women in particular used their
kin and social networks to recruit supporters for rallies and other
community activities. Like the union organizers, the leaders of well-
established nonprofit organizations heavily relied on community brokers such as Elena to recruit and mobilize people for the cause, which
shows that the idiom of kinship and social networks also penetrates the
realms of community politics. This means that, as in the case of work
and family, the realms of community politics and family among low-
income immigrants in places like Santech are closely intertwined
(Hardy-Fanta 1993).

Whereas work, family, and community politics are deeply interrelated in the lives of immigrants in Santech, a disconnection exists between the realms of labor and community politics. Indeed, labor and community activism constituted two separate realms both for the actors who participated in them and for the union and grassroots organizations that supported these collective mobilizations. Thus, while addressing the needs and demands of the low-income immigrants in the region, labor and community politics most often constituted parallel forms of political activism and only rarely intersected. Despite the gap between these two forms of immigrant politics, I have argued that what at first glance might appear to be independent social movements constitutes complimentary expressions of political activism by immigrants in San Jose. Together union and grassroots community politics articulate claims for labor, civil, and political rights that challenge increasingly narrow and exclusionary models of community membership and citizenship imposed from above by the state. As the newcomers engage in both labor and grassroots political movements, they help write another chapter in the history of Silicon Valley, and in the process they fight to transform the meanings of citizenship, membership, and immigrant politics.

Limits to Political Agency

It would be misleading, however, to romanticize the scope and advances of immigrants' activism in Silicon Valley. Thus in this book I have cautioned against the optimistic interpretation of immigrants' labor and community politics at a time when the state is implementing policies aimed at carefully delimiting the boundaries of immigrants' labor, civil, and political rights. As illustrated by the experience of immigrant workers at Sonix, the undocumented status of many immigrants sets up clear structural limits to the gains that labor and other forms of political mobilization can accomplish. Indeed, the INS action that led to the replacement of Sonix's subcontracted undocumented janitors by a new cadre of undocumented Mexican workers can be seen as part of a revolving-door policy by the state that, as Nicholas De Genova argues, increases instability in the industries where undocumented immigrants are employed, aggravates immigrants' vulnerability, and enhances labor exploitation (De Genova 2002: 437–38). In this sense, the role of the state in sorting out, classifying, and defining the legal, labor, and civil rights to which immigrants are entitled is critical and cannot be underestimated (Heyman 1998; Kearney 2003). As Dohan has shown, neither labor unions, hiring halls, nonprofit organizations, nor other institutions that make up the local context in which the everyday lives of many undocumented immigrants unfold can erase the judicial distinction between legal and illegal immigrants imposed by the state, or resolve the private feelings of anxiety that undocumented immigrants constantly experience (2003: 130–38).

Here, the notion of "circles of membership" can shed some light (cited in Heyman 2001: 131). From this perspective, U.S. immigration law can be seen as sponsoring an exclusionary notion of membership with citizens positioned at the center, permanent residents constituting a second layer, and undocumented immigrants positioned in the outer zone (Heyman 2001: 131). In this model, immigration agencies and officers are in charge of guarding access to legal membership, and their actions represent a constant and palpable risk for undocumented immigrants despite the legal right to organize into unions and engage in other forms of collective mobilization. After all, as De Genova has shown, "illegality" is a juridical status imposed from above by the state. The regimes of immigration law that produce this condition of illegality create "spaces of nonexistence" (Susan Coutin cited by De Genova 2002: 427), social spaces in which undocumented immigrants' everyday activities, such as working, driving, and venturing outside their places of work, are transformed into illicit acts.[2] The goal of these exclusionary laws is not to physically exclude immigrants, as their labor is needed, but, as De Genova argues, to "socially include them under conditions of enforced and protracted vulnerability" (2002: 429). Unsurprisingly, in this context, public action by immigrants in both labor and community politics often takes the form of struggles over symbols and categories that challenge this exclusionary model of membership and proposes alternative, more inclusive and democratic models with labor and civil rights for all de facto, rather than de jure, people who make up local communities.

Finally, I have also discussed some of the internal limits that immigrants as political actors in San Jose confront in labor unions and community groups in which they participate. For one thing, there are significant class and cultural differences between immigrants as members of labor unions and community groups, on the one hand, and the political leadership of these organizations, on the other, that cannot be ignored. As illustrated, social class, education, citizenship status, and cultural and political background are some of the differences that distinguish the leadership of labor and community organizations, like

Local 1877 and PACT, respectively, from the rank and file of Mexican immigrants. Just like Mexican workers who joined Local 1877 had to adapt, not always eagerly, to the union's organizational style and culture, so too the Santech residents who joined community organizations like PACT had to adapt to the structure, political style, and organizational culture of this group's community activism. This accommodation process is not without tension reflecting the different priorities, expectations, and organizational and political backgrounds that the newcomers bring to these labor unions and civic organizations. As I have shown here, this affects power within these institutions and how political goals and strategies are decided internally, a process in which rank-and-file immigrants often have lesser influence. As immigrant workers become important actors in these organizations, the form in which class and cultural differences shape the interaction between new immigrants and established unions and diverse community, civil, and political organizations should attract further research in the future.

Epilogue
After the Dot-Com Demise

It is July 2004. After several years, I am back in San Jose to see how changes in the region have affected the people whose lives I portray in this book. I am excited about the opportunity to visit many of my former informants, but also anxious about possibly being unable to find those with whom I have not kept in touch. On the second day in San Jose, I attend a baptism party organized by Anselmo for his newborn child. The day before, while helping him prepare for the party, I had asked Anselmo how he was doing now that he was married and was a father. He told me he was very happy and that he could not convey in words the deep and strong mix of tenderness and other emotions he was experiencing as a new father. But he also told me about his concerns. Since 1996, he said, he had been working as a delivery truck driver for a furniture company in the city of Santa Clara. The problem, he added, was that his driver's license was about to expire in a few months, and that, because he did not have a valid Social Security number, he would not be able to renew it. Without a driver's license, his only option would be to work in the furniture store, where he would make less money than as a truck driver, and move furniture around, which he wants to avoid because of a back injury he suffered while working as a janitor at Sonix.

At the baptism, I see many friends I have not seen for a long time. Everybody seems to be having a good time celebrating the happy occasion, and, after eating, a few start dancing. When I go outside to get some fresh air, I run into Israel, Anselmo's brother. He is with his six-year-old daughter, who is playing with other children. I ask Israel about his work. He responds that he is working as a janitor, as he has since he first came to San Jose in 1993. Yet, he adds, work is pretty slow these days because many companies are laying off people. He says he used to work in a building owned by Tri-Com (a large high-tech company in the region), but that he was relocated to a building in downtown San Jose when that company closed down because of the economic crisis. After a few months in his new location, he explains, his employer has eliminated four janitorial positions to save costs, so now Israel has a heavier workload.

The concerns about work and the future expressed by Anselmo and Israel in this vignette reflect some of the new challenges that several of the individuals described in this book face today. Indeed, since my previous visit to San Jose in 2000, many things have changed in the region. The economic crisis that hit Silicon Valley in 2001 had a dramatic effect on employment. Between the summer of 2000 and January of 2004 alone, the region lost two hundred thousand jobs, pushing one of every six Silicon Valley workers out of work (Nissenbaum 2004). In addition, the aftermath of September 11 fueled a chain of policy changes that dramatically affected immigrants around the country. For example, stronger policing of the U.S.-Mexican border and closer scrutiny of the identities of people traveling domestically greatly curtailed the ability of a large number of undocumented immigrants to visit their relatives either in Mexico or within the United States. As I came back to Silicon Valley, I wondered how all these changes were affecting the workers and families I first met in the 1990s and how they were coping with them. What was the effect on Mexican workers who labored in low-paid jobs in the service sector? How did the post–September 11 political climate affect undocumented immigrants in the region? And how had Mexican labor and community politics evolved in San Jose since the economic crisis?

This epilogue is an attempt to answer these questions. During short-term ethnographic fieldwork in summer 2004, I had the opportunity to talk with several of my former informants and interview a few union officials of Local 1877, government workers, and community organizers whom I had also met previously. This epilogue is based on primary rather than secondary sources, and the interpretations I provide are of a provisional and suggestive nature.

Downsizing Low-Paid Service Jobs

By fall 2001, Silicon Valley was in the midst of a major economic crisis. The downfall of the so-called dot-coms had a dramatic effect on the economy and employment in the region. While unemployment figures in Silicon Valley were considerably lower than those for the state and for the country as a whole during most of the 1990s, they had skyrocketed and surpassed statewide and national levels by the second half of 2001 (Pellow and Sun-Hee Park 2002: 206). For example, on November 2003, official statistics estimated the unemployment rate in Santa Clara County at 7.1 percent, compared to 5.9 percent in the nation and 6.5 percent in California (Konrad 2004). And while more recent statistics seemed to show that the valley might be on a path of economic recovery, the effects of the crisis were apparent during my visit to San Jose. Most attention concerning the effects of the crisis has focused on the high-skilled jobs for which Silicon Valley is internationally known, while no attention has been given to how it affected low-skilled jobs in the region, such as those in the building-cleaning industry. The economic crisis has affected employment and working conditions for Mexican immigrants in this industry in several important ways.

First, after a rapid expansion of industrial parks in the second half of the 1990s, including in San Mateo and other counties in the region at the time of the dot-com frenzy, many high-tech companies in Silicon Valley either closed down or significantly reduced their business starting in late 2001. Many large office buildings have closed down since then, leaving hundreds of custodial workers without jobs as the demand for building-cleaning services—including that generated by large corporations such as Apple, Hewlett-Packard, Tri-Com, and others—declined. Sonix, for example (the company described in chapter 2) was hit hard by the crisis, and it closed down several of its buildings in Cupertino, Sunnyvale, and San Jose, where many of the immigrant janitors depicted in this book had been employed. According to a Local 1877 official, almost half the 250 janitors employed by Sonix in the year 2000 had lost their jobs four years later. Furthermore, the increasing globalization of the high-tech industry over the past few years, which has encouraged large corporations to shift software engineering abroad to low-cost countries like India, will likely continue to reduce the demand for office space in Silicon Valley.

The economic crisis in the building-cleaning sector in Silicon Valley has led to increased competition by cleaning subcontractors in an already highly competitive industry. To survive the hard economic times, cleaning companies fiercely try to outcompete their rivals with lower bids. This they usually accomplish by reducing the number of workers per building, thus increasing the workload for their employees. This trend was already apparent in the 1990s but has since intensified. This strategy is today known as the "skip cleaning system," a system in which janitors are instructed to skip parts of their assigned area in order to allow time for the additional work they are assigned. New janitorial workers particularly suffer from the increasing workload because they believe that to keep their jobs they must clean the entire area assigned to them.

The crisis has also negatively affected the ability of the union representing custodial workers in Silicon Valley to negotiate wage increases on their behalf. After a decade of explosive growth in which the union was able to secure wage increases and better benefits for thousands of janitors in the region—especially for those whose contracts were signed in the mid-1990s, when the economy was booming—the last contract negotiated by Local 1877, in the summer of 2003, incorporated only meager wage increases, which vary between $.10 and $.25 cents per hour per year. Unable to push for better wages in the midst of harsh economic times and to avoid further job losses, the union opted to negotiate to contain health insurance costs paid by workers as part of their contracts, which had risen dramatically from $70.00 to $140.00 a month in the past few years. In the new contract that expires in 2008, union workers' copayment for health insurance has gone down from $150.00 to $30.00 a month, and will remain this amount for the duration of the contract, regardless of rising medical costs. This, according to union officials, represents the equivalent of a raise amounting to $.50 to $.60 per hour per year, which offsets the meager wage increases the union was able to negotiate. Considering the increasing health costs for many union workers in other industries and the fact that many nonunion workers do not have health insurance altogether, this is an important accomplishment.

But perhaps the most dramatic effect of the economic crisis on immigrant janitorial workers has been the increasing turnover rates due to their undocumented status. Unlike in the past, when the turnover was often the result of direct actions by government immigration authorities, today's cleaning companies routinely request that their workers provide documentation of their right to work in the United States. This practice gives contractors a legal basis for replacing workers who have years of seniority with new and equally undocumented janitors. The fake documentation that was considered valid when they were first hired is then used to terminate their contracts. This is a significant labor-cost reduction for these companies because the newly hired workers start at the bottom and do not qualify for full benefits. In the 1990s, whenever a high-tech company in the region switched unionized cleaning contractors, the new company hired most of the workers employed by the former contractor and respected workers' seniority. Today, cleaning contractors seek to increase employee turnover to keep labor costs down and enhance their competitiveness. According to Salvador Busta-mante, the regional vice president of Local 1877, this is most common when workers have several years of seniority in the job and qualify for full benefits and paid vacations. He explained to me,

> One example is eBay, which switched union contractors. In the past, this change used to be just a formality, but now they check workers' docu-ments. Because of that, in the office building of eBay, with the new con-tract, out of twenty-two janitors who were previously working, eighteen were replaced by new workers of Service Performance. . . . It's clear that the motive is not to comply with the [immigration] law, but for economic reasons, given that the new employees start making 80 percent of the master contract wage, and they do not have full benefits until [after] the first year of work. It was by doing this that Service Performance could save up to a hundred thousand dollars with respect the previous cleaning contractor and offered the best bid.

The cases of Don Manuel and Jesús (introduced in chapter 2) illus-trate the effects of some of these trends. In 1995, shortly after losing his job cleaning the office buildings of Sonix, and after a brief stint work-ing in a restaurant, Don Manuel found a new janitorial job cleaning an office building in Fremont. After two years, he was laid off when the company determined that his Social Security number was invalid. He got a new cleaning job for a company contracted to clean the offices of the National Aeronautics and Space Administration in the South Bay Area, where he worked until the year 2000, earning $8.50 an hour. Once again, he lost his job when his employer checked his Social Secu-rity number. He was then hired by Acme, a large cleaning company in the region, to clean the office buildings of Tri-Com, a major electron-ics company in Santa Clara, which later closed down in the midst of the economic crisis. After more than a decade of working as a janitor in many different companies, Don Manuel switched occupations and found a job in the assembly department of a large electronics company that manufactured laser-related products. He felt more satisfied, both because he was earning about $14 an hour (well beyond what he could make as a janitor) and received full benefits and because his new occu-pation seemed more stable than his previous one. Moreover, he felt proud of his new job because it did not carry social stigma like his pre-vious janitorial jobs.

Jesús continued working as a janitor, but his life took some surpris-ing turns. After losing his job at Service International in 1995, he got hired by Acme to clean the offices of a military defense company. He was employed there until the summer of 1999, when this company moved out of Silicon Valley. Shortly afterward, he started working for Clean Source, the company formed when Service International merged with another cleaning firm. Unexpectedly for him, Jesús went back to clean the office buildings of Sonix, where he had previously worked until he lost his job as a result of an INS inspection. This time he was assigned to clean a Sonix building in Santa Clara, since the Cupertino building he had cleaned earlier had closed down after the economic crisis hit. When I asked him about this unexpected turn of events, and whether his former supervisors at Sonix did not remember him losing his job because of his undocumented status, he replied:

> Well I don't know, but I have always used the same [fake] Social Security number since I first started working and haven't changed it at all. You are going to laugh, and I must say that I was personally shocked when, after going back to Sonix, I found out that my former supervisor from this company was now working as a dishwasher there! I asked him in disbelief, "What are you doing here?" And he replied "Jesús, these sons of a bitch have terminated my job and told me that either I move here or leave."

Five months after landing this job, Jesús quit and returned to his hometown in Oaxaca to start his own construction-trucking business. With the twenty-two thousand dollars he had saved since coming to the United States in the early 1990s—by living a rather frugal life in San Jose—he bought himself a truck. However, things did not work as expected, and after eight months, he returned to San Jose to work again as a janitor, this time in a large shopping mall. He liked his current job better than his previous ones, because it was a day job. But, as he explained, his workload increased. To face the economic crisis, his employer reduced the number of janitors working in the mall from fifteen to ten, and Jesús was now solely responsible for maintaining a food-court area with about six hundred chairs, as well as other common areas in the mall. Moreover, he explained, management asked workers to attend daily meetings to learn how to service clients at the mall when they asked for directions or any other questions. "They want us to attend now a daily meeting of fifteen minutes and to attend clients, give them directions if they ask and even walk them to where they want to go. . . . They want to make us, the housekeepers, help customers at the shopping mall. For us, this means more pressure at work."

Many Mexican workers I first met in the early 1990s in San Jose continued working as janitors. Most changed janitorial jobs several times, moving from one company to another, either because their employer lost a contract or because they were laid off for not having proper work documents. Their employment histories were marked by constant instability as they moved horizontally from one company to another, often changing their Social Security numbers or their names, in most cases as a result of their employers using workers' illegal status to provoke a high turnover to reduce labor costs. In the midst of the economic downturn, this became a common practice among cleaning contractors in their efforts to offer the most competitive bids and stay afloat.

Local 1877 Responds to the Crisis

Surprisingly, the union that represents custodial workers in Silicon Valley was not dramatically affected by the economic crisis. While unable to negotiate wage increases for its members, Local 1877 prevented the expansion of nonunion contractors in the region, an important political victory considering not only the economic pressure of the crisis but also the traditional antiunion environment in Silicon Valley. Unlike in previous economic recessions in the 1980s, when nonunion contractors made significant inroads in the industry, Local 1877 was at its peak by the early 2000s and had the political muscle to prevent this from happening again. In 1997, the Building Service Division of Local 399 in Los Angeles merged with Local 1877 in Northern California, and as a result, it emerged as one of the largest service unions in the country, with about twenty-six thousand members. This prepared the union for the harsh economic times that started in 2001, as it had powerful political clout.[1]

Also, the political support built in the region by Local 1877 since the late 1980s, including support by influential political and community leaders, helped the union to deal with the harsh economy of the early 2000s. The union's ability to present the cause of immigrant janitors as an issue of economic and social justice in the local community was critical for its political success. As Salvador Bustamante of Local 1877 commented,

> We have been successful in promoting a good image of janitors, so that today it is not popular to attack this segment of the population. . . . Other unions keep with the old approach of confronting employers and workers, and they focus on economic raises alone of a few cents for their members. . . . But what is novel about our approach is that we explain to the

public why the wage increase is necessary, which basic subsistence needs are going to be covered, to explain to the public the needs of [the working poor] so that they understand.

While the union was successful in advancing the rights and interests of immigrant workers in Silicon Valley, it encountered much stronger resistance in other parts of Northern California. In Sacramento, for example, after the victories in Silicon Valley, Local 1877 launched a Justice for Janitors campaign in 1995 to organize custodial workers in the city. The campaign, which lasted almost five years and unionized about eighteen hundred workers, turned out to be a much tougher battle than union officials anticipated. It demonstrated that locality shapes the political opportunities to respond to structural forces, such as labor subcontracting, differently in different regions, and that the alignment of local political forces in each place plays a central role in determining the outcome of labor union struggles. Comparing the experiences in Sacramento and Silicon Valley, Bustamante commented,

> We made some mistakes in that campaign. We thought that we could use the same model [as in Silicon Valley] there, that we could just transplant it and be successful. . . . Yet something that was vital in Silicon Valley was the political support of the local community and its leaders. In Sacramento it was very different; we did not have that support. Another factor was that the largest cleaning company there had lots of financial resources and very strong political connections with the local establishment and community people, including religious leaders. . . . We had to struggle very hard to win the support of the workers and gain legitimacy in the local community.

Ironically, in Sacramento some of the client companies of nonunionized cleaning contractors unreceptive to the union's campaign were companies that Local 1877 had successfully targeted in Silicon Valley only a few years earlier. For example, Sonix was one of the largest employers of subcontracted janitors in Sacramento. At first I believed that the fact that Sonix was among the largest employers of unionized janitors in Silicon Valley would give the union some leverage in Sacramento. To my surprise, this was not the case. Bustamante said, "It is more difficult to press when you have a relationship with a company than when you don't have it. If you don't have that relationship, you can be more radical. . . . But when you have established a relationship, the preoccupation is not to alienate them, [because] what could then happen to the union workers here [in Silicon Valley]? . . . Well, maybe we limited ourselves." In short, the same corporation responded differently to union pressure depending on the site and the local political environment. This reveals that global companies like Sonix can develop different political responses to the pressure of organized labor depending on their particular political alliances at the local level.

Interestingly, some of the changes in Local 1877 came about as a result of internal pressure to better respond to the needs of members and to the demand for more democracy within the union. Two changes illustrate this trend. First, in order to address the old dilemma of organizing versus serving members, Local 1877 restructured internally by creating two departments, one to attend to work-related grievances and another to organize new members in nonunion companies. It also created a service center to deal more efficiently with workers' grievances, because the stewards system was not strong enough to deal with them in the workplace. This reform was a response to members' complaints that too much time was spent organizing new members and too little attention was paid to the established members.[2]

The union also introduced other changes to strengthen internal democracy. In fact, a common complaint I heard in the field in the 1990s concerned the lack of internal democracy and the absence of change in top leadership positions. Resistant at first, union leaders seem to have become more receptive to this critique. Local 1877 is currently modifying its internal decision-making process. The most significant change is the reactivation of a workers' steward committee, whose members are elected by their peers. The committee is divided into four different groups, which focus on political action, organization, leadership development, and civil and human rights. While this committee has been on the books since 1992, it was not active; only in 2003 did union officials reconsider it. The committee's organization reflects both the increasing demand by rank-and-file immigrant members for access to the union's decision-making structure and the acknowledgment by union officials that they must open positions of power to immigrants, even if this challenges the existing leadership. Reflecting the ambivalence of the union's old guard, Bustamante commented,

> The worst enemy we can have is workers' apathy. I prefer people who are negative but with whom I can talk, [rather] than those who do not care or respond. . . . I want the members of the committee to become leaders, even if they have critical views—at least that is a change. . . . At first I was tempted in the meetings to intervene whenever I thought they were wrong, but I refrained [because] it is part of the process. We have to fol-

low to move beyond our idea that nobody can do things better than us. We need to give them the opportunity.

In short, in the 1990s the powerful combination of a Chicano leadership that had gained experience in the civil rights movement of the 1970s and a base of new immigrants led to the success of Justice for Janitors. Today, some of the immigrant members seem to have evolved greater political consciousness and new skills. These workers are not content to remain in the rank and file but demand access to leadership roles and power within the union. The political future of the union movement might depend on the ability of current leaders to open up access to positions of power and actively incorporate immigrants into the decision-making structure of the organization.

Changes in Santech

Santech also changed in important ways as a result of the economic recession. First, after almost a decade of skyrocketing, housing prices in Santech have come down over the past few years. Housing costs rose dramatically in the mid-1990s at a time of economic boom in the region, and by the end of the decade two-bedroom apartments rented for fifteen hundred dollars a month or more. After the economic slump and the events of September 11, for the first time in more than a decade rents in Santech dropped to twelve hundred dollars a month and less, and the vacancy rate went up. True, many families had to move out of the barrio after their working members lost their jobs. But at the same time, those who were still working, who had lived in overcrowded apartments in Santech for years, were finally able to move into larger apartments and houses in other neighborhoods in San Jose while continuing to live in extended families. And some immigrants living in rented garages or basements finally had the opportunity to rent their own apartments.

But the most important improvements in the barrio were in the housing stock. Many apartment buildings were brought up to legal safety code standards after the city began to force landlords to meet their responsibilities or otherwise face jail sentences. The city also demanded that landlords improve the infrastructure in the area by landscaping the grounds—which are now covered by grass—installing metal fences, and rebuilding the parking lots. Equally important was the reactivation of the homeowners association in the barrio, which had become dormant after Santech apartments were sold to independent property owners. The city of San Jose compelled homeowners, many of whom had become slumlords, to reactivate the association and hire a management company to maintain their properties. It also forced them to hire a private security company to patrol the streets. Today, if something needs to be fixed, residents do not have to deal with reluctant landlords but can request service from the management company, which then bills the property owner. Finally, according to public officials in Santech, drug trafficking and crime rates in the barrio have gone down.

Other people, however, argue that gang-related problems have resurfaced in Santech as a result of the economic crisis. For example, according to Aurora, who was one of the oldest community organizers in PACT, gangs declined in the midst of the economic boom but reemerged in the neighborhood due to the employment recession of the past few years. Criticizing public officials' response to the crisis in communities like Santech, she commented, "[Years ago] we moved from intervention to prevention when things got peaceful. [But] now, because of the shift of the crisis, the thinking is that we have to switch back resources into early intervention [mode] because of the unrest. . . . [Moreover] the money that was used to fund these programs is now going to the state, so there are fewer resources available."

Families Move Out of the Barrio

Many of the families I knew in Santech did not witness any of these changes firsthand. In fact, by the time of my most recent visit, in the summer of 2004, most of them had moved to other neighborhoods in San Jose, and a few had bought their own homes in other cities. For example, some became homeowners in new housing developments in cities like Pittsburg and Modesto, California, and other places where housing costs were considerably lower than in San Jose—often in subdivisions being settled largely by young Latino and other minority families. This homesteading indicates the economic mobility of a small proportion of first-generation immigrants, for whom the American dream has materialized. Other studies have shown a similar process occurring among Mexican farmworkers in rural towns in California (Palerm 1995, 2002; Du Bry 2004). But unlike Mexican immigrants in rural towns, where workplaces and residences are usually within a short distance of each other, immigrants working in cities like San Jose often have to move far away to become homeowners, creating for themselves a long commute between home and work.

Silvia and her family, whom I discussed in chapter 4, illustrate the changes that immigrant families who formerly lived in Santech can experience as a result of homesteading. Shortly after her family moved to Pittsburg in 1999, Silvia, who had worked as a janitor for a nonunion company in San Jose since 1993, asked her employer to relocate her to a place closer to her new home. After being moved first to Fremont and then San Mateo, she was finally assigned to an office building in Pleasant Hill, a town near Pittsburg and outside of Silicon Valley. With the change, however, her wages dropped from $7.00 an hour to $6.75 because, in that city, wages for janitorial workers were lower (wages paid to unionized janitors in the buildings next door ranged from $9.00 to $10.00 an hour depending on seniority).

Meanwhile, her son-in-law still worked two janitorial jobs, one a daytime union job that involved a commute of several hours to Concord, the other a nightshift job at a school in Pittsburg, where he was self-employed. Despite this, Silvia's oldest daughter and son-in-law were satisfied with their new location, because, among other reasons, the market value of their home had increased almost 40 percent since they bought it. Silvia's feelings on this matter were somehow different. First, she was not a homeowner, and recently she had moved out of her daughter's home to a two-bedroom apartment in Pittsburg that she shared with a nephew and niece. She felt that, since her oldest daughter and her son-in-law moved to their own home, they had become more individualistic and materialistic and less concerned about the rest of their relatives. She also felt isolated living in a suburban community and missed her friends and social life in Santech, reflecting a common feeling I found among other women who had moved from inner-city barrios like Santech to suburban neighborhoods far from San Jose. In sum, as Aurora, the former PACT community organizer in Santech, explained to me, most of these families, despite having homesteaded, still lived overcrowded in order to pay the mortgage and often sublet rooms to meet those payments. They also had to commute long hours to work, and they lost the networks and social support they built over the years in San Jose.

Other families were less lucky and still lived in poverty in low-income neighborhoods in San Jose. Carmen, whom I also discussed in chapter 4, still lived in a rented apartment in San Jose, which she shared with eleven persons, including her youngest daughter, her daughter's husband and three children, a cousin who had arrived in town from Mexico in 2003, and two young couples with children who sublet two of the four rooms in the apartment.[3] Her work history over the past few years also reflected the consequences of the economic recession. After receiving her work permit in 1998, Carmen finally became a legal resident in 2002. After that, she went back to work for Santa Clara County as an elder-care worker. This made a major improvement in her financial status: working full-time, she provided care for four elderly people at their homes, and by the year 2000 she earned $10.50 an hour plus generous benefits. But the economic crisis took a toll, as it did for many other women employed in this occupation. In 2003, her job was transferred from Santa Clara County to the state of California under "home supportive services" to reduce labor costs. As a result her wages went down by $.10 an hour and her benefits declined considerably. For example, before this change Carmen's transportation expenses were paid, but afterward they were not; nor was she entitled to a paid vacation or paid holidays. Her working hours were reduced, and at the time I visited, she was working only twenty hours a week. To compensate for the loss, she worked on weekends cleaning the house of one of her former employers.

Meanwhile, her husband, who had abandoned her for a younger woman, left the latter and wanted to come back to Carmen. But Carmen did not want him. She told me that she had been much happier after they parted: "I feel much better since he [her husband] left. I feel I have made a lot of progress since then. I have had plenty of work, I don't have problems with my children at home, and I am happy with all of them, even if they have their own problems." Then she added, "Now he [her husband] wants to come back, but my children don't want me to do it. . . . I now see him as the father of my children but not as my husband any longer."

Some of the most interesting changes I found among the families I met in San Jose in the 1990s have to do with their children. The so-called 1.5-generation immigrants—those who were born abroad but grew up in the United States—faced particular challenges and choices. This was especially the case for those who were still considered undocumented immigrants, which often blocked their access to opportunities for educational and economic mobility. The varying fates of Don Manuel's children illustrate this situation. His oldest son, who was twenty-six years old, had graduated from high school with high grades and was soon accepted by a local public university. However, he could not enroll because of his undocumented status and, disappointed, he quit his studies and took a job as an assistant in an optometry office in a local mall. In contrast, Don Manuel's second son, who was twenty-three years old, was also undocumented but became a legal U.S. resident after marrying a U.S. citizen. He was studying in a public college in San Jose and working for a shipping company that helped pay his tuition. Finally, Don Manuel's only daughter, who was twenty-four years old, also married a U.S. citizen. After becoming a legal resident, she started college and worked part-time for a major health maintenance organization. Illustrating the paramount importance of education to many first-generation immigrant parents, Don Manuel proudly commented, "Well, at least we have given them an education, so that they can work with their brains and not with their hands like us."

That many children of the immigrant families I met in San Jose in the 1990s face difficult choices today is illustrated by the case of Silvia's youngest daughter. Lorena, whom Silvia brought to the United States in 1984 at the age of three, first started working as a janitor in the same company as Silvia in 1998. But being fluent in English and having good typing skills, she was soon hired as a part-time secretary by the insurance company whose offices her mother cleaned. After she graduated from high school, she started working full-time for this company at eight dollars an hour and then obtained several raises because of her performance. However, after two years on the job, her employer found out she was an undocumented worker, and Lorena had to quit. Silvia explained that this was a major blow to her daughter, who, for the first time realized the serious limitations imposed on her future by her immigrant status. A good student in high school, Lorena wanted to go to college and was accepted by San Jose State University, but because she lacked a valid Social Security number she could not enroll.[4]

What happened to the other people portrayed in this book? I was not able to find all my former informants. Luis, one of the janitors described in chapter 2, returned to Mexico after he suffered a work injury and was awarded a monetary compensation. Years later he went back to the Santa Clara Valley, where I lost track of him. Arturo, the frozen-fruit-pop vendor; Laura, the self-employed vendor; and Margarita and her family were no longer in Santech and had left no traces. Others, like Gustavo, the dentist who worked in the informal sector (see chapter 3), moved back to Mexico (he did so in 1998). When I visited Gustavo's family (mother and siblings) in San Jose in 2004, his two children, by then sixteen and twelve years old, were visiting from Mexico. Like Gustavo when he was a child, they often spent the summers in San Jose visiting their family and learning English, preparing them for the future should they decide to return to the United States, where both were born. Earlier, in spring 2000, I had visited Gustavo in the city of Morelia, Michoacán. By then, Gustavo had already opened his own dental clinic, this time as a licensed general dentist and orthodontist in a large office building occupied by numerous medical doctors and others. Barely starting to build a new clientele, he was satisfied with his decision to move back to Mexico and was looking forward to moving his office to his home once it was finished.

Finally, Anselmo, whom I discussed in chapter 2 and at the beginning of this chapter, still lived in San Jose and did not have immediate plans to return to Mexico, despite having worked and lived in the United States as an undocumented immigrant for more than ten years. After he quit working as a janitor in 1996, Anselmo was employed in several jobs. In 1998, he got a job in an electronics company, where he worked in assembly. Suddenly one day the INS raided the company, and as a result, he was deported to Mexico in 1999. Once in Mexico, he visited his mother and family, whom he had not seen for several years. After four months, he went back to San Jose, and at that point he started working as a driver for Sonix, the same company he had worked for as a subcontracted janitor until he lost the job because of his undocumented status. In 2000, he was hired as a truck driver by a furniture company, where he is still employed. Later, in 2002, after many years of living on his own in rented garages shared with roommates, Anselmo moved in with his common-law wife, whom he first met while working as a delivery person for Sonix. In 2003, they had a baby boy, and were living in a modest one-bedroom apartment in San Jose with his wife's seven-year-old daughter. With his driver's license about to expire, Anselmo was worried about the future and his ability to provide for his family. For immigrants like Anselmo, not being able to renew one driver's license has far-reaching economic repercussions.

The Decline of Community Politics

On one of my first days in Santech in 2004, I visit the neighborhood center with Elena, who had volunteered to accompany me. Armando, the director who knows Elena and who has been working there for several years, receives us politely. After I explain the reason for my visit, he starts describing the changes that have taken place in Santech over the past few years. Proudly, he lists improvements, such as housing repairs, landscap-

ing, the injunctions against slumlords by the local authorities, the installation of street traffic signs and lights, the building of a library at Santech
Elementary School, and many others. He also provides me with several
reports, brochures, and newspaper clips that recount some of the problems and changes that Santech has seen over the past few years.

After about forty minutes of conversation, and after thanking him for
his help, Elena and I are about to leave the center when a middle-age Mexican woman holding a baby enters in the office, obviously in distress.
Armando invites her in and asks what he can do for her. Speaking in Spanish, she starts complaining to Armando: her truck was removed from her
parking lot a few minutes earlier by the security company in charge of
patrolling Santech streets. She explains that the truck was correctly parked
in her parking space, and that there was no reason to remove it. When she
complained to the tow truck driver, he told her they were just following
the orders of the neighborhood center and that she should go there.
Armando, who oversees the security company, consults his log to see if, in
a meeting they had held the day before, he had petitioned the company to
remove her truck. Then he tells the woman her truck was not on the list
he had reported and that he does not know what happened. He explains
to her that the policy they follow is to remove any car that does not have
a current registration sticker or that looks inoperable. He adds that there
is nothing he can do at this point, and that she will have to pay the fee to
retrieve her car. Later, he continues, provided that it was her landlord who
called the company to remove her truck, she can sue him in the small
claims court and recover the fee she paid to get her vehicle back.

With tears in her eyes, the woman explains that she does not have the
money to get her truck back and that presently she is out of work. She
repeats that her car was in running condition, that it had a current registration license, and that it was correctly parked in her place. She adds that
a few days before, somebody had tried to steal her truck from her parking space, and that now it is the security company that has towed it away:
"What security are you providing us?" she angrily asks, referring to both
the neighborhood center and the contracted security company. Visibly
embarrassed by the scene unfolding in front of Elena and me, Armando
tells the woman he will personally talk to the security company tomorrow
to find out what happened. Resigned and openly disappointed, the
woman leaves the office still crying.

When she is gone, I ask Armando what criteria the center and the
security company use to determine which vehicles to remove from the
parking lots in Santech. He responds that they must have a current registration sticker in place and be operable; if they determine that a vehicle
is broken down because it has flat tires or is being used for storage, they
remove it because the policy is to remove any object that might indicate
abandonment or deterioration in the neighborhood. When we leave the
office, Elena complains that this is a sign of how the center does not really
care for the people who live in Santech, and that, after she and other

women who previously were active in the community had moved out, things had gotten worse, since there is nobody to fight for people like the woman we just met.

This incident reflects some of the recent changes that have taken place in Santech in the way local authorities address issues of crime control, and the parallel decline of community activism in the neighborhood. In Santech, one of the major effects of the economic crisis in Silicon Valley was the reduction of social and community services and a strong shift in law enforcement. Project Crackdown, originally implemented to combat crime and promote community strength in Santech (see chapter 5), was phased out after years of strong presence and uneven results in the barrio. The neighborhood center, which was in charge of responding to residents' needs and organizing community activities, also reduced its personnel and kept a lower profile in community organizing. With Project Crackdown discontinued, law enforcement was largely outsourced to the management company contracted by the homeowners association, which became responsible for enforcing security in the area through a private security company. Local government workers at the center worked closely with the management company and held responsibility for overseeing its work. As I gathered from my conversation with government workers at the neighborhood center, they subscribed to the theory—generally known as the "broken windows" theory—that it is possible to prevent crime in the neighborhood by having the private security company quickly deal with any apparent signs of deterioration in the streets and public areas, such as abandoned cars, graffiti, and trash.

Meanwhile, the provision of community services and programs in the barrio was left in the hands of nonprofit organizations. Since the late 1990s, the most established of these groups was a religious congregation whose nuns ran several programs in Santech, which taught English as a second language to adults, provided a library for children, conducted youth group activities, collected donated clothes for infants, offered religious services in Spanish, and so forth.

Community meetings organized by city workers have been in decline. Lidia, one of the few remaining residents who originally participated in the government-sponsored meetings when Project Crackdown first arrived in the barrio, commented critically,

> I do not go to the meetings organized by the neighborhood center any longer. They do not help people as in the past, and the programs they used to have, like talks by immigration lawyers and others, have disappeared. Moreover, I feel that the staff at the office is not very nice and

doesn't like Hispanics. They seem bothered if they have to translate into Spanish for us. They should know that here we are all Hispanics and that nobody speaks English! If they don't like to translate or speak Spanish, why do they bother to come to work here? It's been a while since I stopped going to these meetings because of that. . . . But I miss the times when we all came together to the meetings to present our demands and petitions. . . . No, there is not any movement like that any more.

Instead, a new way of addressing the people's social and community needs, based on a partnership between government and the business sector, seemed to be on the rise. Partners (a fictitious name) is a case-management organization funded publicly and by donations from private companies to provide multiple services for low-income families in the neighborhood. Centralizing all services and programs provided by government and nonprofit organizations in Santech into a single hub is one of the central goals of this organization. It mainly focuses on education-related issues for families with children younger than five. Based on the principle that nonprofit organizations should be run more like private businesses, Partners emphasizes the importance of efficiency and accountability and the partnership between the business and the educational communities. It refers to residents as "customers" and to people working with them as "caseworkers." The director of this organization explained to me that, in this model, caseworkers are expected "to bring customers to us," acting as brokers between individual families and the government agencies and private organizations "to help people to navigate the system."

While it might be too soon to interpret the political significance of this change in Santech, it seems to reflect a more general trend in which the city retreats from providing "remedial" services to poor communities and instead focuses on "intervention" programs to reduce crime and enhance social control. Meanwhile, social services and community organizing are left to religious and nonprofit organizations, sending the message that the state is no longer directly responsible for addressing those needs. In this context, organizations like Partners emerge as an alternative to community services; rather than focusing on grassroots organizing, such organizations follow a business management approach that emphasizes efficiency at the individual family or "case" level. This model might involve a depoliticization of community organizing by the implementation of a businesslike approach to community-problem-solving favored by the private sector and the state.

Another factor that explains the decline of political activism in Santech is the fact that former community leaders have moved out of the barrio. The most active community leaders, such as Elena and other women who were deeply engaged in political activism in the 1990s, are no longer in the community, having moved to other neighborhoods in San Jose or to other towns in and outside the region. According to Aurora, a former member of the PACT steering committee, the turnover of leadership is an important problem that grassroots organizations like this one face. An additional factor that accounts for the turnover has to do with the difference in political culture and styles of community organizations like PACT, on the one hand, and Mexican and other Latina immigrant women, on the other. Taking a self-critical perspective, Aurora commented that there was insufficient cultural sensibility in the official leadership of PACT with respect to the expectations of first-generation immigrant women activists. "Relationship building isn't in [PACT's] agenda. [But] that is how trust is built. If you don't invest in relationship building, then it doesn't work. You need to have time for relationship building. . . . Relationship building, developing friendship—that is why people come to the meetings." Further elaborating her thoughts, she said, "We [also] have to distinguish between involving people and engaging them. . . . We need more input from people in identifying [their own needs] and in implementing and evaluating [our programs]. . . . To be honest, PACT officials, rather than people, often decide which issues need to be addressed."

Aurora's comments reflect the need for a less rigid model of community organizing to adapt to the cultural sensitivity of Mexican and other Latino immigrant women who come with a different experience of grassroots mobilizing, one in which trust built on kinship and social connections is a crucial ingredient in community politics. They also reflect the fact that PACT leaders realize immigrant activists want to have a more active role in the internal decision-making process of the organization, including deciding which issues should be addressed by collective action. Her comments seem to indicate that, as in Local 1877, immigrants today are struggling to gain access to positions of leadership and power, pointing to the need for opening up political space for immigrant leaders and increasing internal democracy within grassroots community organizations.

ELENA LEAVES COMMUNITY POLITICS

The turnover of community leadership in Santech is illustrated by the case of Elena, whose role in civic politics I described earlier. After more than fifteen years of community activism, first as an informal leader in

Santech and later as a liaison between one of the local public schools and the community at large, Elena moved from the neighborhood to a suburban community in southern San Jose.[5] Although she moved away from Santech to, as she put it, "bring my children away from the bad influences of gangs and their friends," she acknowledged having paid a high personal price for the change. She felt isolated and disconnected from her people and the community and depressed by her lack of social and community involvement. Confined at home and having no job, she missed the time when she was a community activist in Santech, which gave her the feeling she was doing something for her people. Commenting on how this change affected her life, she said,

> Ever since I moved out of the area [in 2001], I feel sad, because something was taken out of my life. . . . Staying at home, I feel there is something missing. No, no, no, I am not a housewife. I belong to the streets. I feel like a chandelier that illuminates the community when I am outside, and like darkness when I am at home. . . . Honestly, there are few people who are willing to fight for the rights of other people. Many think that you are wasting your time, but one way or another I was able to fill one or two vans with people to go to protests and rallies. And when you get what you were fighting for, then you think, Well done, it was worth the effort. . . . And when you get things done, you feel good!

Isolated from her friends and from community politics and related activities, Elena expressed a sense of social alienation that also illustrated the feelings of other immigrant women who had moved out of Santech to suburban communities in San Jose or other cities. Trying to explain it to me, she added,

> I don't know what happened to me; I don't understand it myself. I had never felt like this in more than twenty years. . . . I don't have contacts with anybody now, with nobody. I lost them. It is as if I had entered a new world. . . . I don't know my neighbors, and that is why there is nothing like knowing your community. That is very important. . . . Living here is killing me, is hurting me a lot—a lot, as you cannot imagine. I get stressed; I don't have money. All my children expect me to bring home money, and when I don't they get angry.

Despite her sense of alienation that came from quitting her political activism and living today in an Anglo suburban neighborhood, Elena was proud of her life. On one occasion, I read to her parts of my description of the political activism she engaged in while living in Santech (chapter 5). After politely listening to my account, she nodded her head as if giving her approval. Then in a more critical tone she asked why I had not included anything about how her life had improved after she split from her husband or the happiness she had finally experienced in the midst of all the problems I recounted when she became romantically involved with a man after that separation. I realized that, to her, this was a part of her life that I had somehow neglected (this happened after I had left San Jose).

But I also realized it had an important political significance: it expressed her sense of liberation and freedom from the traditional patriarchal culture in which she grew up, a liberation that was also part of her personal political agenda, and one that I had not properly captured in my description of her community political activities. In fact, as she explained to me, separating from her husband and starting a new relationship took a lot of courage, as she had to confront the rejection and resentment of her children. With a strong sense of pride and resolution, she commented, "They [the children] prefer to see me back with my ex-husband who beat me, [rather] than being with somebody who treats me well. Well, I am sorry, I am not going to tolerate that any longer." At the time of this writing, Elena was looking for a way to get involved in community-related activities again, as she believed that the fight must continue, to avoid losing victorious terrain, and that returning to grassroots politics would help her regain her self-esteem, enthusiasm, and pride.

Undocumented Immigrants and Driver's Licenses

After several days of trying to find Jesús (whom I discussed in chapter 2), I finally locate him and, over the phone, we decide to meet the next morning. When we meet, Jesús is in good spirits: we are both happy to see each other after several years. Known among his friends for his generosity and for working hard while living with little, he has visibly aged and his hair has turned white.

When we go for lunch after I interview him at his home about the changes in his life over the past few years, I ask him about the driver's license issue, since he had earlier mentioned he had lost his. With a mixture of sadness and anger, he explains to me that he received his driver's license in 1994, a few years after arriving in town, but that when he went to renew it in spring 2004, he was rejected because he did not have a valid Social Security number. He says he still drives to work, but without a license he runs the risks of being fined and losing his car if the police stop him on the road.

Jesús' comments, like those of Anselmo, reflect a common feeling I encountered among the Mexican immigrants I talked to during my visit to San Jose. One issue that constantly emerged in conversation was the then-current debate on whether undocumented immigrants should have the right to get driver's licenses in California. Until 1993, the state of California allowed undocumented immigrants and people with non-immigrant visas to obtain driver's licenses without much trouble. Under the administration of Governor Pete Wilson, however, that changed, and applicants without valid Social Security numbers (or official individual taxpayer identification numbers) could not obtain a driver's license.[6] The prohibition affected thousand of undocumented immigrants, including those who had never had a driver's license in the state before, as well as those who had been issued one in the past but who, under the new law, could not renew it. As a result, today many immigrants are driving to work without licenses and are afraid of being detained by the police and getting their cars impounded. This describes, for example, many who are employed as janitors in nightshift jobs, and for whom public transportation is not available. It is not surprising then that many immigrants I talked to considered the driver's license issue to be one of the most pressing and important problems today.

The inability to obtain a license has also had numerous collateral effects on undocumented immigrants in the region. For example, it has resulted in an increase in the fees many workers without driver's licenses pay to others who give them a ride to work. When their *rites* fail, some nighttime workers, like Silvia, must spend the night in their buildings after finishing work, until the first bus or train starts running in the early morning. Moreover, many immigrants who are driving without a license drive run-down cars in case the police stop them and impound their vehicles, which increases safety risks on public roads. Also, as noted earlier, after September 11, immigrants have found increased restrictions on traveling. Without a license as a standard official identification, many immigrants who in the past could not travel abroad but were able to travel by air to visit relatives in other states, now find themselves confined to their own local communities because air travel has become much more scrutinized than before. As a result, their mobility has been significantly reduced, a sad instance of irony at a time when many immigration scholars have proclaimed that transnational immigrants are increasingly able to circumvent traditional controls of nation-states and move across national boundaries. In fact, the refusal to grant driver's licenses to undocumented immigrants can best be interpreted as being part of what Nicholas De Genova describes as "everyday forms of surveillance, repression, and intimidation" through which the state reinforces undocumented workers' vulnerability as a highly exploitable workforce (2002: 438).

In response to this situation, a number of grassroots organizations, labor unions, and pro-immigrants' rights groups organized public mobilizations and strikes to gather support for an initiative presented to the California legislature to change the current law and allow people who are not eligible for a Social Security number to obtain a driver's license.[7] Thus Local 1877, which represents thousands of janitors who are immigrant workers in Silicon Valley negatively affected by the current law, contributed to the formation of the San Jose Drivers License Action Network, an umbrella of several community, religious, and labor groups, to press for reform of the current legislation to allow immigrants to obtain a driver's license. The network organized several public rallies and meetings with California legislators, chiefs of police departments, the Mexican consul, and other public officials. Rather than couching it as a demand for immigrants' civil rights, this organization chose to use a public discourse that emphasizes the issue of public safety to ensure that all drivers "are properly trained, tested, and insured." As the regional vice president of the union, who is the chair of the network, told me, "We are using a pragmatic approach [as the rationale for the campaign] that focuses on public safety on the road. . . . To present it as a rights issue would not be popular today because of the current political climate. . . . [Yes,] we emphasize the issue of public safety in the roads. They are going to drive anyway, so the question is: What is best for all of us as California citizens? What is more convenient for the public safety of the society as a whole?"

Yet, from his perspective, the issue of driver's licenses was but part of a larger political battle over the labor and civil rights of immigrants. He believed this battle should eventually lead to a structural reform of immigration legislation in order to adjust to the reality of the economic dependence of many industries on undocumented immigrant labor. As he put it,

> The issue of the driver's license is just the tip of the iceberg. . . . Immigration laws need to be reformed in order to regularize the situation of all the people who maintain with their labor these industries, so that they can work and live without fear of being deported, and to avoid abuses by employers who hire them knowing they are undocumented, but who, when they don't need them any longer, use their undocumented status

against them. . . . If these workers are needed to keep industries going, we need to stop the hypocrisy and let them work [legally]. . . . What we need is to reform immigration law to regularize the status of undocumented immigrant workers.

In contrast to the pragmatic approach used by the San Jose Drivers License Action Network in California to frame the public debate on the driver's license issue, immigrants themselves took a more political approach that portrayed it as an issue of social justice and civil rights. Whenever I asked my informants about this problem, they made an explicit connection between their contributions to society through their work and the right to have a driver's license from the state to which they were contributing with their taxes. To them, obtaining a driver's license should not be viewed as a favor, but rather as a basic civil right they earn as local residents with their work and taxes.

A case in point is Jesús, who worked as a janitor in a San Jose shopping mall. Explaining his view on the driver's license issue as we were having lunch, he emphatically commented,

> There is a lot of injustice in this country. This is a country that preaches about human rights to the world, but it does not apply [at home]. We come as immigrants not to ask for a free license, it is not a privilege for us—we come here to work. . . . We are not getting a free license, but we pay for it and for our rights. We are paying taxes, but where are they going? . . . [The bill to allow immigrants get a driver's license] should be approved because we are working; we are not criminals. We are paying taxes, so why don't they then renew our driver licenses? Why not help people who are not a burden to the country?

When I first met Jesús, shortly after he had arrived in the United States, he was openly critical of the Mexican government and its failure to provide opportunities for the poor, which had compelled people like him to leave their families and communities and come work in the United States. More recently, he had changed his views. After years of hard work as an undocumented immigrant in this country, he had come to see the United States not just as a land of work opportunities but also as a land of exploitation, where democracy and what he considered to be basic rights were accessible only to some. He was disenchanted, both because of government policies toward Latino immigrants like him and because of foreign policies that he believed were geared to favor the government's economic interests rather than promoting democracy and freedom abroad. He said:

This is a major problem, the license issue. The other thing the U.S. government is doing is issuing new laws against us immigrants because they think we are all terrorists. Just recently Bush authorized employers to investigate their employees' papers, and the Social Security agency to investigate all the Social Security numbers of people who are working. All these measures are against Latino people, against la Raza. . . . With the crisis we are living, with all these wars and invasions of poor countries, instead of helping them it is hurting them more, and [the president] is putting his own country at risk, not giving his own people access to health care, reducing teachers in public schools, closing help centers [for the needy], all to spend the money on wars, and all for what up until now has been shown to be a lie. . . . They think that just because one doesn't speak English, we don't realize what is going on.

As an undocumented immigrant, Jesús made a direct link between the poor treatment immigrants receive in the country and the U.S. policies toward poor countries abroad. Overall, denying driver's licenses to undocumented immigrants places increasing hardship on their lives, one of the central goals of anti-immigrant groups that support this prohibition. But rather than restricting illegal immigration (and pushing undocumented immigrants out the United States) the prohibition is pushing undocumented immigrants further underground. The result is diminished rather than enhanced public safety for all.

Because of the multiple effects that the inability to obtain driver's licenses has on the lives of thousands of undocumented immigrants in Silicon Valley, the public campaign to change the current law has led to a collaboration of labor and grassroots community groups, which in the past had little contact with each other. Thus, for example, PACT was active in the driver's license campaign and sent representatives to Sacramento to talk to state legislators. This might indicate the beginning of a broader political alliance between labor and community organizations who address issues that are closely related for thousands of immigrant workers and their families. In a political context that distances capital and labor through flexible employment practices, a social movement of this type offers the political potential to bring together labor and civil rights that pertain to the spheres of production and social reproduction and that are of paramount importance to immigrant workers and their families. The struggle over the driver's license issue could advance new forms of solidarity between labor and community groups and rearticulate notions of immigrants' membership in society and entitlement to basic labor and civil rights.

Notes

Introduction

1. This argument goes against common wisdom, which portrays low-wage immigrants in U.S. cities as being in a position of structural vulnerability that makes labor unionization and other forms of civil and political mobilization increasingly difficult. It also highlights the intrinsic contradictions of the new economy in the United States, which, on the one hand, has become increasingly dependent on cheap and flexible immigrant labor and, on the other hand, has built new legal barriers to the labor, civil, and political rights of immigrants, especially the undocumented.

2. Heyman 1998: 172; Wells 1996: 298; Griffith and Kissam 1995: 290; Cornelius 1992; Krissman 1996. Griffith and Kissam (1995), for example, consider the subcontracting of undocumented immigrants by large agribusiness corporations as disguised slavery, debt peonage, paternalism, and patron-client relations. For a discussion of the role of labor contractors who employ immigrant workers in enhancing labor control in agriculture and the industrial sector, see Ortiz 2002.

3. Anthropologists distinguish between families and households. The term *family* refers to a group of persons related by marriage and kinship ties and is, therefore, culturally defined in each society. In contrast, *household* refers to people living under the same roof who contribute to their maintenance and share some consumption activities. While the personnel of families and households often overlap, the two categories must be examined separately because they describe two different groups with distinctive functions and purposes.

4. Chávez 1990, 1992; Briody 1986; Palerm and Urquiola 1993; García 1992. For a detailed discussion of the variety of domestic groups found among Mexican immigrants, see Chávez 1990, 1992.

5. Goldring 1998; Rivera-Salgado 1999; Kearney and Nagengast 1989; Rouse 1992. For example, organizations formed by indigenous Mixtec immigrants

employed as farmworkers in Mexico and the United States defend their labor, political, human, and cultural rights in a context in which they are discriminated against and exploited because of their race, ethnic affiliation, and class status (Rivera-Salgado 1999).

6. Pardo 1998a; Zavella 1987; Hondagneu-Sotelo 1994; Jones-Correa 1998. Some authors have shown that Latino immigrants' politics are shaped by a gender pattern in which men tend to concentrate on and monopolize the leadership of transnational political organizations as a way to enhance their social status, while women tend to be more active in local community politics to enhance the well-being and future of their children and families (Jones-Correa 1998; Goldring 2003).

7. My study does not address the transnational politics of Mexican immigrants, because, in Santech, very few of the people I met were engaged in transnational political activities and organizations. This speaks only about this particular community; however, there is a tendency in contemporary academic studies to focus on transnational political activities, sometimes to the detriment of less formal and visible types of local political activism through which immigrants struggle for civil and membership rights in the host society.

8. An informal approach based on spending long hours with people and engaging in conversations with them is a highly labor-intensive but effective research technique in urban ethnographic fieldwork (Dohan 2003).

9. I was born in Bolivia and grew up in Madrid, Spain. Because of my physical appearance and my Polish last name, people usually thought I was an "American" or *bolillo* (white American). While my appearance made me stand out in Mexican barrios like Santech, my cultural background and native language greatly facilitated my interaction with and acceptance by many of the barrio's residents. It also made me feel comfortable among them, an important factor when conducting intensive ethnographic fieldwork. At the same time, I felt that my *bolillo* appearance also facilitated my interaction with some of the public officials and industry executives I interviewed in the field. Other government officials, however, were more cautious and reserved in our interviews.

1. Mexican Immigrants in Silicon Valley

1. The term was first coined by journalist Don Hoefler in 1971 and soon became incorporated into popular speech (Saxenian 1994: 31)

2. Alesch and Levine 1973: 12. For the history of San Jose's urban development, see Trounstine and Christensen 1982, chap. 4.

3. For example, Our Lady of Guadalupe Parish, founded in 1952 in East San Jose, soon became an important site for labor and community organizing efforts by the Mexican American population, including activists like César Chávez, who at the time was living in Sal Si Puedes, and who later became the emblematic and charismatic leader of farmworkers in California in the 1960s (Pitti 2003: 150–52).

4. Commenting on how the economic transformations in the region affected the Mexican population in the mid-1970s, an astute journalist observed, "During the past 20 years, Santa Clara Valley's agri-business has been rapidly decreasing. Large cultivated areas have given way to urban sprawl; many of our major canneries have moved closer to the source of the fruit supply. This change in our economy has not stopped illegal Mexican immigrants from coming to Santa Clara Valley. They now find jobs as dishwashers and waiters in Mexican restaurants, as gardeners, janitors and construction workers" (Juárez 1976).

5. Martínez Saldaña 1993; Blakely and Sullivan 1989.

6. If we consider San Mateo and Santa Cruz counties, into which Silicon Valley has expanded, the number of janitors is even higher than the population of computer engineers. In 1990, janitors in San Mateo outnumbered engineers by 2,350 workers (4,450 and 2,100 workers, respectively), and janitors in Santa Cruz outnumbered engineers by 830 (1,350 and 520 workers, respectively) (State of California, Employment Development Department 1998).

7. Saxenian 1985; Benner 2002: 75. Alan Hyde locates the early "Defense Period" between 1941 and 1959 (2003: 4).

8. Benner 2002: 50; Saxenian 1994: 25–27. Hyde divides the development of the semiconductor industry into two different phases: an initial stage (1950–1980) of growth and expansion, and a second stage of consolidation and crisis due to foreign competition (1980–1986) (2003: 6–11). Owing much of its early development to government investment in the defense sector, this industry underwent a major crisis in the 1980s as the result of strong competition from Japan. In the 1990s, it reinvented itself by developing and manufacturing state-of-the-art microprocessors and other related products in what became a continuous process of technological innovation (2003: 74–75)

9. Benner 2002: 69; Hyde 2003: 13. In the 1990s, however, the industry experienced unexpected rapid local growth when large multinational corporations in Silicon Valley contracted out the assembly of electronics products to independent companies in the region that, for technological reasons, needed to be close to the research and development centers. According to Benner, there are about three hundred firms in Silicon Valley providing electronics manufacturing services (2002: 67).

10. For example, between December 2000 and October 2001, the valley lost 3.7 percent of its jobs, and by April 2002 unemployment in the region was 7.4 percent (Hyde 2003: 21).

11. Walker and Bay Area Study Group 1990: 33; Benner 2002: 38; Hyde 2003. Employment in Silicon Valley has become increasingly flexible over time due to the growth of labor market intermediaries such as temporary employment, part-time employment, independent contractors, and self-employment. For example, the percentage of the Silicon Valley workforce employed in temporary agencies is twice the national percentage, and up to 40 percent of the region's workforce is involved in nonstandard employment relationships (including not only temporary employment but also part-time employment, independent contractors, and self-employment; Benner 2002: 38). Also, the number of tempo-

rary help agencies in Silicon Valley more than doubled between 1987 and 1997 (Hyde 2003: 148).

12. Benner 2002: 43. Rather than being seen as a radical departure from past practices, local outsourcing in Silicon Valley can be viewed as the next step in the process of decentralization within this industrial district that started in the 1960s, when large high-tech companies began sending manufacturing abroad.

13. Pellow and Sun-Hee Park 2002: 137. Most high-tech companies out-source significant aspects of production, and for a typical personal computer, this ratio has been estimated as 80 percent of total production costs (Hyde 2003: 107). According to Pellow and Sun-Hee Park, piecework—where workers assemble silicon chips and other components that lie at the heart of electronic consumer products—also increased in the 1990s. Like in the garment industry, they maintain, electronics piecework is organized through a pyramid of con-tractors in which the original manufacturing company outsources the work to a first-tier contractor, who, in turn, outsources part of the work to a second-tier contractor, and so on (2002: 159, 165).

14. Chun 2001: 149. Profit rates in electronics manufacturing service firms are rather narrow, averaging 4 to 6 percent, while profit rates in large high-tech companies that contract out work to those firms are 40 percent and higher (Benner 2002: 225).

15. Benner 2002: 225. Chris Benner makes an important distinction between the concepts of work flexibility and employment flexibility. Work flexibility refers to the activities workers perform, the skills required to perform them, and the social organization of production in which such activities are carried out. In contrast, employment flexibility refers to the nature of relationships between employers and employees, including forms of remuneration, benefits, and man-agement practices (2002: 4, 24). From this perspective, in Silicon Valley the pro-liferation of labor market intermediaries since the 1980s, especially temporary work agencies and independent contractors, has been a central mechanism in enhancing employment flexibility in the region. This flexibility has contributed to the high productivity of large high-tech firms and to the financial insecurity of a large segment of workers (2002). Along similar lines, Jennifer Chun argues that employers in Silicon Valley use three forms of labor flexibility to reduce operating costs and respond to fluctuations in a competitive market: *numerical flexibility,* meaning the expansion and contraction of workforces according to changing production needs; *structural flexibility,* meaning the contracting out or outsourcing of operating costs and responsibility to independent contractors; and *functional flexibility,* meaning the enhancement of workers' mobility and cooperation across tasks in the workplace (2001: 129). From a different theoret-ical perspective, Hyde maintains that the heavy use of temporary help agencies and independent contractors in Silicon Valley is not a device to reduce labor costs, but rather a mechanism that facilitates and enhances the rapid and flexi-ble transmission of information and knowledge upon which the cycle of con-stant technological innovation in the region depends (2003: 97).

16. Hossfeld 1988; Blakely and Sullivan 1989; Siegel 1995; Walker and Bay Area Study Group 1990. The existence of a labor market highly bifurcated along

ethnic lines in Silicon Valley has been a constant theme in several studies of this region (e.g., Green 1983; Katz and Kemnitzer 1983; Saxenian 1985; Hossfeld 1988). For a discussion of gender segregation in Silicon Valley's electronics industry, see Hossfeld 1988.

17. Benner 2002: 207–10. According to Hyde, the Santa Clara Valley was one of the few regions in the country where income for the lowest 20 percent of the population declined in the 1990s (2003: 207). Between 1990 and 1998, wages for the lowest paid 25 percent of workers living in Silicon Valley decreased by 14 percent (Sachs, cited by Pellow and Sun-Hee Park 2002: 239n40). In addition, the ratio of annual income of the valley's top hundred executives to that of the average manufacturing worker went from 42:1 in 1991 to 220:1 in 1996 (Hyde 2003: 207).

18. Benner 2002: 217–20. According to a study conducted by Blakely and Sullivan, in 1985 Latinos held almost 80 percent of the clerical and operating jobs in the low-wage service sector (1989: 4). Later, in 1990, Latinos made up 17 percent of the operators and 11 percent of the clerical staff in high-tech firms (Benner 2002: 220).

19. Historically, this was not always the case. In the early 1950s, most electronics firms were unionized by the United Electrical, Machine, and Radio Workers when the high-tech industrialization of the region had just begun (Hyde 2003: 155). Yet by the end of the 1950s, as a result of the cold war repression, the union was routed from the region (Michael Eisenscher, cited by Hyde 2003: 155).

20. Estimates of the ethnic composition of the neighborhood are based on data from the *San Jose City Directory* for the period 1963 to 1992, from interviews with two of San Jose's city housing officials conducted in 1993, and from an interview with a Cambodian social worker who lived in Santech until the mid-1980s.

21. U.S. Bureau of the Census 2000. Census tract figures for Santech are rounded and slightly modified to protect the anonymity of barrio residents.

22. Statistics for the Hispanic population in this area indicate that the average age of this group is 21.5 years and the average household size is six members. However, comparisons between official statistics and my own data must be made with care. First, the official statistical data are from the 2000 census, whereas I made my ethnographic survey in the early 1990s. Second, there is not an exact match between the census tract and Santech: the former encompasses an area larger than this barrio, which has the effect of lowering the average household size in the tract.

23. The amnesty program was part of the Immigration Reform and Control Act approved by Congress in 1986, which allowed undocumented immigrants who could prove continuous residence in the United States since January 1, 1982, and those who worked in agriculture in the country for at least ninety days during specific time periods, to become legal residents.

24. For a detailed study of the difference between licit and illicit income-generating activities in Mexican and Mexican American neighborhoods in San Jose and Los Angeles, see Dohan 2003.

2. The Subcontracting of Mexican Janitors in the High-Tech Industry

1. I contacted most workers at Sonix through their own social networks. Most of the information presented in this chapter comes from informal and lengthy conversations with them, formal open-ended interviews with a sample of about twenty-five janitors subcontracted by Sonix, and twenty structured interviews conducted with ten key informants selected from this group of twenty-five. All interviews were conducted in Spanish, and the quotes used are my own translations. Information regarding work organization and management methods of Sonix and its cleaning contractors was gathered from structured interviews with the top maintenance managers of these companies. While I contacted the janitors directly through personal networks, I contacted managers through formal letters. My relationship with the managers was a formal one, and all interviews were conducted in English. I supplemented this information with data from internal reports by Sonix and its contractors that addressed issues of management practices dealing with custodial workers and the companies' plans to organize janitorial work, which I obtained from these companies' managers. The discussion regarding janitors' participation in labor union activities is based on direct observation, informal interviews, and many hours of conversation with dozens of workers who actively participated in these activities.

2. State of California, Employment Development Department 1998. This building-cleaning industry ranks in the top ten in the county in terms of absolute growth (Pellow and Sun-Hee Park 2002: 209).

3. Mines and Avina 1992: 441. By the early 1970s, all the large building-maintenance contractors were unionized. These contractors formed the Associated Building Maintenance Contractors of Santa Clara Valley to avoid price competition among them and established joint collective bargaining (Johnston 1994: 158).

4. Mines and Avina 1992: 431–35. The restructuring was a two-part process. The first changes occurred when nonunion, midsize janitorial firms took over a significant share of the cleaning market previously in the hands of large, unionized cleaning firms that served large high-tech companies. Later, in the mid-1980s, many high-tech corporations that still employed their own in-house custodial workers also started to contract out their cleaning services to independent janitorial firms (Zlolniski 2001: 269).

5. Moreover, in response to the inroads made by subcontractors, Local 77—the labor union representing custodial workers in the Santa Clara Valley at the time—signed a two-tier master contract in which new employees were subject to a four-year apprenticeship, during which they were paid only a percentage of journeyman wages (70 percent the first year, 80 percent the second year, and so on; Mines and Avina 1992: 442).

6. For an account of the contracting-out trend in Silicon Valley's building-cleaning industry, see Johnston 1994: 146–74; and Mines and Avina 1992.

7. Originally, Local 77 covered the neighboring counties of Santa Clara and San Mateo. In 1987, it merged with Local 18, after which the new Local 1877 also included workers in Alameda and Contra Costa counties (Johnston 1994: 158).

8. Fisk, Mitchell, and Erickson 2000. This was made possible by a change of national leadership in the Service Employees International Union in the mid-1980s that allowed the adoption of new and aggressive organizing strategies—carried out under the slogan "Justice for Janitors"—in Silicon Valley and cities like Saint Louis, Denver, Philadelphia, San Diego, Hartford, and Los Angeles (Johnston 1994: 164–65).

9. In doing so, Local 1877 pursued what Johnston calls a "three-way agreement"—namely, between the contractor and the client firm; the union and the client firm or its association concerning wages and benefits; and between the union and the contractors' association concerning job security, portability of benefits, and other issues (1994: 167).

10. At the time, there was a rumor that Bay-Clean was close to bankruptcy, which I was unable to confirm.

11. While I was not able to obtain much information on this point, my impression was that most supervisors at Bay-Clean were indeed Koreans, whereas most of the janitors were Mexicans. Korean workers were controlled through kinship ties and a paternalistic management style to ensure their loyalty in exchange for favorable treatment, including promotions. Mexican workers were controlled by authoritarian rules, which, though causing a high worker turnover in the company, seemed not to present a major problem, since other undocumented immigrants easily replaced individuals who rejected these rules.

12. At the time, Luis was the president of the club, which facilitated the agreement. The union agreed to pay the team's annual dues in the regional league (about a thousand dollars) and for the player's uniforms.

13. Bay-Clean soon retaliated after some of its workers got involved in the union's campaign. A week after the rally, the company assigned the largest and most difficult areas to clean to those janitors identified as sympathizing with the union's cause. Several workers were asked to show their work authorization cards, and some supervisors tried to talk workers out of the union's campaign. To obstruct the dissemination of information among workers, the company also issued an order forbidding them to leave their buildings during their midnight "lunch" break. These tactics lowered workers' morale; many of them feared losing their jobs or being denounced to the *migra* (INS authorities), which some supervisors had threatened to do.

14. Service International had a thicker and more complex managerial structure than Bay-Clean. This structure included floor workers, foremen, site supervisors, managers, an operation manager, and a branch manager.

15. Reed-Danahay 1993. Reed-Danahay uses the French term *débrouillardise* to refer to all actions that indicate "making do" in such situations, including notions of accommodation and resistance (1993: 224).

16. Despite this, both Luis and Anselmo recognized the overall benefits and positive effects that had come from joining Local 1877. Luis acknowledged that

they were better protected from abuse in the workplace—such as harassment by their supervisors or being fired without a solid reason—than when employed by Bay-Clean, and Anselmo commented that workers like him who represented the union at work were treated with more respect by their supervisors than before.

17. For similar findings, see Dohan 2003: 44.

3. Working in the Informal Economy

1. Moser 1994; and Wilson 1998. For a review of the theories and debates in the literature on the informal economy, see Wilson 1998; Moser 1994; and Rakowski 1994.

2. Castells and Portes 1989. Particularly important to this approach are those informal activities carried out by immigrant workers who appear in official employment statistics as self-employed workers, but who indeed are disguised proletarians whose work serves to reduce labor expenses in the formal sector.

3. If overemphasized, however, this approach runs the risk of romanticizing the informal economy as an alternative, "counterhegemonic" set of entrepreneurial activities by disempowered people, as Wilson (2005) correctly warns us.

4. The ethnographic information presented in this chapter is based on direct interaction with the workers employed in three types of informal activities. These interactions included participant observation, long hours of informal conversations with the participants, and a few structured interviews. I accompanied participants at work on dozens of occasions. This allowed me to document their activities in detail and understand why they chose to work in these informal occupations. It also gave me the opportunity to converse with them at length about how they themselves interpreted the advantages and disadvantages of their informal jobs with respect to work opportunities in the formal sector, a subjective dimension often neglected in studies of the informal economy based on surveys and quantitative research methods.

5. Unlike my interaction with Laura and her husband, my interaction with Arturo was more sporadic and it principally occurred in the streets, the place where I first met him and where I conducted most of my observations about his work.

6. Arturo bought the cards for $1.25 and could sell them at any price and keep the profit.

7. His situation reflects a common dilemma faced by many Mexican and Central American immigrants, who often underestimate the living costs in the United States and overestimate their ability to move ahead (Mahler 1995).

8. From a legal angle, Arturo's status was similar to that of a statutory worker. According to the U.S. Internal Revenue Service, statutory employees are those who work on commission and "who work by the guidelines of the person for whom the work is done, with materials furnished by and returned to that person." In other words, statutory workers are self-employed individuals who

provide services for payment outside of an established place of work, but whose conditions as employees are considered different from self-employed workers and independent contractors (Fernández-Kelly and García 1989: 256). For the purpose of defining labor status, however, Arturo best fits the definition of "employee" as provided by the Supreme Court, according to which it means "common law" employee, one who, on examination of multiple factors, does not, on balance, control the means and manner of his or her employment (Hyde 2003: 120).

9. Otherwise, given the sensitive nature of his business, I believe I would have had a hard time approaching him, much less observing his work up close and documenting it.

10. As a "target earner," Gustavo illustrates the behavior predicted by the new economics of migration. According to these economics, the impetus for migration cannot be reduced to wage differences alone: market failures like the lack of access to credit in the home communities also compel migrants to search elsewhere for opportunities to build capital in order to start their own businesses upon return (Massey et al. 1993: 436–39).

11. Although Gustavo was engaged in a skilled occupation, his dental practice critically depended on the same factors crucial to the survival of those in less skilled occupations in the informal sector, like Laura and Arturo. Namely, he relied on personal relations, close social networks, and trust. Gustavo was located in a familiar Latino neighborhood, and, as a Mexican immigrant like most of his patients, he easily connected with the needs and expectations of his patients. Also, his careful screening of his patients, his habit of checking their referrals, and the rapport he established with them were key to keeping his dental office running.

4. Mexican Families in Santech

1. I use the term *extended family households* to refer to households composed of a nuclear family and other unmarried kin that extend laterally (i.e., with siblings and cousins) or lineally, both up (with a parent or a married couple) and down (with grandchildren; Sanjek 1996: 286). In some cases, however, I have also included under this label households composed of two or more nuclear families whose members are related by kinship, which are often called "multiple family households." My main objective is to distinguish the extended family household—the most common by far in Santech—from simple family households (those composed of married couples with or without children) and no-family households (those made of siblings who live together or persons who are not related by kinship). In addition, extended family households in Santech often included unrelated persons as boarders, usually immigrants from the same hometown, who frequently were described with fictive kinship names (e.g., cousin, uncle, aunt) to emphasize a household ideology of solidarity and mutual rights and obligations.

2. Census statistics seem to confirm my observations, as about 30 percent of the 775 families who live in the area are female-headed (U.S. Bureau of the Census 2000). This is an approximate figure because, as I explained before, there is not an exact match between Santech and the area included in this tract.

3. See, for example, Roberts 1994; Chávez 1992; Selby, Murphy, and Lorenzen 1990; Wood 1981, 1982. As Roger Rouse (1989), who has criticized this approach, argues, a basic assumption of this model is that migration is the outcome of a household economy strategy in which the primary goal is to preserve the unity and viability of the household as a whole. The use of the family strategies model for the study of Mexican immigrant families in the United States has been defended on several grounds. Brian Roberts, for example, argues that it has a renewed heuristic value in a politico-economic context in which immigrants are relegated to the low end of the labor market and excluded from the welfare-state product of neoliberal policies. He maintains that, although individual family members may have conflicting interests and some privileged access to certain resources, immigrant households often pool labor, income, and other material and social resources to cope with poverty (1994: 14–15).

4. Similarly, Victoria Malkin's study of Mexican emigration to New Rochelle criticizes the family strategies approach for interpreting women's decisions and behavior through their role in household reproduction (1998: 16). She proposes instead an actor-oriented approach that analyzes women's choices in light of their own interpretations and practices (1998: 222).

5. Most of the information I present in this chapter was collected by intense participant observation, rather than by questionnaires or structured interviews. I spent many hours visiting, talking, and interacting with these families, as well as participated in many of their day-by-day routines and social activities. While in the field, I visited these and other families on a weekly basis for extended periods of time, often developing a strong and personally rewarding bond with many of their members. I followed these families for several years to obtain a long-term perspective on the changes they experienced and how they dealt with them.

6. Valenzuela 1999; Torres Sarmiento 2002; Menjívar 2000: 218–19. For a discussion of children's labor and other activities that play an important role in the economic and social integration of Mexican and other Latino immigrant families, see Valenzuela 1999.

7. Mexican and other Latino undocumented immigrants often fall prey to unscrupulous people who seek to profit from their desperation to obtain work authorization and residency permits. The underground industry in fake work permits and other false documents rapidly expanded after the passage of the Immigration Reform and Control Act in 1986, which amplified the need to obtain such documents to claim the right to work in the United States. For an ethnographic account of this underground industry, see Mahler 1995.

8. I developed a close relationship with Margarita and her family, whom I visited periodically. Despite all her problems, Margarita always found time to talk with me. I often had the impression that, since I was one of the few people she

knew outside her family, she felt secure enough to vent her problems and complaints, and that doing so served as a safety valve.

9. There were fifteen workers assigned to that building. Twelve of them were hired by the janitorial company that took over the contract, and three of them—those with less seniority in the job, including Alfredo—were laid off.

10. She reported about 50 percent of her earnings, which was paid by check. She received payment for the second half—the unreported work-hours—in cash, an arrangement that she and her employer considered mutually beneficial.

11. In this city with one of the highest median housing costs in the country, and a critical shortage of affordable housing for low-income people, Margarita, like many other families in Silicon Valley, had to wait for several years before gaining access to subsidized housing.

12. This was a common uniform of the Sureño gang in the barrio, largely made up of young, first-generation Mexican immigrants.

13. For a detailed discussion of the types of welfare aid commonly used by Mexican immigrants in a low-income barrio in San Jose, and the ambivalent feelings that welfare generates in a culture that emphasizes self-reliance and hard work, see Dohan 2003, 157–207.

5. Community Politics in the Barrio

1. Most of the ethnographic information I present in this chapter was gathered through participant observation, and hours of informal conversations and interviews with women involved in community politics in Santech. I attended dozens of meetings organized by local residents in the neighborhood, as well as many other reunions and political events in which they participated in conjunction with other groups and nonprofit organizations. I followed, observed, and participated in these political campaigns from the beginning and spent many hours talking to the other people who participated in them. Because I already knew many of the women who were leaders and activists, entering into this important aspect of their lives seemed like the natural thing to do. Participating in and documenting the community and political activities of the people of Santech turned out to be one of the most exciting and rewarding experiences I had while in the field.

2. Before Project Crackdown, Santech had a long history as a focus of government programs, starting about fifteen years after this barrio was built. In the mid-1980s, the San Jose city government came up with a housing-loan program designed to curb the rapid deterioration of housing in Santech. The program consisted of generous loans to property owners to bring their buildings up to official safety standards. The program did not produce the expected results and was cancelled by city officials in 1988. One year later, the San Jose Department of Housing launched another, more aggressive housing rehabilitation loan initiative, funded by the federal and city governments, that allowed landlords to borrow up to sixty thousand dollars interest free to fix their blighted apart-

ments. This program too was canceled shortly after it began because few owners applied for loans and because city officials themselves were divided about whether government money should be used to subsidize unscrupulous landlords who abused their tenants.

3. According to a city official from the San Jose Department of Housing whom I interviewed, Santech was catalogued as having a high incidence of blight, drugs, and crime, to the point that "the area no longer functioned as a neighborhood" and needed immediate police attention. The quote refers to an internal document authored by the city of San Jose titled "Neighborhood Revitalization Strategy" (1992), in which Santech is categorized as part of the group "Neighborhood IV," referring to the most dilapidated neighborhoods in San Jose.

4. A parish-based organization, PACT is part of a nationwide Jesuit-founded network (Pacific Institute for Community Organizations) that largely adopted strategies developed by Saul Alinsky, a pioneer in community organizing. PACT's central goal was to promote organizing in neighborhoods inhabited by low-middle- and working-class residents in San Jose, and by the early 1990s it had become the largest, most influential and vocal grassroots community group in the city.

5. The grassroots political mobilization of Santa Clara Valley women to challenge urban growth in San Jose and foment neighborhood community participation is not new and goes back at least to the 1970s. For a history of women's grassroots politics in the region at the time, see Johnston 1994: 88–112.

6. Funding for the project was secured from the San Jose City Council, the school district to which Santech Elementary School belonged, and a few local nonprofit organizations, including PACT.

7. Interestingly, in her brief discussion of immigrant women's politicization, Caroline Brettell (commenting on Wenona Giles's work on Portuguese women in London) reports that the movement these women started became bureaucratized with time as they lost control over it (2003: 192). To my knowledge, the issue of how and when immigrant women's political activity becomes more formal and disengaged from everyday life has received scant attention.

Conclusion

1. These authors, however, go well beyond this principle and extract other, more controversial conclusions. According to Waldinger and Lichter, immigrant networks tend to expand both horizontally and vertically. Horizontal expansion (or exclusionary closure) prevents members of other groups from taking those jobs. Vertical expansion (or usurpationary closure) hampers the ability of managers to control the hiring process and constrains managerial authority. But what the authors interpret as the exclusionary effects of immigrants' networks can be alternatively interpreted as managerial business decisions to take better control of the workforce. More important, in their effort to

untangle the laws governing the micro dynamics of the recruiting, hiring, and firing of workers laboring in low-paid occupations in Southern California, Waldinger and Lichter underestimate the larger politico-economic forces that govern the process. These forces most often shift the balance of power to the side of management and away from immigrants and their networks, no matter how socially dense the latter might be.

2. De Genova 2002: 427. For additional discussion of how the policing of the workplace and public spaces disciplines undocumented immigrants and exacerbates their sense of vulnerability, see Rouse 1992.

Epilogue

1. The largest increase of union members in the Santa Clara Valley took place between 1992 and 1994, at the height of the Justice for Janitors campaign in Silicon Valley. Before that, the union represented about 35 percent of workers employed in the industry. Today it represents close to 75 percent (in Santa Clara and San Mateo counties).

2. Despite this structural change and greater efficiency in responding to members needs, Local 1877 still falls short in the financial and human resources needed to attend to all its members. As Bustamante explained, the union has about sixty-five hundred members in Silicon Valley and only four union representatives to visit all sites, which makes it difficult to keep up.

3. Shortly before my visit to San Jose, Carmen's oldest daughter, her daughter's husband, and their four children moved to Minnesota in search of better work opportunities and a lower cost of living.

4. To deal with thousands of similar cases, the California legislature in 2001 approved AB 540, a provision that allows immigrant students, including the undocumented, to attend college providing they meet certain requirements. The requirements of AB 540 include having studied in a California high school for three or more years, having graduated from a California high school (or having passed the General Educational Development test), and having filled out an affidavit stating that the student has applied for or plans to apply for legal residence as soon as he or she is able to do so. In Lorena's case the law came too late. Although she still wants to go to college, she is now married and has a baby girl, and she works full-time in the cafeteria of an elder-care clinic. Unable to obtain a driver's license because of her undocumented status, she cannot drive to college after work in the evenings. These cases seem to echo some common problems that adolescent immigrants often confront as a result of factors such as poverty, legal instability, and lack of incentives to improve their education (Menjívar 2000: 229).

5. Elena had worked as a liaison between 1996 and 2000, after which she worked as a "community action specialist" in another program to promote college attendance by Latino students, until 2002, when the program was discontinued because of a lack of funds.

6. As of September 2004, nearly forty states plus the District of Columbia required drivers to prove legal residency before they could be issued a driver's license, according to the National Immigration Law Center based in Los Angeles. Most of California's neighbors, however, including Oregon, Washington, Utah, and Hawaii, did not have this requirement (*New York Times*, August 29, 2004).

7. The initiative, headed by Senator Gilbert Cedillo of Los Angeles, would allow non–U.S. citizens to obtain a driver's license if they provide an Individual Taxpayer Identification Number and two additional forms of identification. This would not be completely novel, as many legal immigrants who do not qualify for a Social Security number are issued driver's licenses in California and other states using an Individual Taxpayer Identification Number. The bill was approved by the California legislature on August 31, 2004, but vetoed by Governor Arnold Schwarzenegger on September 22 of the same year. At the time of this writing, several Latino and pro-immigrant-rights organizations are planning boycotts and public demonstrations to protest the governor's decision.

References

Adler, Rachek H.

    2004. *Yucatecans in Dallas, Texas.* Boston: Pearson.

Alarcón, Rafael.

    2000. "Skilled Immigrants and Cerebreros: Foreign-Born Engineers and Scientists in the High-Technology Industry of Silicon Valley." In *Immigration Research for a New Century: Multidisciplinary Perspectives,* ed. Nancy Foner, Rubén G. Rumbaut, and Steven J. Gold, pp. 301–21. New York: Russell Sage Foundation.

Alesch, Daniel J., and Robert A. Levine.

    1973. *Growth in San Jose: A Summary Policy Statement.* Report Prepared for the National Science Foundation. Santa Monica, CA: Rand.

Benería, Lourdes, and Martha Roldán.

    1987. *The Crossroads of Class and Gender: Industrial Homework, Subcontracting, and Household Dynamics in Mexico City.* Chicago: University of Chicago Press.

Benner, Christopher C.

    1998. "Win the Lottery or Organize: Traditional and Non-Traditional Labor Organizing in Silicon Valley." *Berkeley Planning Journal* 12: 50–71.

    2000. "Navigating Flexibility: Labor Markets and Intermediaries in Silicon Valley." Ph.D. diss., University of California, Berkeley.

    2002. *Work in the New Economy: Flexible Labor Markets in Silicon Valley.* Malden, MA: Blackwell Publishing.

Blakely, E., and S. Sullivan.

    1989. *The Latino Workforce in Santa Clara County: The Dilemmas of High Technology Change on a Minority Population.* Santa Clara, CA: Latino Issues Forum of Santa Clara County.

Blim, Michael L.

1992. "Introduction: The Emerging Global Factory and Anthropology." In *Anthropology and the Global Factory*, ed. Frances Abrahamer Rothstein and Michael L. Blim, pp. 1–30. New York: Bergin and Garvey.

Bonacich, Edna.

2000. "Intense Challenges, Tentative Possibilities: Organizing Immigrant Garment Workers in Los Angeles." In *Organizing Immigrants: The Challenge for Unions in Contemporary California*, ed. Ruth Milkman, pp. 130–49. Ithaca: Cornell University Press.

Bonacich, Edna, and Richard P. Appelbaum.

2000. *Behind the Label: Inequality in the Los Angeles Apparel Industry.* Berkeley: University of California Press.

Borjas, George J.

1994. "The Economics of Immigration." *Journal of Economic Literature* 32, no. 4: 1667–1718.

1996. "The New Economics of Immigration." *Atlantic Monthly* 278, no. 5: 72–80.

Brettell, Caroline B.

2000. "Theorizing Migration in Anthropology: The Social Construction of Networks, Identities, Communities, and Globalscapes." In *Immigration Theory: Talking across Disciplines*, ed. Caroline B. Brettell and James F. Hollifield, pp. 97–135. New York: Routledge.

2003. *Anthropology and Migration: Essays on Transnationalism, Ethnicity, and Identity.* Walnut Creek, CA: AltaMira Press.

Briody, Elizabeth K.

1986. *Household Labor Patterns among Mexican Americans in South Texas: Buscando Trabajo Seguro.* New York: AMS Press.

Burawoy, Michael.

2000. Introduction to *Global Ethnography: Forces, Connections, and Imaginations in a Postmodern World*, ed. Michael Burawoy et al., pp. 1–40. Berkeley: University of California Press.

Castells, Manuel, and Alejandro Portes.

1989. "World Underneath: The Origins, Dynamics, and Effects of the Informal Economy." In *The Informal Economy: Studies in Advanced and Less Developed Countries*, ed. Alejandro Portes, Manuel Castells, and Laura Benton, pp. 11–37. Baltimore: Johns Hopkins University Press.

Chávez, Leo R.

1990. "Coresidence and Resistance: Strategies for Survival among Undocumented Mexicans and Central Americans in the United States." *Urban Anthropology* 19, no. 1–2: 31–61.

1992. *Shadowed Lives: Undocumented Immigrants in American Society.* Fort Worth: Holt, Rinehart, and Winston.

Chinchilla, Norma S., and Nora Hamilton.

2001. "Doing Business: Central American Enterprises in Los Angeles." In

Asian and Latino Immigrants in a Restructuring Economy: The Meta-morphosis of Southern California, ed. Marta Lopez-Garza and David R. Diaz, pp. 188–214. Stanford: Stanford University Press.

Chun, Jennifer JiHye.

   2001. "Flexible Despotism: The Intensification of Insecurity and Uncertainty in the Lives of Silicon Valley's High-Tech Assembly Workers." In *The Critical Study of Work: Labor, Technology, and Global Production,* ed. Rick Baldoz, Charles Koeber, and Philip Kraft, pp. 127–54. Philadelphia: Temple University Press.

Clark, Margaret.

   1970. *Health in the Mexican-American Culture: A Community Study.* 2nd ed. Berkeley: University of California Press.

Comaroff, Jean, and John L. Comaroff.

   2001. "Millennial Capitalism: First Thoughts on a Second Coming." In *Millennial Capitalism and the Culture of Neoliberalism,* ed. Jean Comaroff and John L. Comaroff, pp. 1–56. Durham: Duke University Press.

Cornelius, Wayne A.

   1992. "From Sojourners to Settlers: The Changing Profile of Mexican Immigration to the United States." In *U.S.-Mexico Relations: Labor Market Interdependence,* ed. J. Bustamante, C. Reynolds, and R. Hinojosa-Ojeda, pp. 155–95. Stanford: Stanford University Press.

Cranford, Cynthia.

   2000. "Aquí Estamos y No Nos Vamos!": *Justice for Janitors* in Los Angeles and New Citizenship Claims." Paper presented at the seminar "Migrantes Mexicanas en Contextos Transnacionales: Trabajo, Familia y Actividades Politico-Comunitarias," organized by the Chicano/Latino Research Center, University of California, Santa Cruz, and Centrode Investigaciones y Estudios Superiores en Antropología Social, Ajijic, Jalisco, México, March 22–24.

Cross, John C.

   1998. *Informal Politics: Street Vendors and the State in Mexico.* Stanford: Stanford University Press.

De Genova, Nicholas P.

   2002. "Migrant 'Illegality' and Deportability in Everyday Life." *Annual Review of Anthropology* 31: 419–47.

Delgado, Héctor L.

   1993. *New Immigrants, Old Unions: Organizing Undocumented Workers in Los Angeles.* Philadelphia: Temple University Press.

Delgado-Gaitán, Concha.

   2001. *The Power of Community: Mobilizing for Family and Schooling.* Lanham, MD: Rowman and Littlefield.

Dennis, Dion.

   1995. "Brave New Reductionism: TQM as Ethnocentrism." *Education Policy Analysis Archives* 3, no. 9: 1–12.

Dohan, Daniel.
  2003. *The Price of Poverty: Money, Work, and Culture in the Mexican American Barrio*. Berkeley: University of California Press.

Du Bry, Travis Anthony.
  2004. "The New Pioneers of Mecca: Farm Laborers in the California Desert." Ph.D. diss., University of California, Riverside.

Durrenberger, Paul, and Suzan Erem.
  1999. "The Abstract, the Concrete, the Political, and the Academic: Anthropology and a Labor Union in the United States." *Human Organization* 58, no. 3: 305–12.

Dwyer, Daisy, and Judith Bruce, eds.
  1988. *A Home Divided: Women and Income in the Third World*. Stanford: Stanford University Press.

English-Lueck, J. A.
  2002. *Cultures@Silicon Valley*. Stanford: Stanford University Press.

Fernández-Kelly, P., and Anna M. García.
  1989. "Informalization at the Core: Hispanic Women, Homework, and the Advanced Capitalist State." In *The Informal Economy: Studies in Advanced and Less Developed Countries,* ed. Alejandro Portes, Manuel Castells, and Laura Benton, pp. 247–264. Baltimore: Johns Hopkins University Press.

Fisk, Catherine, Daniel Mitchell, and Christopher Erickson.
  2000. "Union Representation of Immigrant Janitors in Southern California: Economic and Legal Challenges." In *Organizing Immigrants: The Challenge for Unions in Contemporary California,* ed. Ruth Milkman, pp. 199–224. Ithaca: Cornell University Press.

Flores, William Vincent.
  1987. "The Dilemma of Survival: Organizational Dependence, Conflict, and Change in a Chicano Community." Ph.D. diss., Stanford University.

Foner, Nancy.
  1999. "Anthropology and the Study of Immigration." *American Behavioral Scientist* 42, no. 9: 1268–70.

Franklin-McKinley School District.
  1993. "Master Plan for Economic Development." Manuscript. Franklin-McKinley School District, San Jose.

García, Víctor.
  1992. "Surviving Farm Work: Economic Strategies of Mexican and Mexican American Households in a Rural Californian Community." Ph.D. diss., University of California, Santa Barbara.

Goldring, Luin.
  1998. "The Power of Status in Transnational Social Fields." In *Transnationalism from Below,* ed. Michael Peter Smith and Luis Eduardo Guarnizo, pp. 165–95. New Brunswick: Transaction Publishers.
  2003. "Gender, Status, and the State in Transnational Spaces: The Gender-

ing of Political Participation and Mexican Hometown Associations." In *Gender and U.S. Immigration: Contemporary Trends,* ed. Pierrette Hondagneu-Sotelo, pp. 341–58. Berkeley: University of California Press.

González de la Rocha, Mercedes.
1994. *The Resources of Poverty: Women and Survival in a Mexican City.* Oxford: Blackwell Publishers.

Green, Susan S.
1983. "Silicon Valley's Women Workers: A Theoretical Analysis of Sex-Segregation in the Electronics Industry Labor." In *Women, Men, and the International Division of Labor,* ed. Jane Nash and María Fernández-Kelly, pp. 273–331. Albany: State University of New York Press.

Grey, Mark A.
1999. "Immigrants, Migration, and Worker Turnover at the Hog Pride Pork Packing Plant." *Human Organization* 58, no. 1: 16–27.

Griffith, David, and Ed Kissam.
1995. *Working Poor: Farmworkers in the United States.* Philadelphia: Temple University Press.

Hardy-Fanta, Carol.
1993. *Latina Politics, Latino Politics: Gender, Culture, and Political Participation in Boston.* Philadelphia: Temple University Press.

Heyman, Josiah McC.
1998. "State Effects on Labor Exploitation." *Critique of Anthropology* 18, no. 2: 157–80.
2001. "Class and Classification at the U.S.-Mexico Border." *Human Organization* 60, no. 2: 128–40.

Hondagneu-Sotelo, Pierrette.
1994. *Gendered Transitions: Mexican Experiences of Immigration.* Berkeley: University of California Press.

Hossfeld, Karen.
1988. "Divisions of Labor, Divisions of Lives: Immigrant Women Workers in Silicon Valley." Ph.D. diss., University of California, Santa Cruz.
1990. "'Their Logic against Them': Contradictions in Sex, Race, and Class in Silicon Valley." In *Women Workers and Global Restructuring,* ed. Kathryn Ward, pp. 149–78. Ithaca, NY: ILR Press.

Hyde, Alan.
2003. *Working in Silicon Valley: Economic and Legal Analysis of a High-Velocity Labor Market.* Armonk, NY: M. E. Sharpe.

Ibarra, María de la Luz.
2000. "Mexican Immigrant Women in the New Domestic Labor." *Human Organization* 59, no. 4: 452–64.

Johnston, Paul.
1994. *Success While Others Fail: Social Movement Unionism and the Public Workplace.* Ithaca, NY: ILR Press.

Jones-Correa, Michael.
   1998. "Different Paths: Gender, Immigration, and Political Participation."
   International Migration Review 32, no. 2: 326–49.

Juárez, Luis.
   1972. "Fruit Harvest Awoke Sleepy S.J. of '40s." *Opinion,* September 10.
   1975. "Cannery Job Opportunities Shrink with Urbanization." *Opinion,*
   September 21.
   1976. "Illegal Immigrants 'In Season.'" Mexican-American Notes, *San Jose
   Mercury News,* July 4.

Katz, Naomi, and David S. Kemnitzer.
   1983. "Fast Forward: The Internationalization of Silicon Valley." In *Women,
   Men, and the International Division of Labor,* ed. Jane Nash and María
   Fernández-Kelly, pp. 332–45. Albany: State University of New York Press.

Kearney, Michael.
   2003. "The Classifying and Value Filtering Missions of Borders." *Journal of
   Theoretical Anthropology.*

Kearney, Michael, and Carole Nagengast.
   1989. *Anthropological Perspectives on Transnational Communities in Rural
   California.* Working Group on Farm Labor and Rural Poverty, Working
   Paper No. 3. Davis: California Institute for Rural Studies, February.

Kenney, Martin, ed.
   2000. *Understanding Silicon Valley: The Anatomy of an Entrepreneurial
   Region.* Stanford: Stanford University Press.

Konrad, Rachel.
   2004. "Stalled Economy Dominates Schwarzenegger's Trip to Silicon Valley." *Associated Press,* February 6, 2004.

Krissman, Fred.
   1996. "California Agribusiness and Mexican Farmworkers (1942–1992): A
   Binational Agricultural System of Production/Reproduction." Ph.D.
   diss., University of California, Santa Barbara.

Lamphere, Louise.
   1992. "Introduction: The Shaping of Diversity." In *Structuring Diversity:
   Ethnographic Perspectives on the New Immigration,* ed. Louise Lamphere,
   pp. 1–34. Chicago: University of Chicago Press.

Lamphere, Louise, Guillermo Grenier, and Alex Stepick.
   1994. Introduction to *Newcomers in the Workplace: Immigrants and the
   Restructuring of the U.S. Economy,* ed. Louise Lamphere, Alex Stepick,
   and Guillermo Grenier, pp. 1–21. Philadelphia: Temple University Press.

Lamphere, Louise, Alex Stepick, and Guillermo Grenier, eds.
   1994. *Newcomers in the Workplace: Immigrants and the Restructuring of the
   U.S. Economy.* Philadelphia: Temple University Press.

Lee, Chong-Moon, William F. Miller, Marguerite Gong Hancock, and Henry
S. Rowen.

2000. *The Silicon Valley Edge: A Habitat for Innovation and Entrepreneurship.* Stanford: Stanford University Press.

López, Steven H.
2000. "Contesting the Global City: Pittsburgh's Public Service Unions Confront a Neoliberal Agenda." In *Global Ethnography: Forces, Connections, and Imaginations in a Postmodern World,* ed. Michael Burawoy et al., pp. 268–98. Berkeley: University of California Press.

López-Garza, Marta.
2001. "A Study of the Informal Economy and Latina/o Immigrants in Greater Los Angeles." In *Asian and Latino Immigrants in a Restructuring Economy: The Metamorphosis of Southern California,* pp. 141–68. Stanford: Stanford University Press.

Mahler, Sarah J.
1995. *American Dreaming: Immigrant Life on the Margins.* Princeton: Princeton University Press.

Malkin, Victoria.
1998. "Gender and Family in Transmigrant Circuits: Transnational Migration between Western Mexico and the United States." Ph.D. diss., University College London.

Markusen, Ann.
1996. "Sticky Places in Slippery Space: A Typology of Industrial Districts." *Economic Geography* 72, no. 3: 293–313.

Martínez Saldaña, Jesús.
1993. "At the Periphery of Democracy: The Binational Politics of Mexican Immigrants in Silicon Valley." Ph.D. diss., University of California, Berkeley.

Massey, Douglas S., Joaquín Arango, Graeme Hugo, Ali Kouaouci, Adela Pellegrino, and J. Edward Taylor.
1993. "Theories of International Migration: A Review and Appraisal." *Population and Development Review* 19, no. 3: 431–66.

Matthews, Glenna.
2003. *Silicon Valley, Women, and the California Dream: Gender, Class, and Opportunity in the Twentieth Century.* Stanford: Stanford University Press.

Menjívar, Cecilia.
2000. *Fragmented Ties: Salvadoran Immigrant Networks in America.* Berkeley: University of California Press.

Milkman, Ruth.
2000. Introduction to *Organizing Immigrants: The Challenge for Unions in Contemporary California,* ed. Ruth Milkman, pp. 1–24. Ithaca: Cornell University Press.

———, ed. 2000. *Organizing Immigrants: The Challenge for Unions in Contemporary California,* ed. Ruth Milkman. Ithaca: Cornell University Press.

Milkman, Ruth, and Kent Wong.

2000. "Organizing the Wicked City: The 1992 Southern California Drywall Strike." In *Organizing Immigrants: The Challenge for Unions in Contemporary California,* ed. Ruth Milkman, pp. 169–98. Ithaca: Cornell University Press.

Mines, Richard, and Jeffrey Avina.

1992. "Immigrants and Labor Standards: The Case of California Janitors." In *U.S.-Mexico Relations: Labor Market Interdependence,* ed. Jorge Bustamante, Clark Reynolds, and Raúl Hinojosa-Ojeda, pp. 429–48. Stanford: Stanford University Press.

Moore, Joan, and Raquel Pinderhughes.

1993. Introduction to *In the Barrios: Latinos and the Underclass Debate,* pp. xi–xxxix. New York: Russell Sage Foundation.

Moser, Caroline O.

1994. "The Informal Sector Debate, Part 1: 1970–1983." In *Contrapunto: The Informal Sector Debate in Latin America,* ed. Cathy A. Rakowski, pp. 11–29. Albany: State University of New York Press.

Nissenbaum, Dion.

2004. "Silicon Valley Revival? Back in the Fast Lane?" *State Net California Journal* 61, no. 17 (April 1, 2004).

O'Connor, Mary.

1990. "Women's Networks and the Social Needs of Mexican Immigrants." *Urban Anthropology* 19, no. 1: 81–98.

Ortiz, Sutti.

2002. "Laboring in the Factories and in the Fields." *Annual Review of Anthropology* 31: 395–417.

Palerm, Juan V.

1995. "Policy Implications of Community Studies." Paper presented at the conference "Changing Face of Rural California," Pacific Grove, California.

2002. "Immigrant and Migrant Farm Workers in the Santa Maria Valley." In *Transnational Latina/o Communities: Politics, Processes, and Cultures,* ed. Carlos Vélez-Ibañez and Anna Sampaio, pp. 247–72. Lanham, MD: Rowman and Littlefield.

Palerm, Juan V., and Jose Ignacio Urquiola.

1993. "A Binational System of Agricultural Production: The Case of the Mexican Bajio and California Agribusiness." In *Mexico and the United States: Neighbors in Crisis,* ed. Daniel G. Aldrich Jr. and Lorenzo Meyer, pp. 311–367. San Bernardino: Borgo Press.

Pardo, Mary S.

1998a. *Mexican American Women Activists: Identity and Resistance in Two Los Angeles Communities.* Philadelphia: Temple University Press.

1998b. "Gendered Citizenship: Mexican American Women and Grassroots Activism in East Los Angeles, 1986–1992." In *Chicano Politics and Society in the Late Twentieth Century,* ed. David Montejano, pp. 58–79. Austin: University of Texas Press.

Parker, Mike, and Jane Slaughter.
1988. "Management by Stress." *Technology Review* 91, no. 7: 36–44.

Pellow, David Naguib, and Lisa Sun-Hee Park.
2002. *The Silicon Valley of Dreams: Environmental Injustice, Immigrant Workers, and the High-Tech Global Economy.* New York: New York University Press.

Pessar, Patricia R.
1999. "The Role of Gender, Households, and Social Networks in the Migration Process: A Review and Appraisal." In *The Handbook of International Migration: The American Experience,* ed. Charles Hirschman, Philip Kasinitz, and Josh De Wind, pp. 53–70. New York: Russell Sage Foundation.

Pitti, Stephen J.
1998. "Quicksilver Community: Mexican Migrations and Politics in the Santa Clara Valley, 1800–1960." Ph.D. diss., Stanford University.
2003. *The Devil in Silicon Valley: Northern California, Race, and Mexican Americans.* Princeton: Princeton University Press.

Portes, Alejandro.
1995. "Economic Sociology and the Sociology of Immigration: A Conceptual Overview." In *The Economic Sociology of Immigration: Essays on Networks, Ethnicity, and Entrepreneurship,* ed. Alejandro Portes, pp. 1–41. New York: Russell Sage.

Raijman, Rebeca.
2001. "Mexican Immigrants and Informal Self-Employment in Chicago." *Human Organization* 60, no. 1: 47–55.

Rakowski, Cathy.
1994. "The Informal Sector Debate, Part 2: 1984–1993." In *Contrapunto: The Informal Sector Debate in Latin America,* ed. Cathy A. Rakowski, pp. 31–50. Albany: State University of New York Press.

Reed-Danahay, Deborah.
1993. "Talking about Resistance: Ethnography and Theory in Rural France." *Anthropological Quarterly* 66, no. 4: 221–46.

Rivera-Salgado, Gaspar.
1999. "Mixtec Activism in Oaxacalifornia: Transborder Grassroots Political Strategies." *American Behavioral Scientist* 42, no. 9: 1439–58.

Roberts, Brian.
1994. "Informal Economy and Family Strategies." *International Journal of Urban and Regional Research* 18, no. 1: 6–23.

Rosaldo, Renato, William V. Flores, and Blanca Silvestrini.
1993. "Identity, Conflict, and Evolving Latino Communities: Cultural Citizenship in San Jose, California." Research report.

Rouse, Roger C.

1989. "Mexican Migration to the United States: Family Relations in the Development of a Transnational Migrant Circuit." Ph.D. diss., Stanford University.

1992. "Making Sense of Settlement: Class Transformation, Cultural Struggle, and Transnationalism among Mexican Migrants in the United States." In *Towards a Transnational Perspective on Migration,* ed. Linda Basch, Cristina Blanc-Szanton, and Nina Glick Schiller, pp. 25–52. Annals of the New York Academy of Sciences. Vol. 645. New York: New York Academy of Sciences.

Sánchez, George J.

1984. "Adaptation to Conquest: The Mexican Community of San Jose, 1845–1880." Stanford Center for Chicano Research. Working Paper Series No. 4. Stanford University.

Sanjek, Roger.

1996. *Encyclopedia of Social and Cultural Anthropology.* Ed. Alan Barnard and Jonathan Spencer. New York: Routledge.

Sassen, Saskia.

1989. "New York City's Informal Economy." In *The Informal Economy: Studies in Advanced and Less Developed Countries,* ed. Alejandro Portes, Manuel Castells, and Laura Benton, pp. 60–77. Baltimore: Johns Hopkins University Press.

1994. "The Informal Economy: Between New Developments and Old Regulations." *Yale Law Journal* 103: 2289–2304.

1999. "Whose City Is It? Globalization and the Formation of New Claims." In *The Urban Movement: Cosmopolitan Essays on the Late-20th-Century City,* ed. Robert A. Beauregard and Sophie Body-Gendrot, pp. 99–118. Thousand Oaks: Sage Publications.

Saxenian, AnnaLee.

1985. "Silicon Valley and Route 128: Regional Prototypes or Historic Exceptions?" In *High Technology, Space, and Society,* ed. Manuel Castells, pp. 81–105. Urban Affairs Annual Reviews, vol. 28. Beverly Hills: Sage.

1994. *Regional Advantage: Culture and Competition in Silicon Valley and Route 128.* Cambridge: Harvard University Press.

1999. *Silicon Valley's New Immigrant Entrepreneurs.* San Francisco: Public Policy Institute of California.

Scott, James.

1985. *Weapons of the Weak: Everyday Forms of Peasant Resistance.* New Haven: Yale University Press.

Selby, Henry, Arthur D. Murphy, and Stephen A. Lorenzen.

1990. *The Mexican Urban Household: Organizing for Self-Defense.* Austin: University of Texas Press.

Sherman, Rachel, and Kim Voss.

2000. "'Organize or Die': Labor's New Tactics and Immigrant Workers." In

Organizing Immigrants: The Challenge for Unions in Contemporary California, ed. Ruth Milkman, pp. 81–108. Ithaca: Cornell University Press.

Siegel, Lenny.
  1995. "Las Nuevas Tecnologías y la Polarización de la Fuerza Laboral en Silicon Valley." In *California: Problemas Económicos, Políticos y Sociales,* ed. Rosa Cusminsky, pp. 153–67. México: Universidad Nacional Autónoma de México.

State of California, Employment Development Department.
  1998. "Santa Clara County: Occupations with Greatest Growth, 1995–2000." *Projections and Planning Information, Labor Market Information Division.* San Francisco.

Staudt, Kathleen.
  1998. *Free Trade? Informal Economies at the U.S.-Mexico Border.* Philadelphia: Temple University Press.

Stepick, Alex.
  1989. "Miami's Two Informal Sectors." In *The Informal Economy: Studies in Advanced and Less Developed Countries,* ed. Alejandro Portes, Manuel Castells, and Laura Benton, pp. 111–31. Baltimore: Johns Hopkins University Press.

Tapia, Javier.
  1995. "Making a Living: The Microeconomics of U.S. Mexican Households." *Urban Anthropology* 24, no. 3–4: 255–80.
  1996. "Juntos y Separados: Cultural Complexity in U.S. Mexican Households." In *Chicanas and Chicanos in Contemporary Society,* ed. Roberto M. De Anda, pp. 75–86. Boston: Allyn and Bacon.

Torres Sarmiento, Socorro.
  2002. *Making Ends Meet: Income-Generating Strategies among Mexican Immigrants.* New York: LFB Scholarly Publishing LLC.

Trounstine, Philip, and Terry Christensen.
  1982. *Movers and Shakers: The Study of Community Power.* New York: St. Martin's Press.

U.S. Bureau of the Census.
  1990. *Census of Population and Housing Characteristics,* Table 3. Washington, DC.
  2000. *Profile of General Demographic Characteristics.* Summary file 1 and Table DP-1. Washington, DC.

Valenzuela, Abel.
  1999. "Gender Roles and Settlement Activities among Children and Their Immigrant Families." *American Behavioral Scientist* 42, no. 4: 720–42.

Van Maanen, John.
  1988. *Tales of the Field: On Writing Ethnography.* Chicago: University of Chicago Press.

Vélez-Ibáñez, Carlos.
  1988. "Networks of Exchange among Mexicans in the U.S. and Mexico:

Local Level Mediating Responses to National and International Transformations." *Urban Anthropology* 17, no. 1: 27–51.

1993. "U.S. Mexicans in the Borderlands: Being Poor without the Underclass." In *In the Barrios: Latinos and the Underclass Debate*, pp. 195–220. New York: Russell Sage Foundation.

Waldinger, Roger, Chris Erickson, Ruth Milkman, Daniel J. B. Mitchell, Abel Valenzuela, Kent Wong, and Maurice Zeitlin.

1996. *Helots No More: A Case Study of the Justice for Janitors Campaign in Los Angeles*. Working Paper No. 15. Los Angeles: Lewis Center for Regional Policy Studies, School of Public Policy and Social Research, University of California.

Waldinger, Roger, and Michael I. Lichter.

2003. *How the Other Half Works: Immigration and the Social Organization of Labor*. Berkeley: University of California Press.

Walker, Dick, and Bay Area Study Group.

1990. "The Playground of US Capitalism? The Political Economy of the San Francisco Bay Area in the 1980s." In *Fire in the Hearth: The Radical Politics of Place in America*, ed. Mike Davis, Steven Hiatt, Marie Kennedy, Susan Ruddick, and Michael Sprinker, pp. 3–82. New York: Verso.

Wells, Miriam J.

1996. *Strawberry Fields: Politics, Class, and Work in California Agriculture*. Ithaca: Cornell University Press.

2000. "Immigration and Unionization in the San Francisco Hotel Industry." In *Organizing Immigrants: The Challenge for Unions in Contemporary California*, ed. Ruth Milkman, pp. 109–29. Ithaca: Cornell University Press.

Wilson, Tamar Diana.

1998. Introduction. *Latin American Perspectives* 25, no. 2: 3–17.

2005. *Subsidizing Capitalism: Brickmakers on the U.S.-Mexican Border*. SUNY Series in the Anthropology of Work. New York: State University of New York Press.

Wolf, Eric R.

1982. *Europe and the People without History*. Berkeley: University of California Press.

Wood, Charles.

1981. "Structural Changes and Household Strategies: A Conceptual Framework for the Study of Rural Migration." *Human Organization* 40, no. 4: 338–44.

1982. "Equilibrium and Historical-Structural Perspectives on Migration." *International Migration Review* 16, no. 2: 298–319.

Zabin, Carol.

2000. "Organizing Latino Workers in the Los Angeles Manufacturing Sector: The Case of American Racing Equipment." In *Organizing Immi-*

grants: The Challenge for Unions in Contemporary California, ed. Ruth Milkman, pp. 150–68. Ithaca: Cornell University Press.

Zavella, Patricia.

1987. *Women's Work and Chicano Families: Cannery Workers of the Santa Clara Valley.* Ithaca: Cornell University Press.

1995. "Living on the Edge: Everyday Lives of Poor Chicano/Mexican Families." In *Mapping Multiculturalism,* ed. Avery F. Gordon and Christopher Newfield, pp. 362–88. Minneapolis: University of Minnesota Press.

Zlolniski, Christian.

1994. "The Informal Economy in an Advanced Industrialized Society: Mexican Immigrant Labor in Silicon Valley." *Yale Law Journal* 103, no. 8: 2305–35.

2000. "Etnografía de trabajadores informales en un barrio de inmigrantes mexicanos en el Silicon Valley." *Revista Mexicana de Sociología* 62, no. 2: 59–87.

2001. "Unskilled Immigrants in High-Tech Companies: The Case of Mexican Janitors in Silicon Valley." In *The International Migration of the Highly Skilled: Demand, Supply, and Development Consequences in Sending and Receiving Countries,* ed. Wayne Cornelius, Thomas J. Espenshade, and Idean Salehyan, pp. 265–87. San Diego: Center for Comparative Immigration Studies, University of California, San Diego, 2001.

2003. "Labor Control and Resistance of Mexican Immigrant Janitors in Silicon Valley." *Human Organization* 62, no. 1: 39–49.

Zlolniski, Christian, with Juan-Vicente Palerm.

1996. *Working but Poor: Mexican Immigrant Workers in a Low-Income Enclave in San Jose.* Chicano/Latino Policy Project, Working Paper 4, no. 2. University of California, Berkeley.

Index

Page numbers in italics refer to illustrations.

Text:	10/13 Galliard
Display:	Galliard
Compositor, printer, and binder:	Sheridan Books, Inc.
Illustrator:	Bill Nelson
Indexer:	Roberta Engleman